Cambridge Lower Secondary

Maths

STAGE 8: STUDENT'S BOOK

Michele Conway, Belle Cottingham, Alastair Duncombe, Mike Fawcett, Caroline Fawcus, Deborah McCarthy, Sarah Sharratt, Fiona Smith

Series Editors: Michele Conway, Alastair Duncombe, Caroline Fawcus, Sarah Sharratt

Collins

William Collins' dream of knowledge for all began with the publication of his first book in 1819.

A self-educated mill worker, he not only enriched millions of lives, but also founded a flourishing publishing house. Today, staying true to this spirit, Collins books are packed with inspiration, innovation and practical expertise. They place you at the centre of a world of possibility and give you exactly what you need to explore it.

Collins. Freedom to teach.

Published by Collins
An imprint of HarperCollins*Publishers*
The News Building
1 London Bridge Street
London
SE1 9GF

Browse the complete Collins catalogue at
www.collins.co.uk

MIX
Paper from
responsible sources
FSC™ C007454

FSC
www.fsc.org

This book is produced from independently certified FSC paper to ensure responsible forest management.

For more information visit:
www.harpercollins.co.uk/green

British Library Cataloguing in Publication Data
A catalogue record for this publication is available from the British Library.

Authors: Michele Conway, Belle Cottingham, Alastair Duncombe, Mike Fawcett, Caroline Fawcus, Deborah McCarthy, Sarah Sharratt, Fiona Smith
Series editors: Michele Conway, Alastair Duncombe, Caroline Fawcus, Sarah Sharratt
Publisher: Celia Wigley/Elaine Higgleton
Commissioning editor: Karen Jamieson/Lisa Todd
Editorial manager: Wendy Alderton
Project manager: Karthikeyan at Jouve
Copyeditor and collator: Alison Bewsher
Proofreader: Marie Taylor
Answer checker: Gillian Rich
Illustrator: Ann Paganuzzi
Cover designer: Gordon MacGilp
Cover illustrator: Maria Herbert-Liew
Typesetter: Jouve India Private Limited
Production controller: Sarah Burke
Printed and bound by: Grafica Veneta SpA in Italy

Acknowledgements

The publishers gratefully acknowledge the permission granted to reproduce the copyright material in this book. Every effort has been made to trace copyright holders and to obtain their permission for the use of copyright material. The publishers will gladly receive any information enabling them to rectify any error or omission at the first opportunity.

All photographs used under licence from Shutterstock except p 187 World History Archive / Alamy Stock Photo

All exam-style questions and sample answers have been written by the authors.

Introduction

The *Collins Lower Secondary Maths* Stage 8 Student's Book covers the Cambridge Lower Secondary Mathematics curriculum framework through 9 topic-based units, broken down into 36 chapters. The series is designed to illustrate concepts and provide practice questions at a range of difficulties to allow you to build confidence on a topic.

The authors have included plenty of worked examples in every chapter. These worked examples will lead you, step-by-step, through the new concepts, with clear and detailed explanations. Where possible, links have been made between topics, encouraging you to build on what you know already, and to practise mathematical concepts in a different context. You will learn to develop mental maths strategies, spot patterns and improve your ability to solve mathematical problems.

Every chapter has these helpful features:
- 'Starting point': to remind you of what you know already and why this will be helpful in the new chapter

- 'This will also be helpful when …': to let you know where you will use this mathematics in the future

- 'Hook': to get you interested in the new topic through an activity or game

- 'Key terms' boxes: to identify new mathematical words you need to know in that chapter, and provide a definition

- Worked examples: to show you how to address questions with both formal and informal (diagrammatic) explanations provided

- Clear topic headings: so that you can see what you are going to be learning in each section of the chapter

- 'Tip' boxes: to give you guidance on the possible methods and common errors

- 'Develop' questions (shown as a blue question number): to encourage you to think more deeply about the ideas you have been learning in this chapter and practising in this exercise

- 'Challenge' questions (shown as a red question number): to help you to think beyond the ideas covered in this chapter, and stretch you to apply the concepts in a different context

- 'Think about' boxes: to suggest areas of the mathematics that you might want to consider in more detail

- 'Discuss' boxes: to encourage you to talk about mathematical ideas with a partner or in class

- 'End of chapter reflection': to help you think about how well you have understood the ideas in the chapter, so that you can monitor your own progress.

We hope that you find this approach enjoyable and engaging as you progress through your mathematical journey.

The series editors

Contents

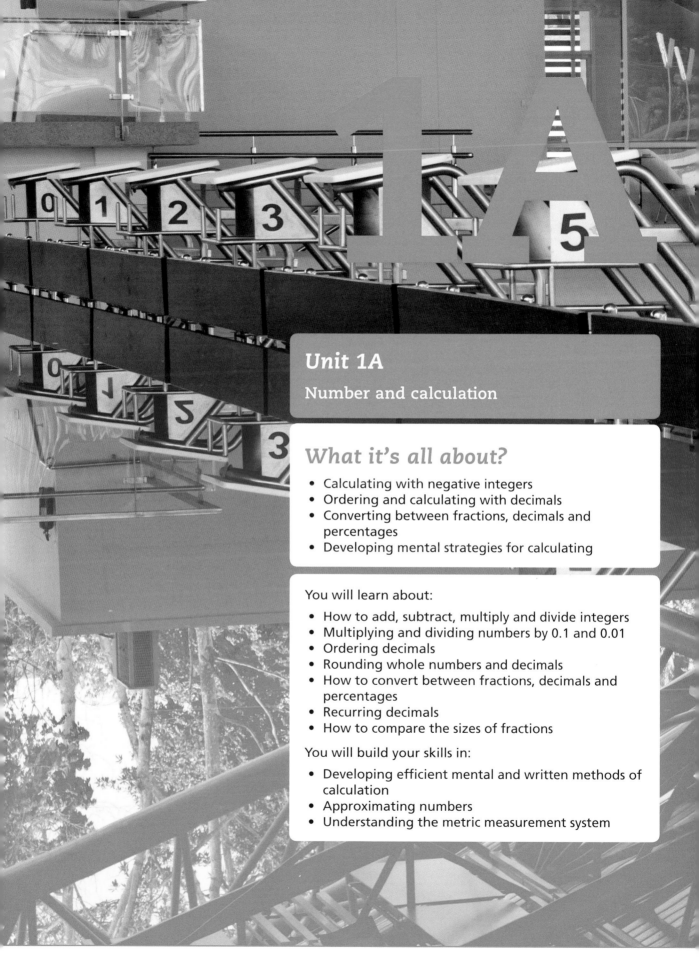

Unit 1A

Number and calculation

What it's all about?

- Calculating with negative integers
- Ordering and calculating with decimals
- Converting between fractions, decimals and percentages
- Developing mental strategies for calculating

You will learn about:

- How to add, subtract, multiply and divide integers
- Multiplying and dividing numbers by 0.1 and 0.01
- Ordering decimals
- Rounding whole numbers and decimals
- How to convert between fractions, decimals and percentages
- Recurring decimals
- How to compare the sizes of fractions

You will build your skills in:

- Developing efficient mental and written methods of calculation
- Approximating numbers
- Understanding the metric measurement system

Negative numbers

You will learn how to:
• Add and subtract integers.
• Multiply and divide integers.

Starting point

Do you remember …?

• how to use facts to multiply and divide?
  For example, if $2 \times 17 = 34$, what is $34 \div 17$?

• how to use place value to multiply and divide?
  For example, if $18 \div 2 = 9$, what is $180 \div 2$?

• how to test for divisibility?
  For example, is 1024 divisible by 3?

• how to add and subtract integers in context?
  For example, if the temperature is –2°C and drops by 5°C what is the new temperature?

• how to work out when a division problem will leave a remainder?

This will also be helpful when you:

• perform different calculations with bigger integers.

Hook

Here are five positive integer cards.

Work in pairs. Follow these rules. Experiment to get at least six different integer answers.

• Create number sentences using all the numbers exactly once, for example, $10 \div 5 \times 2 + 8 - 1$.
• Each number sentence must use each of these four operations: +, –, × and ÷
• You may use brackets.
• Which were the biggest and smallest answers?

Tip

You need to remember the order of operations (BIDMAS).

Adding and subtracting integers

Key terms

An **integer** is a whole number, whether positive, negative or zero.

Positive numbers are greater than zero.

Negative numbers are less than zero. They have a minus sign before the number.

Multiplication, division, addition and subtraction are four **operations**.

Worked example 1

Calculate:

a) −7 + 5   b) 3 + −5   c) −3 − −8

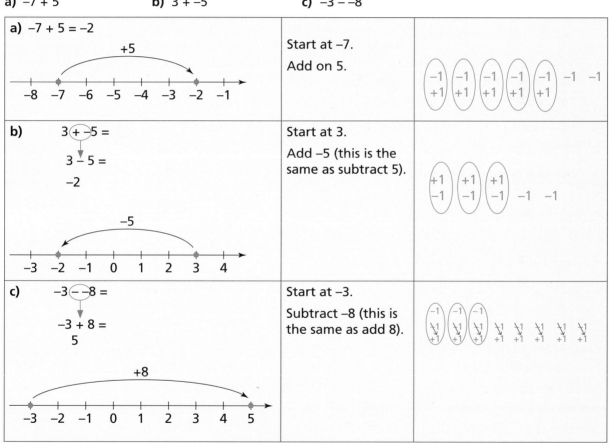

Exercise 1   1–8

1 Draw a number line to show the numbers from −10 to +10. Mark the answer to each problem on your number line.

a) −8 + 2   b) 1 + −3   c) 5 + −1

2 Work out:

   a) $7 - 9$ b) $6 - 4$ c) $4 - 7$

   d) $-5 - 3$ e) $-4 - 7$ f) $-8 - 6$

   g) $-12 + 9$ h) $-8 + 12$ i) $-16 + 19$

3 Calculate:

   a) $5 - +3$ b) $7 + -4$ c) $-3 + -2$

   d) $4 - -8$ e) $-6 + -7$ f) $5 - -8$

   g) $-2 - -6$ h) $7 - +9$ i) $9 - -9$

   j) $-5 + -9$ k) $-8 - -9$ l) $-7 + -2$

4 Write your own integer questions that give the following answers, using only the numbers 8, −10 and −5.

   a) 3   b) −2   c) −18   d) 5

5 In a magic square, all the rows, columns and diagonals should add up to the same total. Complete this magic square.

> **Tip**
>
> First find the sum of the diagonal.

2		
	−5	6
		−12

6 Benji says that $-35 - 12 = 47$ because two negatives make a positive.

Explain why Benji is wrong.

7 Work out the missing numbers.

   a) $28 + \underline{\quad} = 12$

   b) $50 + \underline{\quad} = 27$

   c) $\underline{\quad} + -35 = -200$

8 Explain whether the following is true or false.

When you subtract a negative integer from another negative integer, the answer is always negative.

9 Use a calculator to work these out.

   a) $145 - -254$

   b) $-829 + -764$

   c) $45 - -199$

Multiplying and dividing integers

Work out:

a) 2×-3 b) -4×-5 c) $-15 \div 3$ d) $-24 \div -8$

a) $2 \times -3 = -6$ -3 -3 -7 -6 -5 -4 -3 -2 -1 0 1	You need to work out 2 lots of –3.	(–1 –1 –1) (–1 –1 –1)
b) $-4 \times -5 = 20$	You can use these rules to work these out: positive × positive = positive positive × negative = negative negative × positive = negative negative × negative = positive	$+ \times + = +$ $+ \times - = -$ $- \times + = -$ $- \times - = +$
c) $-15 \div 3 = -5$	How many threes make –15? $3 \times -5 = -15$ So $-15 \div 3 = -5$	(–1 –1 –1 –1 –1) (–1 –1 –1 –1 –1) (–1 –1 –1 –1 –1) –15 split into 3 groups
d) $-24 \div -8 = 3$	How many negative eights make –24? $-8 \times 3 = -24$ So $-24 \div -8 = 3$	(–1 –1 –1 –1 –1 –1 –1 –1) (–1 –1 –1 –1 –1 –1 –1 –1) } –24 (–1 –1 –1 –1 –1 –1 –1 –1)

Exercise 2   1–8

1 The temperature changes by –2°C every hour. What is the total change in temperature after 7 hours?

2 Work out:

a) -4×4 b) 5×-7 c) -5×9 d) -10×-2

e) -3×6 f) 7×5 g) -8×-4 h) 5×-11

3 The answer to a question is –10.

Give two possible questions using multiplication, and two using division.

4 Which is the odd one out? Give a reason for your answer.

8 × –4   –9 × 1   –4 × –4   –5 × 3

5 Write true or false for each calculation. If it is false, correct it.

a) –7 × 9 = –63   **b)** –49 ÷ 7 = 7   **c)** 25 ÷ –5 = 5

d) –18 ÷ –3 = 6   **e)** 6 × –8 = 48   **f)** –7 × 4 = –28

6 Write two multiplication calculations and two division calculations that give each answer.

a) –9   **b)** 8   **c)** –12

7 Use Excel to make a multiplication table like the one below. If you do not have Excel, you can copy this one. Shade positive numbers in blue, negative numbers in yellow and zero in grey. Describe any patterns you notice.

×	–3	–2	–1	0	1	2	3
3							
2							
1							
0							
–1							
–2							
–3							

8 Work out the missing numbers.

a) ___ × –4 = –28   **b)** –6 × ___ = –30   **c)** ___ × –3 = 12

9 Use a calculator to work out:

a) 38 × –69   **b)** –87 × 6   **c)** 4050 ÷ –50

d) 9126 ÷ –3   **e)** –189 ÷ –3   **f)** –341 × 214

> **Think about**
>
> How can you use multiplication tables to help you work out multiplication and division involving negative integers?

End of chapter reflection

You should know that ...	You should be able to ...	Such as ...
Integers are whole numbers. Negative integers are less than 0 and have a minus sign.	Add, subtract, multiply and divide integers.	
In addition and subtraction: $+ \; + \; = \; +$ $+ \; - \; = \; -$ $- \; + \; = \; -$ $- \; - \; = \; +$		$36 + {-4}$ $-8 + 5$ $-2 + {-7}$ $16 - {-2}$ $-23 - 2$ $-37 - {-10}$
In multiplication: $+ \times + \; = \; +$ $+ \times - \; = \; -$ $- \times + \; = \; -$ $- \times - \; = \; +$		-15×3 $9 \times {-4}$ $-12 \times {-8}$
The same applies to division.		$56 \div {-2}$ $-75 \div 3$ $-54 \div {-6}$

Place value and rounding

You will learn how to:

- Read and write positive integer powers of 10; multiply and divide integers and decimals by 0.1 and 0.01.
- Order decimals, including measurements, making use of the =, ≠, > and < signs.
- Round whole numbers to a positive integer power of 10, e.g. 10, 100, 1000 or decimals to the nearest whole number or one or two decimal places.

Starting point

Do you remember …?

- how to interpret decimal notation and place value?

  For example, what is the value of the 5 in 0.75?

- how to multiply and divide whole numbers and decimals by 10, 100 or 1000?

  For example, what is 64.3 ÷ 10?

- how to order decimals including measurements, changing these to the same units?

  For example, put these in order of size, smallest first: 550 cm, 5 m, 0.58 km.

- how to round whole numbers to the nearest 10, 100 or 1000 and decimals, including measurements, to the nearest whole number or one decimal place?

  For example, round 18.4 litres to the nearest litre.

This will also be helpful when you:

- multiply and divide integers and decimals by decimals.

Hook

In Stage 7, you worked with **square numbers**.

$1 \times 1 = 1$ You say 'one squared' or '1 to the power of 2' 1^2

$2 \times 2 = 4$ You say 'two squared' or '2 to the power of 2' 2^2

$3 \times 3 = 9$, and so on.

Can you arrange all of the numbers below in a line so that if you add any number to its neighbour, the sum is a square number?

14   29   9   16   2   7   20   35

Can you always make a line containing all the numbers whichever number you start with?

Can you arrange all the numbers in a circle so that if you add any number to its neighbour, the sum is a square number?

Can you find a completely different set of eight numbers which you can arrange in a line so that if you add any number to its neighbour, the sum is a square number?

Tip

14 + 2 = 16 and 2 + 7 = 9.

Powers of ten; multiplying and dividing by 0.1 and 0.01

Key terms

10^5 means $10 \times 10 \times 10 \times 10 \times 10$

The number 5 is the **index** or **power** of 10.

Worked example 1

a) What is the value of 10^7?

b) Write 10 000 as a power of ten.

a) $10^7 = 10\,000\,000$

b) $10\,000 = 10 \times 10 \times 10 \times 10$

$= 10^4$

Multiplying a number by 0.1 is the same as multiplying the number by $\frac{1}{10}$.

Multiplying by $\frac{1}{10}$ is the same as dividing by 10.

This means that multiplying a number by 0.1 is the same as dividing the number by 10.

In the same way, multiplying a number by 0.01 is the same as dividing the number by 100.

Dividing by 0.1 means finding how many tenths are in the number. Each unit has 10 tenths so to find how many tenths are in the number, you multiply the number by 10.

Dividing a number by 0.1 is the same as multiplying the number by 10.

Dividing by 0.01 means finding how many hundredths are in the number. Each unit has 100 hundredths so to find how many tenths are in the number, you multiply the number by 100.

Dividing a number by 0.01 is the same as multiplying the number by 100.

Worked example 2

a) Multiply 15 by 0.1 b) Multiply 0.15 by 0.01

c) Divide 15 by 0.1 d) Divide 0.15 by 0.01

a) $15 \times 0.1 =$ $15 \div 10 = 1.5$	Multiplying by 0.1 is the same as dividing by 10.	
b) $0.15 \times 0.01 =$ $0.15 \div 100 = 0.0015$	Multiplying by 0.01 is the same as dividing by 100.	
c) $15 \div 0.1 =$ $15 \times 10 = 150$	Dividing by 0.1 is the same as multiplying by 10.	
d) $0.15 \div 0.01 =$ $0.15 \times 100 = 15$	Dividing by 0.01 is the same as multiplying by 100.	

Exercise 1 1–7, 9–10

1) Write as powers of 10:

   a) 10×10 b) $10 \times 10 \times 10$ c) $10 \times 10 \times 10 \times 10 \times 10 \times 10$

2) Write the following numbers as powers of ten.

   a) 100 b) 10 000 c) one million d) 1 000 000 000

3) Write as integers:

   a) 10^3 b) 10^5 c) 10^7

4) Write these numbers in order of size, smallest first.

   10^4 1000 10^5 1 000 000

5) **Vocabulary feature question**

   Match the numbers with the same value.

10^6	Ten
Ten to the power of 1	One hundred thousand
10^5	Ten thousand
Ten to the power of four	One million

6 Computer memory is measured in kilobytes (KB), megabytes (MB), gigabytes (GB) and terabytes (TB). Many manufacturers state that $1KB = 10^3$ bytes and $1MB = 10^3$, etc. But is this correct? Does 1MB equal 10^3 KB or 1024 KB? Use the internet to find out which of these is actually correct.

7 Work out:
   a) 3×0.1 b) 15×0.1 c) 0.2×0.1 d) 1.5×0.1
   e) 3×0.01 f) 15×0.01 g) 0.2×0.01 h) 1.5×0.01

8 Use your calculator to find the value of:
   a) 1.4×0.1 b) 2.56×0.1 c) 0.128×0.1
   d) 1.4×0.01 e) 2.56×0.01 f) 0.128×0.01

9 Work out:
   a) $0.6 \div 0.1$ b) $0.6 \div 0.01$ c) $1.52 \div 0.1$ d) $1.52 \div 0.01$
   e) $0.025 \div 0.1$ f) $16 \div 0.1$ g) $0.27 \div 0.01$ h) $0.0065 \div 0.01$

10 a) Look at your answers to question 7. Does multiplication always make a number bigger?
   b) Look at your answers to question 9. Does division always make a number smaller?

11 Complete the following:
   a) $4 \times$ _____ $= 0.4$ b) $1.2 \times$ _____ $= 0.12$ c) $7.8 \times$ _____ $= 0.078$
   d) $9 \div$ _____ $= 90$ e) $6.2 \div$ _____ $= 620$ f) _____ $\div 0.01 = 4.85$

Comparing and ordering decimals

Key terms

Symbol	Meaning	Example
=	is equal to	$3 + 4 = 7$
≠	is not equal to	$3 + 4 \neq 6$
<	is less than	$6 < 7$
>	is greater than	$-6 > -7$

Worked example 3

Write the correct symbol, < or >, between each pair of numbers or measurements.
   a) 0.64   0.67   b) 0.8   0.74   c) −0.8   −0.74
   d) 0.00645   0.0007   e) 10 cm   99 mm

a)	0	.	6	4	Start with the highest place value (furthest digit to the left) and compare the digits in each decimal place. Work from left to right.	ruler: 0.60 0.64 0.67 0.70
	0	.	6	7		
0.64 < 0.67						

b)	0	.	8	0	Write 0.8 as 0.80 to make the decimals easier to compare.	ruler: 0.70 0.74 0.80
	0	.	7	4		
0.8 > 0.74						

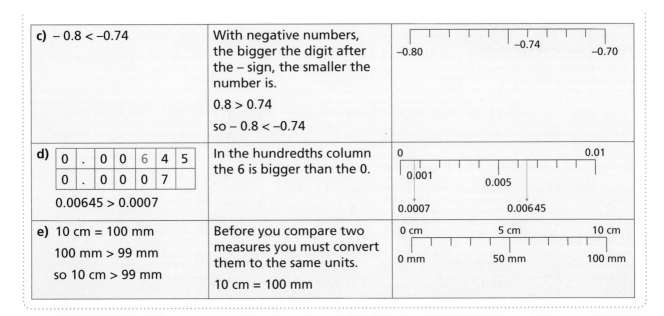

| c) − 0.8 < −0.74 | With negative numbers, the bigger the digit after the − sign, the smaller the number is.

0.8 > 0.74

so − 0.8 < −0.74 | |

| d) | In the hundredths column the 6 is bigger than the 0. | |

| 0 | . | 0 | 0 | 6 | 4 | 5 |
| 0 | . | 0 | 0 | 0 | 7 | |

0.00645 > 0.0007

| e) 10 cm = 100 mm

100 mm > 99 mm

so 10 cm > 99 mm | Before you compare two measures you must convert them to the same units.

10 cm = 100 mm | |

Tip

When comparing two measures it is usually easier to convert larger units to smaller units, so if you are comparing a number of metres to a number of kilometres you would usually convert the km to m.

Exercise 2 1–6

1 Which of these four signs (= < > ≠) could you put in the space between each pair of numbers to make a correct number statement? Some pairs have more than one correct answer.

a) 0.23   0.35
b) 0.53   0.49
c) 0.53   0.53
d) 0.000 65   0.001
e) 85 mm   0.96 cm
f) 2316 m   1.96 km
g) 3.6 m   2500 cm

2 Which is the largest number in each set?

a) 2.6 2.45 2.59
b) 0.345 0.435 0.297
c) 0.034 0.025 0.0057

3 Which of the measures in each pair is larger?

a) 2.45 m 1345 cm
b) 360 g 0.350 kg
c) 0.385 mm 0.04 cm

4 Write each set of numbers in order of size, largest first.

a) 0.382   0.415   0.427   0.384   0.392
b) 0.0215   0.00793   0.1   0.0206   0.0008

5 Write the correct symbol < or > between each pair of numbers to make a true number statement.

a) 0.75   0.68
b) 0.038   0.004
c) 0.06   0.0578

6 Write down one number which could go in each space to make correct number statements.

a) 0.7 < _____ < 0.9   b) 0.64 < _____ < 0.66   c) 0.8 < _____ < 0.9   d) 0.24 > _____ > 0.23

Key terms

Rounding is a form of **approximation** which means that a number is written to a given accuracy.

Round 42 to the nearest ten means to write 42 as the multiple of 10 that it is nearest to, which is 40.

Did you know?

When you round 42 to the nearest 10 you must not write 42 = 40 as this is not true. 42 does not equal 40 but it is approximately equal to 40. There is a special sign for 'approximately equal to' and it looks like this $\approx$.

Tip

Rounding to the nearest 10 will give a number ending in at least one zero.
Rounding to the nearest 100 will give a number ending in at least two zeros.
Rounding to the nearest 1000 will give a number ending in at least three zeros.

Rounding to 1 decimal place (written 1 d.p.) will give a number with one digit after the decimal point.
Rounding to 2 decimal places (written 2 d.p.) will give a number with two digits after the decimal point.

Worked example 4

a) Round 3845:

   i) to the nearest 1000   **ii)** to the nearest 100   **iii)** to the nearest 10.

b) Round 3.845:

   i) to the nearest whole number   **ii)** to 1 decimal place   **iii)** to 2 decimal places.

a) i)

Th	H	T	U
3	(8)	4	5
4	0	0	0

3845 to the nearest 1000 is 4000.

Thousands have 3 zeros so you need to cut off the 8, 4 and 5 and replace them by zeros. As the first number you cut off is an 8, which is over 5, you add 1 to the number before it so the 3 becomes a 4.

ii)

Th	H	T	U
3	8	(4)	5
3	8	0	0

3845 to the nearest 100 is 3800.

Hundreds have 2 zeros so you need to cut off the 4 and the 5 and replace them with zeros. As the first number you cut off is less than 5, you do not need to do anything else.

iii)

Th	H	T	U
3	8	4	(5)
3	8	5	0

3845 to the nearest 10 is 3850.

Tens have one zero so you need to cut off the 5 and replace it with a zero. As the number cut off is a 5, you add 1 to the number before it.

b) i)

U	•	1 d.p.	2 d.p.	3 d.p.
3	•	8̸	4̸	5̸
4				

3.845 to the nearest whole number is 4.

The nearest whole number means you want no numbers after the decimal point. The first number cut off is 8, which is bigger than 5, so you add 1 to the previous number.

(number line: 3 — 3.5 — 4, with 3.845 marked near 4)

ii)

U	•	1 d.p.	2 d.p.	3 d.p.
3	•	8	4̸	5̸
3	•	8		

3.845 to one decimal place is 3.8.

One decimal place means you cut off all the numbers after the first decimal place. The first number cut off is less than 5 so no further action is needed.

(number line: 3.8 — 3.85 — 3.9, with 3.845 marked)

iii)

U	•	1 d.p.	2 d.p.	3 d.p.
3	•	8	4	5̸
3	•	8	5	

3.845 to two decimal places is 3.85.

Two decimal places means you cut off all the numbers after the second decimal place. The first number cut off is 5 so add 1 to the number before it.

(number line: 3.84 — 3.845 — 3.85, with 3.845 marked)

Exercise 3   1–4, 6–7

1 Copy and complete the following table rounding the numbers to the accuracy stated.

	To the nearest 1000	To the nearest 100	To the nearest 10
a) 3432			
b) 8627			
c) 84352			
d) 167546			
e) 824			

2 Copy and complete the following table rounding the numbers to the accuracy stated.

	To the nearest whole number	To 1 d.p.	To 2 d.p.
a) 3.423			
b) 6.157			
c) 0.6466			
d) 11.091			
e) 155.568			

14   Unit 1A: Number and calculation

3 Round each of these times, given in seconds, to 1 d.p.

   a) 28.9092 s   **b)** 55.0481 s   **c)** 100.2448 s

Discuss

What is 485 correct to the nearest thousand?

4 Use a calculator to do these calculations. Write the answers correct to two decimal places.

   a) $1 \div 3$ **b)** $5 \div 16$ **c)** $8 \div 9$ **d)** $15 \div 19$

5 Jana is asked to write 0.2354 correct to 2 d.p. She gives an answer of 0.23.

   a) Is her answer correct?

   b) Explain your answer to part a).

6 Jack starts with a number with two decimal places. He rounds his number to 1 d.p. His answer is 7.2.

   a) Give four possible values for the number he started with.

   b) Compare answers with the person next to you. Were there any other possible values for Jack's starting number?

7 In this chapter you have seen one form of rounding where you round up 5s. This is just one method. Other methods round down 5s or round up and down alternate 5s. Use the internet to find out more about different types of rounding from websites such as 'Maths is Fun'.

8 **Vocabulary feature question**

Complete the text using words from the box.

| thousand | round | hundred | places | decimal |
| zero | rounding | calculator | correct | |

_____ is a type of approximation. If you divide two numbers on a _____, you sometimes get an answer with too many decimal _____ to be useful and then you _____ your answer to a particular accuracy, often _____ to 1 or 2 _____ places.

You can round numbers to powers of 10 such as to the nearest ten, _____, thousand or even million. If you round a number to the nearest 10, the rounded number will end in at least one _____. If you round a number to the nearest _____ the rounded number will end in at least three zeros.

End of chapter reflection

You should know that ...	You should be able to ...	Such as ...
$10^0 = 1$ $10^1 = 10$ $10^2 = 10 \times 10 = 100$ $10^3 = 10 \times 10 \times 10 = 1000$ etc.	Read and write positive integer powers of 10.	What is 10 to the power of 5? What is the value of 10^3?
Multiplying by 0.1 is the same as dividing by 10. Multiplying by 0.01 is the same as dividing by 100. Dividing by 0.1 is the same as multiplying by 10. Dividing by 0.01 is the same as multiplying by 100.	Carry out multiplication and division of whole and decimal numbers by 0.1 and 0.01.	Work out: **a)** 3.2×0.1 **b)** 0.73×0.01 Work out: **a)** $9.1 \div 0.1$ **b)** $0.54 \div 0.01$
You can use these signs =, ≠, > and < to show relative sizes of decimals, including measurements.	Order decimals including measurements.	Place the correct sign (<, > or =) between these pairs of numbers. **a)** 0.04718 ___ 0.41078 **b)** −3.201 ___ −3.301
You can round whole numbers to a positive integer power of 10, e.g. 10, 100, 1000 or round decimals to the nearest whole number or one or two decimal places.	Round numbers to a given degree of accuracy.	Round 31.8913 to 2 d.p.

Fractions, decimals and percentages

You will learn how to:
- Find equivalent fractions, decimals and percentages by converting between them.
- Convert a fraction to a decimal using division; know that a recurring decimal is a fraction.
- Order fractions by writing them with common denominators or dividing and converting to decimals.

Starting point

Do you remember …?

- the equivalence of fractions and decimals?

  For example, can you convert $\frac{1}{4}$ to a decimal, and 0.75 to a proper fraction?

- how to simplify fractions?
- how to convert between fractions and decimals?
- how to compare two or more simple fractions?

This will also be helpful when you:

- multiply and divide fractions.
- want to simplify calculations involving fractions and decimals.

Hook

Look at these three shapes:

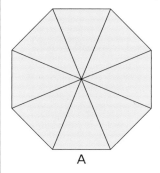 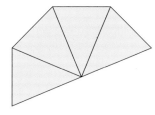

A   B   C

- How many of shape B are needed to make up shape A?
- How many of shape C are needed to make up shape A?
- Express the size of B as a **fraction** of A, and the size of C as a fraction of A.

  Then express them as **percentages**.

- Can you create your own question like this by dividing a different regular polygon into triangles?

Key terms

The **numerator** of a fraction is the number above the fraction line.

The **denominator** of a fraction is the number below the fraction line.

Converting between fractions, decimals and percentages

Worked example 1

Find the decimal and percentage equivalent to $\frac{3}{20}$.

Decimal		
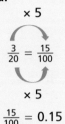 $\times 5$ $$\frac{3}{20} = \frac{15}{100}$$ $\times 5$ $$\frac{15}{100} = 0.15$$ **Percentage** $$0.15 \times 100 = 15$$ 15%	One way to convert a fraction to a decimal is to find an equivalent fraction with a denominator of 10, 100 or 1000. To convert a decimal to a percentage, multiply by 100.	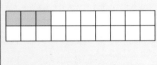 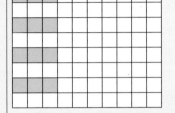

Worked example 2

Find the decimal and fraction equivalent to 12.5%.

Decimal $$12.5 \div 100 = 0.125$$ **Fraction** $$12.5\% = \frac{12.5}{100}$$ $\times 10$ $$\frac{12.5}{100} = \frac{125}{1000}$$ $\times 10$ $\div 5 \quad \div 25$ $$\frac{125}{1000} = \frac{25}{200} = \frac{1}{8}$$ $\div 5 \quad \div 25$	To convert a percentage to a decimal, divide by 100. Remember, percentage means 'parts per hundred'. To convert a percentage to a fraction, write it as a fraction with a denominator (bottom) of 100. Use equivalent fractions to make sure that you don't have a decimal as the numerator of the fraction. Remember to simplify your answer if possible.

Discuss

How could you have found $\frac{1}{8}$ in worked example 2 with fewer calculation steps?

What is the smallest number of calculation steps you could have used?

Key terms

Equivalent means equal in value.

$0.5 = 50\% = \frac{5}{10} = \frac{1}{2}$

These are equivalent decimals, percentages and fractions.

Exercise 1

1 Convert the following decimals to percentages.

a) 0.65   b) 0.12   c) 0.9   d) 0.225   e) 0.168

f) 0.075   g) 0.018   h) 0.105   i) 1.35   j) 4.2

2 Convert the following percentages to decimals.

a) 63%   b) 70%   c) 27%   d) 17.5%   e) 9%

f) 23.8%   g) 6.7%   h) 20.5%   i) 139%   j) 190%

3 Convert the following percentages to fractions.
Simplify your fractions if possible.

a) 30%   b) 35%   c) 24%   d) 58%   e) 95%

f) 56%   g) 96%   h) 12.5%   i) 37.5%   j) 32.4%

4 Convert the following fractions to percentages.

a) $\frac{13}{25}$ b) $\frac{17}{20}$ c) $\frac{9}{25}$ d) $\frac{7}{40}$ e) $\frac{19}{40}$

5 **Discuss**

How many different methods can you think of to convert $\frac{8}{20}$ from a fraction to a percentage?

Which is the most efficient method?

Is this always the most efficient method for converting a fraction to a percentage?

6 Convert the following decimals to fractions.
Simplify your fractions if possible.

a) 0.8   b) 0.24   c) 0.375   d) 0.96   e) 0.1875

7 Convert the following fractions to decimals by using equivalent fractions.

Discuss

Why was it harder to convert some of the fractions to decimals than others? How did you do it?

a) $\frac{3}{4}$ b) $\frac{7}{25}$ c) $\frac{9}{20}$

d) $\frac{11}{40}$ e) $\frac{3}{8}$

8 Which of the following fractions are between 0 and 0.25?
Show how you know.

a) $\frac{3}{8}$ b) $\frac{3}{20}$ c) $\frac{9}{25}$ d) $\frac{7}{40}$ e) $\frac{3}{25}$

f) Can you think of any other methods to answer this question? Which method is the most efficient?

9 **a)** Chen is converting 8.5% to a decimal.

Here is his working:

$8.5\% = 0.85$

He has made an error in his working.

Explain what the error is and correct the working.

b) Blessy is converting $\frac{17}{25}$ to a decimal.

Here is her working:

$\frac{17}{25} = \frac{17+75}{25+75} = \frac{92}{100} = 0.92$

She has made an error in her working.

Explain what the error is and correct the working.

10 **a)** Write a decimal number that is between $\frac{5}{8}$ and $\frac{6}{8}$.

Show how you found your answer.

b) Find the decimal number that is exactly halfway between $\frac{5}{8}$ and $\frac{6}{8}$.

Show how you found your answer.

11 An advertisement says:

"17 out of 20 people prefer Butterfree!"

What percentage of people prefer Butterfree?

12 Yousef works out that he spends 15% of his spare time playing computer games. What fraction of his spare time is this?

13 A cinema has 250 seats. On one night, 185 people buy tickets to watch a movie. What percentage of the seats are filled?

14 Brindusa and Salma have collected some data about the favourite sports of students in their class.

Brindusa calculates that 35% of the students like football best.

Salma calculates that $\frac{3}{8}$ of the students like hockey best.

Which sport is more popular, football or hockey?

Key terms

A **recurring** decimal has a repeating digit or pattern of digits.

For example, is 0.55555…, is 0.344444…, is 1.575757…

Recurring and terminating decimals

Worked example 3

Express each of the following fractions as a decimal and as a percentage.

a) $\frac{3}{8}$ **b)** $\frac{7}{9}$

a) $\frac{3}{8} = 3 \div 8$	To change a fraction to a decimal, divide the top number (the numerator) by the bottom number (the denominator).
$$\begin{array}{r} 0\ .\ 3\ 7\ 5 \\ 8\overline{)\,3\ .\ {}^{3}0\ {}^{6}0\ {}^{4}0} \end{array}$$ $0.375 \times 100 = 37.5$ $0.375 = 37.5\%$	To convert a decimal to a percentage, multiply by 100.
b) $\frac{7}{9} = 7 \div 9$	
$$\begin{array}{r} 0\ .\ 7\ 7\ \dots \\ 9\overline{)\,7\ .\ {}^{7}0\ {}^{7}0\ {}^{7}0} \end{array}$$ $\frac{7}{9} = 0.777\dots$ $\quad = 0.\dot{7}$ $0.\dot{7} \times 100 = 77.\dot{7}$ $0.\dot{7} = 77.\dot{7}\%$	First convert the fraction to a decimal by dividing the numerator by the denominator. To convert the decimal to a percentage, multiply by 100.

Think about

How do we know when a decimal will recur? How can we recognise this from our division calculation?

Key terms

A **terminating decimal** has a finite number of decimal places. It does not go on forever. It terminates (ends).

A **recurring decimal** has digits that keep going forever and repeat in a pattern. We put dots or a bar above the part that repeats.

$0.\dot{2}$ or $0.\overline{2}$ means $0.2222\dots$ – the 2 keeps repeating.

$0.\dot{1}\dot{2}$ or $0.\overline{12}$ means $0.121212\dots$ – 1 and 2 keep repeating.

All terminating decimals and recurring decimals are equivalent to fractions.

Exercise 2   1–3

1 Use division to convert these fractions to decimals. Show your workings.

   a) $\frac{3}{5}$ b) $\frac{3}{8}$ c) $\frac{7}{8}$ d) $\frac{5}{16}$ e) $\frac{9}{16}$

2 Use division to convert these fractions to recurring decimals.

   a) $\frac{1}{3}$ b) $\frac{1}{6}$ c) $\frac{1}{9}$ d) $\frac{1}{12}$

3 Maya says,

'Any fraction with a denominator of 6 gives a recurring decimal.'

Is Maya correct?

Explain your answer.

4 Investigate the recurring decimals that are equivalent to $\frac{1}{7}, \frac{2}{7}, \frac{3}{7}, \frac{4}{7}, \frac{5}{7}, \frac{6}{7}$.

Describe any pattern that you see.

5 Are the following statements always true, sometimes true or never true?

Give reasons for your answers.

a) A decimal can be written as a fraction.

b) If a fraction in its simplest form has an odd denominator, then it will be a recurring decimal.

c) If a fraction in its simplest form has an even denominator, then it will be a terminating decimal.

d) If a fraction in its simplest form has a denominator that is a multiple of 10, then it will be a terminating decimal.

6 Use a spreadsheet. Create a table that shows the patterns that these fractions create when you convert them to decimals.

a) thirds

b) sevenths

c) ninths

d) elevenths

e) any other prime number denominator.

7 | Think about

We have learnt about decimals that terminate, for example, 0.34.

We have learnt about decimals that recur, for example, 0.3333…

Can you find any examples of decimals that do not terminate, but do not recur?

Ordering fractions

Worked example 4

Write these fractions in order from smallest to largest.

a) $\frac{11}{12}, \frac{3}{4}, \frac{7}{8}$

b) $\frac{2}{7}, \frac{14}{25}, \frac{4}{11}$

a) 12: 12, <u>24</u>, 36…	First look at the denominators: 12, 4, 8.
4: 4, 8, 12, 16, 20, <u>24</u>…	Find the lowest common multiple (LCM) of the denominators.
8: 8, 16, <u>24</u>, 36…	Use this as a common denominator.
LCM of 12, 4 and 8 = 24	
$\times 2 \qquad \times 6 \qquad \times 3$ $\frac{11}{12} = \frac{22}{24} \qquad \frac{3}{4} = \frac{18}{24} \qquad \frac{7}{8} = \frac{21}{24}$ $\times 2 \qquad \times 6 \qquad \times 3$	Write each of the fractions over the common denominator.
$\frac{18}{24} \qquad \frac{21}{24} \qquad \frac{22}{24}$	Put the fractions in order from the smallest to the largest.
$\frac{3}{4} \qquad \frac{7}{8} \qquad \frac{11}{12}$	Rewrite as the original fractions.
b) $\frac{2}{7} \longrightarrow 2 \div 7 = 0.2857\ldots$ $\frac{14}{25} \longrightarrow 14 \div 25 = 0.56$ $\frac{4}{11} \longrightarrow 4 \div 11 = 0.3636\ldots$	Change all the fractions to decimals by dividing the numerator by the denominator.
$\frac{2}{7} \qquad \frac{4}{11} \qquad \frac{14}{25}$	Put the fractions in order from the smallest to the largest by considering the decimals they are each equivalent to.

Think about

Why did we use equivalent fractions to order the fractions in the part a) and equivalent decimals to order the fractions in part b)?

If you are not sure why, then try to order the fractions in each part using the other method.

1 Use this fraction wall to help you put the following sets of fractions in order from smallest to largest.

$\frac{1}{2}$				$\frac{1}{2}$			
$\frac{1}{3}$			$\frac{1}{3}$			$\frac{1}{3}$	
$\frac{1}{4}$		$\frac{1}{4}$		$\frac{1}{4}$		$\frac{1}{4}$	
$\frac{1}{5}$		$\frac{1}{5}$		$\frac{1}{5}$	$\frac{1}{5}$		$\frac{1}{5}$
$\frac{1}{6}$	$\frac{1}{6}$		$\frac{1}{6}$	$\frac{1}{6}$		$\frac{1}{6}$	$\frac{1}{6}$
$\frac{1}{7}$	$\frac{1}{7}$	$\frac{1}{7}$	$\frac{1}{7}$	$\frac{1}{7}$	$\frac{1}{7}$		$\frac{1}{7}$

a) $\frac{2}{3}$ $\frac{4}{5}$ $\frac{3}{7}$ **b)** $\frac{5}{7}$ $\frac{1}{3}$ $\frac{2}{5}$

2 Ritesh and Jamal had a competition to see who could keep a spinner going the longest. They each recorded their times:

	Ritesh	Jamal
Round 1	$5\frac{1}{2}$ minutes	5.755 minutes
Round 2	$5\frac{3}{4}$ minutes	5.589 minutes
Round 3	$5\frac{1}{4}$ minutes	5.289 minutes

Work out who won each round.

3 Use equivalent fractions to compare these pairs of fractions.

Write in the correct symbol <, > or =.

a) $\frac{5}{8}$ ☐ $\frac{7}{16}$ **b)** $\frac{5}{14}$ ☐ $\frac{2}{7}$ **c)** $\frac{3}{4}$ ☐ $\frac{2}{3}$ **d)** $\frac{5}{6}$ ☐ $\frac{7}{9}$

e) $\frac{5}{6}$ ☐ $\frac{3}{4}$ **f)** $\frac{4}{9}$ ☐ $\frac{5}{12}$ **g)** $\frac{9}{24}$ ☐ $\frac{3}{8}$ **h)** $\frac{9}{14}$ ☐ $\frac{13}{21}$

4 Use converting to decimals to compare the fractions in each pair.

Write in the correct symbol <, > or =.

a) $\frac{5}{8}$ ☐ $\frac{2}{3}$ **b)** $\frac{1}{3}$ ☐ $\frac{2}{5}$ **c)** $\frac{9}{11}$ ☐ $\frac{5}{6}$ **d)** $\frac{4}{5}$ ☐ $\frac{7}{9}$

5 Compare the fractions in each pair using <, > and =.

You can use equivalent fractions or converting to decimals.

a) $\frac{2}{7}$ ☐ $\frac{5}{12}$ **b)** $\frac{7}{8}$ ☐ $\frac{8}{9}$ **c)** $\frac{5}{7}$ ☐ $\frac{3}{5}$ **d)** $\frac{5}{8}$ ☐ $\frac{17}{20}$

Think about

When is it easier to use equivalent fractions and when is it easier to use converting to decimals?
Can you find some fractions that are difficult to order using equivalent fractions?
Can you find some fractions that are difficult to order using converting to decimals?

6 Which is larger?

a) $\frac{7}{8}$ or 0.885   b) $\frac{7}{12}$ or 0.585   c) $\frac{13}{16}$ or 0.76

7 Put each set of fractions in order from smallest to largest.

a) $\frac{3}{5}$ $\frac{4}{10}$ $\frac{5}{8}$

b) $\frac{2}{3}$ $\frac{7}{9}$ $\frac{5}{6}$

c) $\frac{2}{9}$ $\frac{1}{5}$ $\frac{3}{11}$

8 Find the missing number to make these statements true.
None of your answers should include an improper (top heavy) fraction.

a) $\frac{3}{4} < \frac{\square}{8}$ b) $\frac{3}{4} < \frac{\square}{6}$ c) $\frac{5}{8} > \frac{\square}{3}$ d) $\frac{5}{7} < \frac{\square}{8}$

Is there more than one correct answer for some of these questions?

9 Which fraction is exactly halfway between $\frac{2}{5}$ and $\frac{1}{7}$? You can use a calculator to help you.

10 Vocabulary feature question

Complete the text using words from the box. Some words may be used more than once.

recurring	numerator	denominator	terminating
bar	equivalent fractions	division	dots

All fractions are equivalent to either a _____ decimal or a _____
decimal. A recurring decimal has one or more numbers in the decimal part that repeat; this can
be shown by _____ or a _____ above the numbers that repeat.

We can compare the size of fractions by using _____ to convert the fraction to a
decimal or _____.

To convert a fraction to a decimal by division, we divide the _____ of the
fraction by the _____ of the fraction.

End of chapter reflection

You should know that ...	You should be able to ...	Such as ...
A percentage is a fraction with a denominator of 100. A decimal is a fraction with a denominator that is a power of ten, written with a decimal point.	Find equivalent fractions, decimals and percentages by converting between them.	Express as decimals: a) 32%　　　b) $\frac{7}{20}$ Convert to percentages: a) $\frac{24}{25}$　　　b) 0.045 Write the following as fractions: a) 11%　　　b) 0.23
You can convert a fraction to a decimal by dividing the numerator by the denominator. A terminating decimal has a finite number of decimal places. A recurring decimal has a repeating pattern in its decimal places.	Convert a fraction to a decimal using division. Order fractions by writing with common denominators or dividing and converting to decimals.	Write $\frac{3}{8}$ as a decimal. Write $\frac{7}{9}$ as a decimal. Which is greater: 0.48 or $\frac{8}{15}$? Which fraction is exactly halfway between $\frac{3}{4}$ and $\frac{3}{5}$? Put these fractions in order from smallest to largest: $\frac{5}{7}$　$\frac{1}{3}$　$\frac{2}{5}$

Mental methods

You will learn how to:
- Use known facts to derive new facts, e.g. given $20 \times 38 = 760$, work out 21×38.
- Recall simple equivalent fractions, decimals and percentages.
- Recall relationships between units of measurement.

Starting point

Do you remember …?

- your multiplication facts up to 10×10?
  For example, write down 7×6, 8×9.

- how to convert simple fractions into decimals and percentages?
  For example, write down the decimals and percentages equivalent to $\frac{1}{2}$, $\frac{1}{4}$, $\frac{1}{10}$ and $\frac{1}{100}$.

- how to use the multiplication facts you know to derive other multiplication and division facts?
  For example, $9 \times 10 = 90$, $90 \div 10 = 9$, $90 \div 9 = 10$.

- how to change the order of numbers in addition and multiplication calculations without changing the calculation?
  For example, $2 \times 4 \times 50 = 2 \times 50 \times 4$.

This will also be helpful when you:

- multiply and divide fractions and simple decimals.

- calculate simple percentages of a quantity.

Hook

This is a game for 2 players.

You will need:

- a 6-sided dice

- two sets of 16 counters, each set of a different colour.

5%	0.2	$\frac{1}{20}$	1%
$\frac{1}{3}$	$\frac{1}{2}$	$\frac{1}{5}$	0.33
65%	0.3	0.5	60%
$\frac{1}{100}$	30%	$\frac{13}{20}$	0.6

How to play:

Take turns to roll the dice.

  If you roll an even number, pick a box from the grid.

  If you roll an odd number, the other player chooses a box for you.

Find a fraction, decimal or percentage equivalent to the value in your box.

Cover both boxes with a counter.

The winner is the person that uses the most counters.

Deriving new facts

Key terms

When you **derive** an answer, you work it out using what you already know.

Fractions, decimals and percentages are **equivalent** if they have the same value. For example, 0.5 is equivalent to $\frac{5}{10}$ or $\frac{1}{2}$.

A **percentage** represents the number of parts per hundred. For example, 13% means 13 parts per hundred or $\frac{13}{100}$.

Worked example 1

$379 + 1457 = 1836$

Use this fact to work out:

a) $379 + 1458$ **b)** $579 + 1457$

a) $379 + 1458$ $379 + 1457 = 1836$ $379 + 1458$ $= 379 + (1457 + 1)$ $= 1836 + 1$ $= 1837$ $379 + 1458 = 1837$	Start with the fact that you are given. Compare the calculation you want to work out to the fact. 1458 is 1 more than 1457, the rest of the sum is the same. To find the total, add 1 to 1836.	
b) $579 + 1457$ $379 + 1457 = 1836$ $579 + 1457$ $= (200 + 379) + 1457$ $= 200 + 1836$ $= 2036$ $579 + 1457 = 2036$	Start with the fact that you are given. Compare the calculation you want to work out to the fact. 579 is 200 more than 379, the rest of the sum is the same. To find the total, add 200 to 1836.	

Worked example 2

$10 \times 49 = 490$ and $490 \div 10 = 49$

Use these facts to work out:

a) 11×49 **b)** $490 \div 5$

a) 11×49 $10 \times 49 = 490$ $11 \times 49 =$ $= 10 \times 49 + 1 \times 49$ $= 490 + 49 = 539$ $11 \times 49 = 539$	Start with the fact that you are given. 10 groups of 49 make 490. 11 groups of 49 is one more group of 49 than 10 groups of 49. To find the total, add 49 to 490.	

b) $490 \div 5$ $490 \div 10 = 49$ $490 \div 5 = 49 \times 2$ $49 \times 2 = 98$ $490 \div 5 = 98$	Start with the fact that you are given 490 is 10 groups of 49. When you divide by 5, each part is two times bigger than when you divide by 10. To find the answer, multiply 49 by 2.	490 49 49 49 49 49 49 49 49 49 49 490 49 49 49 49 49 49 49 49 49 49 98 98 98 98 98 490 98 98 98 98 98

Exercise 1   1–9

1 Given that $458 + 2061 = 2519$, work out:

   a) $455 + 2061$ **b)** $358 + 2061$ **c)** $428 + 2061$

   d) $2061 + 450$ **e)** $2051 + 448$ **f)** $456 + 2063$

2 Given that $\$16.99 + \$8.67 = \$25.66$, work out:

   a) $\$25.66 - \$8.67$ **b)** $\$25.66 - \$16.99$ **c)** $\$16.95 + \$8.67$

3 Given that $1567 - 598 = 969$, work out:

   a) $1568 - 598$ **b)** $1567 - 599$ **c)** $2567 - 598$

   d) $1567 - 698$ **e)** $1567 - 498$ **f)** $1566 - 597$

4 Given that $18 \times 17 = 306$, work out:

   a) 19×17 **b)** 36×17 **c)** $306 \div 18$ **d)** $306 \div 17$

5 Given that $150 \times 16 = 2400$, work out:

   a) $2400 \div 16$ **b)** $2400 \div 150$ **c)** 150×8 **d)** 15×16

6 $87 \times 40 = 3480$

   Write down a related fact for each of these answers.

   a) 3567 **b)** 3520 **c)** 348 **d)** 1740

7 Isla multiplies 25 by 29 using this method:

   $25 \times 29 = 25 \times 30 - 25 = 725$.

   Use Isla's method to work out:

   a) 23×19 **b)** 32×29 **c)** 19×43 **d)** 39×25

8 Use the fact $28 \times 39 = 1092$ to find the missing numbers in these related calculations.

   a) $\ldots\ldots \times \ldots\ldots = 1120$ **b)** $\ldots\ldots \times \ldots\ldots = 1131$

   c) The answer to a related fact is 546. Write down one possible fact for this answer.

   d) The answer to a related fact is 2184. Write down two possible facts for this answer.

9 Given that $50 \times 20 = 1000$, Jake calculates 50×19 as follows:

   $50 \times 19 = 1000 - 20 = 980$.

   Is Jake correct? Explain your answer.

10 The selling price of a toy is $23. After a new advertisement the sales are predicted to increase by 100 units each month for the next 6 months.

Use a **spreadsheet** to calculate the sales for the next 6 months.

How would you modify the spreadsheet if the increase of sales was 50 units for the first 3 months, then 150 units for the next 3 months.

Equivalent fractions, decimals and percentages

Worked example 3

a) Write a percentage and decimal equivalent to $\frac{4}{5}$.

b) Write a fraction and percentage equivalent to 1.5.

c) Write a percentage and decimal equivalent to $\frac{2}{3}$.

a) $\frac{1}{5} = 20\%$ $\frac{4}{5} = 4 \times 20\% = 80\%$ $80\% = \frac{80}{100} = 0.8$ $\frac{4}{5} = 80\% = 0.8$	Use what you know about percentage and decimal equivalents to $\frac{1}{5}$ to write a percentage equivalent to $\frac{4}{5}$. $\frac{4}{5}$ is 4 lots of $\frac{1}{5}$, so you need to multiply 20% by 4 to find an equivalent percentage. To find an equivalent decimal, divide the percentage by 100.	$\frac{4}{5}$ | $\frac{1}{5}$ | $\frac{1}{5}$ | $\frac{1}{5}$ | $\frac{1}{5}$ | 80% | 20% | 20% | 20% | 20% | 0.8 | 0.2 | 0.2 | 0.2 | 0.2 |
b) $1.5 = 1 + 0.5$ $\quad = 1 + \frac{1}{2}$ $\quad = 1\frac{1}{2}$ $1.5 = 100\% + 50\% = 150\%$ $1.5 = 1\frac{1}{2} = 150\%$	Use what you know about 0.5 to write a fraction equivalent to $1 + 0.5$. Use the fact that $1 = 100\%$ and $0.5 = 50\%$ to find an equivalent percentage.	1.5 | 1 | 0.5 | $1\frac{1}{2}$ | 1 | $\frac{1}{2}$ | 150% | 100% | 50% |
c) $\frac{1}{3} = 33\frac{1}{3}\%$ $\frac{2}{3} = 66\frac{2}{3}\%$ $\frac{1}{3} = 0.\dot{3}$ $\frac{2}{3} = 0.\dot{6}$	Use what you know about percentage equivalents to $\frac{1}{3}$ to write a percentage equivalent to $\frac{2}{3}$. $\frac{2}{3}$ is 2 lots of $\frac{1}{3}$, so you need to multiply $33\frac{1}{3}\%$ by 2 to find an equivalent percentage. Use what you know about decimal equivalents to $\frac{1}{3}$ to write a decimal equivalent to $\frac{2}{3}$. $\frac{2}{3}$ is 2 lots of $\frac{1}{3}$, so you need to multiply $0.\dot{3}$ by 2 to find an equivalent decimal.	$\frac{1}{3}$ | $\frac{1}{3}$ | $33\frac{1}{3}\%$ | $33\frac{1}{3}\%$ | $\frac{2}{3}$ $66\frac{2}{3}\%$ $\frac{1}{3}$ | $\frac{1}{3}$ | $0.\dot{3}$ | $0.\dot{3}$ | $\frac{2}{3}$ $0.\dot{6}$

1 Write these fractions as percentages and decimals.

    a) $\frac{2}{5}$ **b)** $\frac{2}{3}$ **c)** $\frac{7}{20}$ **d)** $\frac{4}{25}$

    e) $\frac{6}{5}$ **f)** $\frac{5}{4}$ **g)** $\frac{11}{20}$ **h)** $\frac{13}{25}$

2 Use >, < or = to complete the following statements.

    a) 35% ⬚ 0.35   **b)** 8% ⬚ 0.8   **c)** $\frac{2}{3}$ ⬚ 60%   **d)** $\frac{1}{25}$ ⬚ 0.25

    e) $\frac{7}{10}$ ⬚ 0.07   **f)** $\frac{3}{20}$ ⬚ 15%   **g)** 1.2 ⬚ 120%   **h)** $2\frac{1}{2}$ ⬚ 250%

3 Write each of the following decimals as fractions and as percentages.

    a) 0.28   **b)** 0.3   **c)** 1.25   **d)** 2.8

4 Copy and complete this table.

	Fraction	Percentage	Decimal
a)	$\frac{3}{20}$		
b)		70%	
c)			0.45
d)	$1\frac{1}{3}$		
e)			1.02
f)	$\frac{31}{50}$		
g)			1.7

5 Are these statements true or false? Explain your answers.

    a) 0.22 = 2.2%   **b)** 1.25 = $1\frac{1}{4}$ **c)** 1.9 = 109%

6 Which of these is the odd one out? Explain your answer.

    5% $\frac{5}{10}$ 0.05

7 Use the digits 1, 2, 3, 4, 5, 6 only once to make two true statements.

    $1\frac{⬚}{⬚} = 1.⬚\dot{6}$ $\frac{⬚}{2⬚} = ⬚6\%$

8 Lottie knows that $\frac{3}{4}$ = 75%.

    To find $\frac{3}{8}$, she multiples 75% by 2.

    Is Lottie correct? Explain your answer.

Units of measurement

Length 1 km = 1000 m 1 m = 100 cm 1 cm = 10 mm	Mass 1 tonne = 1000 kg 1 kg = 1000 g	Capacity 1 litre = 1000 ml
Area 1 m² = 10 000 cm² 1 cm² = 100 mm²	Time 1 day = 24 hours 1 hour = 60 minutes	Angles 1 whole turn = 360°

Exercise 3   1–10

1 Complete these statements about units of length.

    a) 1 km = ___ m   **b)** 1 m = ___ cm   **c)** 1 cm = ___ mm   **d)** 1 m = ___mm

2 Complete these conversions.

    a) 1 tonne = ___ kg   **b)** 1 l = ___ ml   **c)** 1 cm² = ___ mm²   **d)** 1 m² = ___cm²

3 True or false? Correct the statements that are not true.

    a) 1 km = 1000 m   **b)** 1 cm = 100 mm   **c)** 1 litre = 100 ml

    d) 1 hour = 60 seconds   **e)** 1 tonne = 100 kg   **f)** 1 whole turn = 100°

4 Write in the missing units.

    a) 1 day = 24 ___   **b)** 1 cm² = 100___   **c)** $\frac{1}{10}$ cm = 1___   **d)** 1000 kg = 1 ___

5 Use >, < or = to make the following comparisons true.

    a) 1 litre ☐ 100 ml   **b)** 1 km ☐ 1000 m

    c) 1 tonne ☐ 1000 g   **d)** $\frac{1}{4}$ of a turn ☐ 90°

Think about

When you convert units of measure, what rule do you follow for working out when to divide and when to multiply?

6 Complete the following statements.

    a) To convert 100 m to cm, (multiply/divide) by 100.

    b) To convert 100 mm to cm, (multiply/divide) by 10.

    c) To convert 100 ml to litres, (multiply/divide) by 1000.

    d) To convert 100 m to km, (multiply/divide) by 1000.

7 Which of these is the odd one out? Explain your answer.

1 km   100 metre   1 cm²

8 Which of these is the odd one out? Explain your answer.

1 tonne   1 ml   1 kg

9 Use six of the following cards only once to make two true statements.

tonne	kg	1000	g	10 000	m²	100 000	cm²

☐☐ = 1☐   1☐ = ☐☐

10 Alice says:

1 m = 100 cm

1 m² = 100 cm²

Victor says $\frac{1}{60}$ of an hour = 1 second.

a) Explain the mistakes they have made. Correct them.

b) Work in pairs. Write two statements about measurements that have a mistake. Ask your friend to correct them.

End of chapter reflection

You should know that …	You should be able to …	Such as …
Known facts can be used to work out other related calculations. This can include calculations involving addition, subtraction, multiplication or division.	Use known facts to derive new facts.	Given 20 × 38 = 760, work out 21 × 38. Given 3335 − 1899 = 1436, calculate 3335 − 2899.
You can find equivalent fractions, decimals and percentages in simple cases and that you can use these to derive new facts.	Recall simple equivalent fractions, decimals and percentages.	$\frac{\square}{\square}$ = 0.4 = ___ % $\frac{5}{4}$ = ___ = ___ %
10 mm = 1 cm 100 cm = 1 m 1000 m = 1 km 1000 ml = 1 l 1000 g = 1 kg 1000 kg = 1 tonne 360° = a full turn 60 seconds = 1 minute 60 minutes = 1 hour 24 hours = 1 day 100 mm² = 1 cm² 10 000 cm² = 1 m²	Recall relationships between units of measurement.	How many cm are there in 1 m? How many m are there in 1 km? Is 200° less than half a turn?

1B

Unit 1B
Algebra and geometry

What it's all about?

- Forming and simplifying expressions
- Sequences and functions
- Geometry of parallel lines, triangles and quadrilaterals
- Midpoints

You will learn about:

- The different roles of letters in algebra
- Simplifying expressions, including use of power notation and brackets
- Using rules to generate sequences
- Different ways to represent a function
- Properties of quadrilaterals, triangles and congruent shapes
- Corresponding and alternate angles
- Finding the coordinates of the midpoint of a line segment

You will build your skills in:

- representing relationships between variables using algebra
- manipulating algebraic expressions
- identifying and using spatial relationships in 2 dimensions

Expressions

You will learn how to:
- Understand that letters play different roles in equations, formulae and functions; understand the meanings of *formula* and *function*.
- Understand that algebraic operations, including brackets, follow the same order as arithmetic operations; use index notation for small positive integer powers.
- Construct linear expressions.
- Simplify or transform linear expressions with integer coefficients; collect like terms; multiply a single term over a bracket.

Starting point

Do you remember ...?

- that letters can be used to represent unknown numbers or variables?

  For example, I think of a number, n, and add 3, my answer is 19. Write an equation for the number, n.

- the difference between a term, an expression and an equation?

  For example, is $3n + 1 = 13$ a term, an expression or an equation?

- how to find a power of 10?

  For example, what is the value of 10^3?

- that multiplication and division are performed before addition and subtraction?

  For example, work out $27 - 12 \div 3$.

- how to simplify expressions by collecting like terms?

  For example, simplify $2a + 3a - a$.

- how to multiply a constant over a bracket?

  For example, expand $4(n - 3)$.

This will also be helpful when you:

- substitute into expressions and formulae.
- solve linear equations.
- simplify and construct more complex expressions.
- factorise expressions by writing them with brackets.

Hook

The diagram shows a number pyramid.

The expression in each box is the sum of the expressions in the two boxes below it.

- Complete the number pyramid to find the expression in the top box.
- What other expressions can you get in the top box by rearranging the four expressions in the bottom row?
- Can you find four new expressions to put into the bottom row that make the top expression equal to $21n + 7$?

Equations, formulae and functions

Key terms

An **expression** connects numbers and variables with mathematical operations (such as $+$, $-$, $\times$ and $\div$). For example, $\frac{x}{2} + 2y - 5$. The value of this expression can be found for any given values of x and y.

An **equation** contains an equals sign $=$. It is a statement that shows that the two expressions on either side of the equals sign are equal. For example, $7x - 1 = x + 5$. In this equation, the letter x has a particular value that can be found ($x = 1$).

A **formula** is a type of equation that expresses the relationship between certain variable quantities. For example, area of rectangle = length × width or $A = ab$. The value of A can be found for any given values of a and b.

A **function** is a relationship that maps a set of input values to a set of output values. Each input should map to exactly one output value. For example, $x \mapsto 20 - x$. This relationship between the input (x) and output (y) could also be expressed as $y = 20 - x$.

Worked example 1

Is each of these an expression, an equation, a formula or a function?

a) $5n + 2 = 17$ **b)** $n \mapsto 5n$ **c)** $4(2a + b)$

d) $V = abc$, where V = volume, a = length, b = width and c = height

a) equation	$5n + 2 = 17$ contains an equals sign and the letter, n, represents a particular value that could be found ($n = 3$).	
b) function	$n \mapsto 5n$ is a function that maps each input value, n, to the value that is 5 times larger ($5n$).	
c) expression	$4(2a + b)$ is an expression containing a bracket. If the brackets are expanded, the expression is equivalent to $8a + 4b$.	
d) formula	$V = abc$ is a formula. It expresses the relationship between the volume of a cuboid and the cuboid's measurements.	

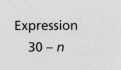

Exercise 1

1 Is each of these an expression, an equation, a formula or a function?

    a) $17 - 3m$　　　**b)** charge $= 25 \times$ number of hours　　　**c)** $5n = 35$

    d) $n \mapsto 2n + 1$　　**e)** $\frac{a}{4} + 2b - 3$　　　　　　　　　　　　　**f)** $x \mapsto \frac{x}{2}$

2 In which of these does n represent a particular fixed value?

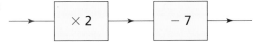

Expression	Function
$30 - n$	$n \mapsto 2n$

Equation	Formula
$2n - 3 = 7$	The cost, $\$C$, of buying n books is $C = 12n$

3 Which of these are functions?

    a) $t \mapsto 11 - t$　　**b)** $y + 2x - 3$　　**c)** $h + 5 = 2h$　　**d)** $x \mapsto 3x + 7$

4 Write the output of each function machine using the input letter shown.

    a)

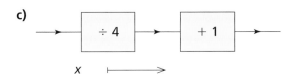

    b)

    c)

5 **a)** Use the internet to find:

      i) a formula for the average speed of an object from the distance it travels and the time it takes

      ii) a formula for the area of a trapezium

      iii) Euler's formula connecting the number of faces, edges and vertices of a 3D object.

    b) Can you find any other interesting formulae?

6 Nafisa says that $17 = 24 - n$ is a function. Explain why Nafisa is incorrect.

7 Decide if these statements are true or false. Try to explain each of your answers.

    a) An equation always contains an addition (+) or a subtraction (−) sign.

    b) An equation always contains an equals sign (=).

    c) If there is an equals sign (=) in an algebraic relationship, then it must be an equation.

Algebraic operations and index notation

Key terms

Powers can be used to simplify algebraic expressions when terms are multiplied. For example, n^3 means $n \times n \times n$.

The number 3 is called the power or **index** and it shows how many times n must be multiplied by itself.

Algebraic operations must follow the same order as those in arithmetic. The order in which operations must be applied is summarised as **BIDMAS**:

	Brackets first
then	**P**owers (or **I**ndices)
then	**D**ivision and **M**ultiplication
and finally	**A**ddition and **S**ubtraction

> **Did you know?**
>
> BIDMAS is sometimes known as BODMAS.

Worked example 2

a) Simplify $t \times t \times t \times t$.

b) Simplify $2 \times y \times y \times y$.

c) In the expression $4(u + 3)$, which operation is done to u first, $\times 4$ or $+ 3$?

a) t^4	t is multiplied by itself 4 times.	$t \times t \times t \times t = t^4$ 4 t's multiplied together
b) $2y^3$	y is multiplied by itself 3 times and then this is multiplied by 2.	$2 \times y \times y \times y = 2y^3$ 3 y's multiplied together
c) + 3 is done first as this is the operation in brackets.	The order of operations is BIDMAS so the operation in brackets is done first.	$u \longrightarrow \boxed{+\ 3} \longrightarrow \boxed{\times\ 4} \longrightarrow 4(u + 3)$

Exercise 2

1 Simplify each expression using powers.

    a) $h \times h \times h \times h$ **b)** $a \times a \times a$ **c)** $e \times e \times e \times e \times e$

    d) $j \times j$ **e)** $q \times q \times q \times q \times q \times q$ **f)** $n \times n \times n \times n \times n \times n \times n$

2 Match each expression to its simplified form.

A [$w \times w \times w$]   P [$3w^2$]

B [$w + w + w$]   Q [$6w$]

C [$3 \times w \times w$]   R [w^3]

D [$2w + 2w + 2w$]   S [$3w$]

3 Simplify using powers:

a) $4 \times r \times r$ **b)** $5 \times f \times f \times f$ **c)** $2 \times m \times m \times m \times m$

4 In each part, write down the part of the calculation that is performed first.

a) $3x + 5$ multiplication or addition

b) $\frac{x}{4} - 2$ division or subtraction

c) $2(x - 4)$ multiplication or brackets

d) $4a^3$ multiplication or power

e) $(x - 2)^2$ bracket or power

5 Here are two expressions:

$(4a)^2$ and $4a^2$

Are these two expressions equal? If not, how do they differ?

6 Convince a friend that $n^2 \times n^4$ is the same as n^6.

Tip

Think about what n^2, n^4 and n^6 mean.

Simplifying and expanding expressions

Worked example 3

Simplify:

a) $6p - 3q + 3 - 4p - 2q$

b) $4a^2 + 3a - 2a^2 - 9a$

c) $4n \times 2n$

a) $6p - 3q + 3 - 4p - 2q$ $= 6p - 4p - 3q - 2q + 3$ $= 2p - 5q + 3$	Identify the terms in p: $6p - 4p = 2p$ Identify the terms in q: $-3q - 2q = -5q$ Identify the constant terms, here just 3. Combine to get $2p - 5q + 3$	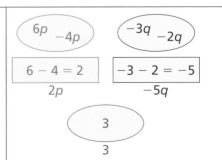

| **b)** $4a^2 + 3a - 2a^2 - 9a$
 $= 4a^2 - 2a^2 + 3a - 9a$
 $= 2a^2 - 6a$ | Identify the terms in a^2:
 $4a^2 - 2a^2 = 2a^2$
 Identify the terms in a:
 $3a - 9a = -6a$
 Combine to get $2a^2 - 6a$ | $4a^2 \quad -2a^2$ $\qquad$ $3a \quad -9a$
 $4 - 2 = 2$ $\qquad$ $3 - 9 = -6$
 $2a^2$ $\qquad\qquad$ $-6a$ |
| **c)** $4n \times 2n$
 $= 4 \times 2 \times n \times n$
 $= 8n^2$ | Multiply together the numbers and the letters and then combine. | $4 \times 2 = 8$ $\qquad$ $n \times n = n^2$
 8 $\qquad\qquad$ n^2
 $8n^2$ |

Think about

Does it matter in what order the terms in $2p - 5q + 3$ are written?

How else could the expression be written?

Worked example 4

Expand the brackets:

a) $n(n - 3)$ $\qquad$ **b)** $5p(2p + 3q)$

| **a)** $n(n - 3) = n^2 - 3n$ | Multiply both the terms inside the bracket by the term on the outside. | | n | $-$ | 3 |
 n | n^2 | $-$ | $3n$ |
| **b)** $5p(2p + 3q)$
 $= 10p^2 + 15pq$ | Multiply both terms inside the bracket by $5p$.
 $5p \times 2p = 5 \times 2 \times p \times p = 10p^2$
 $5p \times 3q = 5 \times 3 \times p \times q = 15pq$ | | $2p$ | $+$ | $3q$ |
 $5p$ | $10p^2$ | $+$ | $15pq$ |

Exercise 3

1 Simplify:

   a) $5n + 4 - 3n + 1 + 2n$ $\qquad$ **b)** $4a - 3b + 6a - 5b$

   c) $7u - 2 + u + 11 - 3u$ $\qquad$ **d)** $8t + 2 - 5t - 12$

   e) $e + 4f + 3e - 2f - 6f$ $\qquad$ **f)** $6g - 3h - 2g + 4h + 2$

   g) $9 + 4u - 4 - 7u + 3$ $\qquad$ **h)** $3 - 2r + q + 4 - 5r - 7q$

   i) $8c - 13 + 4d - 6c + d - 2 - 2c$ $\qquad$ **j)** $6a - 4b + 7c - b - 2c - 11a$

   k) $9a^2 - 3a + a^2 + 2a + 3$ $\qquad$ **l)** $4r - 9 - 6r^2 + 4 + 2r^2 - r$

2 Simplify:

a) $7 \times 6p$

b) $v \times 3 \times 6$

c) $5 \times 2p \times 3$

d) $5d \times d$

e) $7f \times 4f$

f) $9u \times 6u$

g) $4x \times 2 \times 5x$

h) $3 \times 5m \times 3m$

i) $8y \times 4z$

j) $a \times ab$

> **Discuss**
>
> The answer is $12a^2$. What could have been multiplied?

3 Expand the brackets:

a) $7(2a + 3b)$

b) $y(y + 9)$

c) $n(n - 6)$

d) $c(4c + 3d)$

e) $3g(g - 4)$

f) $5r(2r + 11)$

g) $6p(3p - 2q + 4)$

h) $2tu(6t - 3v)$

4 a) Find three equal pairs of expressions.

$6r(2r + 3)$	$8r^2 + 18r$	$3r(4r + 3)$	$6r + 9$
$2r(4r + 9)$	$12r^2 + 9r$	$8r + 18$	$12r^2 + 18r$

b) Write an equivalent expression for each of the two remaining expressions.

5 Expand and then simplify each expression.

a) $5(2t + 5) - 3t$

b) $6 + 3(2x - 7) + x$

c) $9(4m - n) + 3n$

d) $8(3e + f) - 4e - 11f$

6 Complete each statement correctly.

a) $6h + \ldots\ldots\ldots + \ldots\ldots\ldots + 7 = 8h + 11$

b) $2h - \ldots\ldots\ldots + \ldots\ldots\ldots + 4k = 5h + k$

c) $7c + \ldots\ldots\ldots - \ldots\ldots\ldots + 11 = 15 - 3c$

d) $5y - 4 - \ldots\ldots\ldots + \ldots\ldots\ldots = 1 - y$

e) $6h \times \ldots\ldots\ldots = 48h^2$

f) $\ldots\ldots\ldots \times 6n = 30n^2$

g) $4 \times \ldots\ldots\ldots \times 2k = 16k^2$

h) $\ldots\ldots\ldots(5p - \ldots\ldots\ldots) = 45p^2 - 18p$

7 Explain the mistake that has been made in each expansion.

a) $4(2n + 5) = 6n + 20$

b) $t(t + 3) = 2t + 3t$

c) $3r(2r - 5) = 6r^2 - 5$

8 Expand and simplify:

a) $3(4q - 7) + 2(9 - q)$

b) $2t(t - 5) - t^2 + 6t$

c) $4w(3w + x) + w - 5wx - w^2$

d) $3y(3y - 2) + 2y(7 - y)$

Worked example 5

A shop sells two different packets of biscuits.

Small	Large
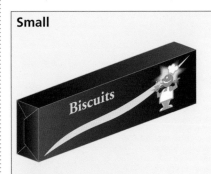	
Contains n biscuits Cost x dollars	Contains 10 more biscuits than a small packet Cost y dollars

Sara buys 3 small packets and 2 large packets.

Find an expression for:

   a) the total cost

   b) the total number of biscuits.

a) $3x + 2y$ dollars	The cost of 3 small packets is $3 \times x = 3x$ dollars. The cost of 2 large packets is $2 \times y = 2y$ dollars.		x	x	x	y	y	
			$3x$			$2y$		
			$3x + 2y$					

b) $3n + 2(n + 10)$ $= 3n + 2n + 20$ $= 5n + 20$	A large packet contains 10 more biscuits than a small packet. So a large packet contains $n + 10$ biscuits. 2 large packets will contain $2(n + 10) = 2n + 20$ biscuits.	n	n	n	$n + 10$	$n + 10$
		$3n$			$2n + 20$	
		$5n + 20$				

Exercise 4

1 Form a simplified expression for the perimeter of each shape. All lengths are measured in centimetres.

a)

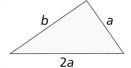

b)

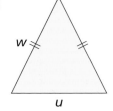

c)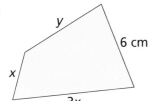

d)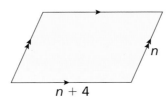

2 A plant pot costs \$x. A plant costs \$w.

Find an expression for:

a) the difference between the cost of a plant pot and the cost of a plant

b) the total cost of a plant pot and 8 plants.

3 The image shows the costs of tickets at a cinema.

Write down an expression for:

a) the cost of 4 adult tickets

b) the total cost of 2 child tickets and 1 adult ticket

c) the total cost of 3 child tickets, 4 student tickets and 2 adult tickets

d) the amount of change from \$50 if 3 adult tickets are bought.

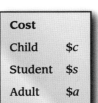

Cost	
Child	\$c
Student	\$s
Adult	\$a

4 A pizza costs \$p plus the cost of the toppings. Each topping costs \$t.

a) Find the cost of a pizza with 2 toppings.

b) Freddie orders a pizza with 3 toppings. Gina orders a pizza with 1 topping. Find the total cost of the two pizzas.

5 Martha has 2 litres of water. She fills 4 glasses. Each glass holds g litres of water. Write an expression for the amount of water she has left.

6 A baker has y grams of flour. A loaf of bread uses 400 grams of flour. How much flour does the baker have left after making n loaves?

7 A shop sells three types of badge.

A **red** badge has mass r grams.

The mass of a **blue** badge is 4 grams more than the mass of a red badge.

The mass of a **green** badge is three times the mass of a blue badge.

Find, in terms of r, an expression for:

a) the mass of a green badge

b) the total mass of 5 blue badges

c) the total mass of 6 red badges and 2 green badges.

8 Liam has m pens. Malik has twice as many pens as Liam. Noor has 3 more pens than Malik.

Omar has twice as many pens as Noor. Find an expression in terms of m for:

a) the number of pens than Noor has

b) the number of pens that Omar has

c) the difference between the number of pens Omar and Liam have

d) the total number of pens the four children have.

9 A packet contains n balloons. Nat buys 3 packets of balloons and shares them equally between 10 people. How many balloons does each person receive?

10 Cakes are sold in three different packs.

Small packs contain c cakes.

Medium packs contain 4 more cakes than a small pack.

Large packs contain three times as many cakes as a small pack.

a) Safee buys $6c + 12$ cakes. Which packs could she have bought?

b) Thimba buys $9c + 4$ cakes. He buys 5 packs in total. Which packs does he buy?

11 Amol, Bea and Cadi are saving money for a holiday.

They start with $\$b$ in a bank account.

They **each** save $\$n$ each week.

The holiday costs $2000.

What does each of these expressions represent in this context?

a) $2000 - b$ b) $3n$ c) $2000 - b - 3nw$

End of chapter reflection

You should know that ...	You should be able to ...	Such as ...
A formula is a type of equation that gives the relationship between variable quantities. A function is a rule that maps an input value to a corresponding output value.	Recognise expressions, equations, functions and formulae.	A shop uses this rule to calculate the charge, $\$C$, of delivering n items: $C = 15 + 3n$ Is this an expression, an equation, a function or a formula?
The order for performing operations in algebra and arithmetic is given by BIDMAS.	Recognise the order in which operations are performed.	In the expression $3(g - 2)$, which operation is done to g first: $- 2$ or $\times 3$?
An index (or power) tells you how many times a letter is multiplied together.	Write expressions in index form.	Write $p \times p \times p$ as a power of p.
You can simplify an expression by collecting together like terms.	Simplify an expression involving positive and negative terms.	Simplify: $14x - 9y - 6x - 3 + y$
You can expand a bracket by multiplying all the terms inside the bracket by the expression on the outside.	Expand a bracket.	Expand: $5f(2f - 3)$
You can construct expressions using letters to represent unknown quantities.	Form an expression to represent a situation.	A tank contains t litres of water. Every hour n litres of water is taken out. Write an expression for the amount of water in the tank after 5 hours?

Sequences and functions

You will learn how to:

- Generate terms of a linear sequence using term-to-term and position-to-term rules; find term-to-term and position-to-term rules of sequences, including spatial patterns.
- Express simple functions algebraically and represent them in mappings.

Starting point

Do you remember …?

- how to continue simple integer sequences?
  For example, what is the 7th term in the sequence that begins 11, 20, 29, 38…?

- how to describe a simple integer sequence using a term-to-term rule?
  For example, what is the term-to-term rule for the sequence 5, 15, 45, 135, …?

- how to describe the general term for spatial patterns?
  For example, what is the rule for finding the number of circles in any pattern in the sequence below?

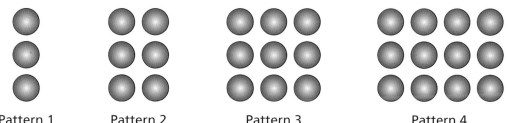

Pattern 1   Pattern 2   Pattern 3   Pattern 4

- how to work with functions expressed in words or symbols, or shown as mapping diagrams?
  For example, what is the output when 6 is used as the input for the function $x \mapsto 3x + 5$?

This will also be helpful when you:

- learn how to write an algebraic expression for any term in the sequence.
- find the inverse of a function.

Hook

Eloa and Mancio receive money each birthday.

> Eloa receives $7.50 on her first birthday.
> The amount she receives increases by $1.50 each year.

> The amount (in $) Mancio receives on each birthday is given by the formula
> 0.5 × age + 11

- How much money does Eloa receive on each of her first five birthdays?
- Who receives the most money on their 10th birthday?
- Who receives the most money in total for their first 10 birthdays?

Generating sequences

Did you know?

Some sequences occur naturally in nature. Search the internet to find out how sunflowers and pineapples are related to the Fibonacci sequence.

Key terms

A **linear sequence** is one that increases or decreases by the same amount each time.

A linear sequence can be described by a **term-to-term** rule or by a **position-to-term** rule.

A linear sequence is also known as an arithmetic sequence.

Worked example 1

a) The first term of a sequence is 4.7.

   The term-to-term rule is '**subtract 0.4**'.

   Find the 5th term.

b) The position-to-term rule of a different sequence is '**multiply by 3 and then add 2**'.

   Find the first 3 terms of this sequence.

c) Here are the first four terms of a sequence: 4, 9, 14, 19, …

   Complete the position-to-term rule for the sequence.

   'Multiply by ….. and then subtract ….. '

a) The 5th term is 3.1.	The term-to-term rule tells you how to go from one term to the next. Here you subtract 0.4 every time.	1st term: 4.7, 4.3, 3.9, 3.5, 5th term: 3.1 (−0.4 each time)
b) The first 3 terms are 5, 8, 11.	To get the 1st term, apply the rule 'multiply by 3 and add 2' to 1. To get the 2nd and 3rd terms, apply the rule to 2 and 3.	Position number → × 3 → + 2 → Term in sequence: 1 ×3 3 +2 5; 2 ×3 6 +2 8; 3 ×3 9 +2 11
c) The position-to-term rule is 'multiply by 5 and then subtract 1'.	The terms in the sequence increase by 5 each time, so the sequence is based on the 5 times table. To get the terms in the sequence, you then need to subtract 1.	Position number → 5 × table → Term in sequence: 1 ×5 5 −1 4; 2 ×5 10 −1 9; 3 ×5 15 −1 14; 4 ×5 20 −1 19

Worked example 2

Here are the first four patterns in a sequence.

  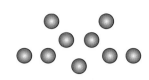 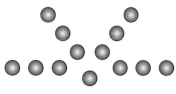

Pattern 1   Pattern 2   Pattern 3   Pattern 4

a) Write down the term-to-term rule for the sequence.

b) Find the position-to-term rule for the number of circles in any pattern.

c) Work out the number of circles in Pattern 15.

a)	The term-to-term rule is **add 4**.	Find the number of circles in each of the patterns. To go from one pattern to the next, 4 circles are added.	Pattern 1 → Pattern 2 → Pattern 3 → Pattern 4 : 1, 5, 9, 13 (+4, +4, +4)
b)	The position-to-term rule is '**multiply by 4 and then subtract 3**'.	The terms in the sequence increase in 4s, so the terms are related to numbers in the 4 times table. The terms in the sequence are 3 less than the 4 times table.	Pattern number / 4 × table / Term in sequence: 1 × 4 = 4, − 3 = 1; 2 × 4 = 8, − 3 = 5; 3 × 4 = 12, − 3 = 9; 4 × 4 = 16, − 3 = 13
c)	15 × 4 − 3 = 57	Apply the position-to-term rule to 15.	Pattern number / 4 × table / Term in sequence: 15 × 4 = 60, − 3 = 57

Exercise 1   1–8, 10–13

1 Write down the next three terms in each sequence.

a) 67, 78, 89, 100, …

b) 101, 95, 89, 83, …

c) −17, −13, −9, −5, …

d) 19, 14, 9, 4, …

e) 1.2, 1.5, 1.8, 2.1, …

f) 3.2, 2.8, 2.4, 2, …

g) $2\frac{1}{2}$, 4, $5\frac{1}{2}$, 7,…

h) $\frac{1}{7}$, $\frac{5}{7}$, $\frac{9}{7}$, $\frac{13}{7}$,…

2 Write down the term-to-term rule for each sequence and use it to find the 7th term each time.

a) 130, 118, 106, 94, …

b) 19, 28, 37, 46, …

c) 17, 11, 5, −1, …

d) −25, −18, −11, −4, …

e) 3.1, 3.6, 4.1, 4.6, …

f) $3\frac{1}{2}$, $3\frac{1}{4}$, 3, $2\frac{3}{4}$, …

3 Use the given information to find the required term in each of these sequences.

a) 1st term = 3.2, term-to-term rule = add 0.4   Find the 4th term.

b) 1st term = 2.8, term-to-term rule = subtract 0.3   Find the 5th term.

c) 1st term = $\frac{1}{10}$, term-to-term rule = add $\frac{3}{10}$ Find the 5th term.

d) 4th term = 5.3, term-to-term rule = add 0.6   Find the 1st term.

e) 8th term = −15, term-to-term rule = subtract 9   Find the 3rd term.

4 The rule for generating a sequence is:

term in sequence = 3 × position number + 7.

Find the terms that are in the following positions:

a) position 1   b) position 4

c) position 10   d) position 20

5 Find the first five terms in the sequences generated by these **position-to-term rules**:

a) multiply by 4   b) multiply by 9

c) multiply by 3 and then add 4   d) multiply by 5 and then subtract 3

e) divide by 2 and then add 5   f) divide by 5 and then add 2

> **Think about**
>
> Does the position to term rule 'multiply by 3 and then add 4' give a different sequence to the rule 'add 4 and then multiply by 3'?

6 How are these sequences related to the numbers in the 7 times table?

a) 8, 15, 22, 29, …   b) 17, 24, 31, 38, …

c) 5, 12, 19, 26, …   d) 1, 8, 15, 22, …

7 Copy and complete the table.

Sequence	Position-to-term rule	10th term
3, 6, 9, 12, …	multiply by …..	
5, 6, 7, 8, …	add …..	
6, 10, 14, 18, …	multiply by 4 and add …..	
9, 11, 13, 15, …	multiply by ….. and add …..	
7, 14, 21, 28, …		
2, 8, 14, 20, …		
10, 13, 16, 19, …		
11, 20, 29, 38, …		

8 Here is some information about three sequences.

Juan's sequence	Laila's sequence	Dominik's sequence
The position-to-term rule is **'multiply by 4 and add 3'.**	The position-to-term rule is **'multiply by 6 and subtract 10'.**	The term-to-term rule is **'subtract 6'.**

a) Find the 20th term in Juan's sequence.

b) Laila says, "The 6th term in my sequence is greater than the 6th term in Juan's sequence." Show that Laila is wrong.

c) The 4th term in Laila's sequence is equal to the 4th term in Dominik's sequence. Find the 1st term in Dominik's sequence.

9 Makato and Dai save some money each month.

The amount that Makato saves each month is given by the formula

$$6 \times \text{month number} + 20.$$

The amount Dai saves in the first month is $12.50.

She increases the amount she saves by $7.50 per month.

They save money each month for two years.

a) Set up a spreadsheet to find the amount of money Makato and Dai save every month over the two years. The first few rows of a possible spreadsheet are shown.

	A	B	C
1	Month number	Makato	Dai
2	1	= 6 * A2 + 20	12.50
3	2	= 6 * A3 + 20	= C2 + 7.50
4	3		

> **Tip**
> You can use the SUM function to add up all the numbers in a column of a spreadsheet.

b) Who saves more money in total over the two years? How much more does this person save?

10 Here are some of the patterns in a sequence made from squares.

a) Draw Pattern 3.

b) Find the term-to-term rule for the sequence.

c) Work out the number of squares needed to make Pattern 7.

 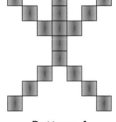

Pattern 1   Pattern 2   Pattern 3   Pattern 4

11 For each of these spatial patterns:

• Draw the next diagram.

• Find how many squares are needed to make Pattern 7.

• Find the position-to-term rule to find the number of squares in any diagram.

• Find the number of squares in Pattern 25.

a)

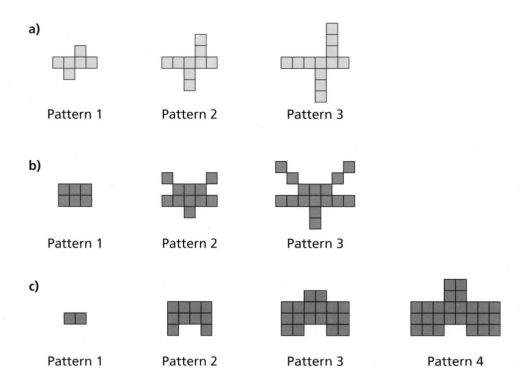

Pattern 1   Pattern 2   Pattern 3

b)

Pattern 1   Pattern 2   Pattern 3

c)

Pattern 1   Pattern 2   Pattern 3   Pattern 4

12 These three patterns are made from circular tiles. The patterns are the first three terms in a sequence.

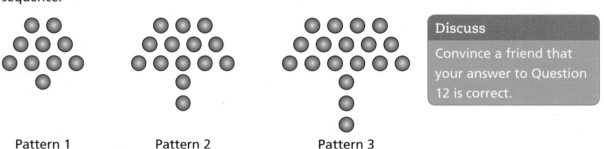

Pattern 1   Pattern 2   Pattern 3

> **Discuss**
>
> Convince a friend that your answer to Question 12 is correct.

How many tiles are needed to make Pattern 100?

13 Here are the first three patterns in a sequence formed from blue and yellow tiles.

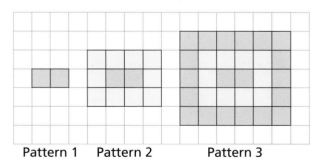

Pattern 1   Pattern 2   Pattern 3

> **Tip**
>
> Think about what length and width the 50th rectangle will be.

Find the total number of tiles in Pattern 50.

Functions and mappings

Key terms

A function can be represented in different ways:

As a **number machine**

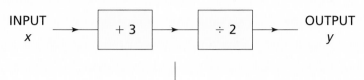

INPUT x → [+ 3] → [÷ 2] → OUTPUT y

Algebraically

$$x \longmapsto \frac{x + 3}{2}$$

or as a formula

$$y = \frac{x + 3}{2}$$

Add 3 then divide by 2

As an **input-output table**

INPUT	OUTPUT
1	2
2	2.5
3	3

As a **mapping diagram**

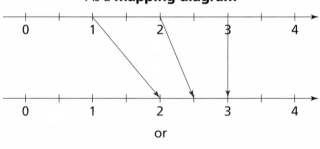

or

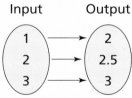

| Input | Output |

The input-output table for a function is shown below.

Input	Output
1	−1
2	2
3	5
4	8

a) Describe in words the rule that maps each input value to the corresponding output value.

b) Write a formula to connect the output, y, with the input value, x.

a) The rule is 'multiply by 3 and then subtract 4'.	The difference between the input values is 1 and the difference between the output values is 3. This tells you that the first part of the rule is 'multiply by 3'. To map 4 to 8, the entire rule must be 'multiply by 3 and then subtract 4'.	input values are 1 apart output values are 3 apart
b) The function can be written as the formula $y = 3x - 4$.	The rule can be shown as a number machine. When x is fed through the number machine, the output is the expression $3x - 4$. We write this as $x \mapsto 3x - 4$ or $y = 3x - 4$.	INPUT x → ×3 → $3x$ → −4 → OUTPUT $y = 3x - 4$

Exercise 2

1 Here are some functions expressed as number machine. Express each function algebraically in the form $x \mapsto$

a)

b)

c)

d)

e)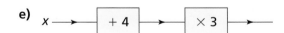

f) x → −5 → ÷4 →

2 Here are some functions. For each function:
- draw the matching number machine
- complete an input-output table.

Input, x	Output, y
1	
2	
3	
4	

a) $x \mapsto 5x + 4$ **b)** $y = 7x - 2$ **c)** $y = \frac{x}{2} + 1$

d) $x \mapsto 4(x - 3)$ **e)** $y = 5(x + 6)$ **f)** $x \mapsto \frac{3x}{2}$

3 a) Find the outputs when 0, 1, 2 and 3 are used as the inputs in the function

$$x \mapsto 2(x - 1).$$

b) Show your answers to part a) on a mapping diagram.

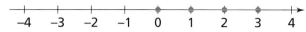

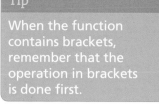

Tip

When the function contains brackets, remember that the operation in brackets is done first.

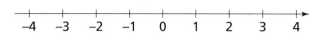

4 A function is represented by the number machine:

$$\text{INPUT } x \longrightarrow \boxed{\times 10} \longrightarrow \boxed{-9} \longrightarrow y \text{ OUTPUT}$$

a) Find the output, y, when the input is $x = 0.3$.

b) Find the input when the output is $y = 31$.

c) Write the relationship between the input, x, and output, y, as a formula.

5 Copy and complete the table.

	Function	Formula	Mapping diagram
a)	$x \mapsto \dfrac{x+1}{4}$	$y = \dfrac{x+1}{4}$	15, 27, 5 →
b)	$x \mapsto \dfrac{x-5}{3}$		14, 38, 95 →
c)		$y = \dfrac{2x}{5}$	10, 35, 45 →
d)	$x \mapsto \dfrac{4x-8}{6}$		11, 20, 3.5 →

6 Match each function to the corresponding number machine.

A → [2] → [+ 1] → [× 3] →

B → [+ 1] → [× 2] → [÷ 3] →

C → [+ 1] → [× 2] → [÷ 3] →

D → [÷ 3] → [+ 1] → [× 2] →

$x \longmapsto \dfrac{2x + 1}{3}$ W

$x \longmapsto \dfrac{2(x + 1)}{3}$ X

$x \longmapsto 2\left(\dfrac{x}{3} + 1\right)$ Y

$x \longmapsto 3(2x + 1)$ Z

7 For each number machine:
- Express the relationship between the input and output as a formula.
- Find the output when the input is 11.

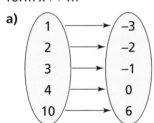

a) INPUT $x \rightarrow$ [× 6] → [− 4] → [÷ 2] → y OUTPUT

b) INPUT $x \rightarrow$ [+ 1] → [× 2] → [÷ 6] → y OUTPUT

c) INPUT $x \rightarrow$ [+ 4] → [÷ 3] → [+ 7] → y OUTPUT

8 Find the function that corresponds to each of these mapping diagrams. Give each answer in the form $x \mapsto \ldots$

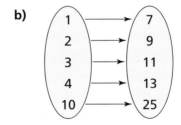

a)
| 1 → −3 |
| 2 → −2 |
| 3 → −1 |
| 4 → 0 |
| 10 → 6 |

b)
| 1 → 7 |
| 2 → 9 |
| 3 → 11 |
| 4 → 13 |
| 10 → 25 |

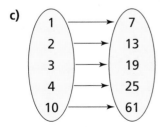

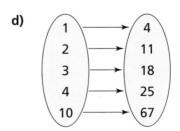

c)
| 1 → 7 |
| 2 → 13 |
| 3 → 19 |
| 4 → 25 |
| 10 → 61 |

d)
| 1 → 4 |
| 2 → 11 |
| 3 → 18 |
| 4 → 25 |
| 10 → 67 |

9 Here is a mapping diagram for a function. Find the missing value.

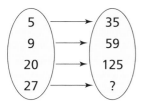

10 Vocabulary feature question

Find the mathematical words that match these definitions.

The number or expression that comes out of a number machine when something is fed in.	O _____
A relationship between input numbers and output numbers	F _____
A diagram that shows the relationship between some input numbers and the corresponding output numbers	M _____ D _____
An algebraic way to give the relationship between inputs and outputs.	F _____

End of chapter reflection

You should know that ...	You should be able to ...	Such as ...
A linear sequence can be defined by a term-to-term rule or a position-to-term rule.	Use and find a term-to-term rule of a linear sequence. Use and find a position-to-term rule of a linear sequence. Use term-to-term and position-to-term rules in connection with spatial patterns.	Find the 8th term of the sequence that begins 16, 10, 4, ... Find the position-to-term rule of a sequence that begins 16, 20, 24, ... Find a rule for the number of dots in any pattern in this sequence:
Functions can be specified in several ways, including as number machines and algebraically.	Find an algebraic rule that matches a number machine. Find a formula that matches a mapping diagram.	A function is defined by the number machine $\rightarrow$ +7 $\rightarrow$ ÷5 $\rightarrow$ Write this function in the form $x \mapsto$ .... For the mapping diagram, write the relationship between the inputs (x) and outputs (y) as a formula. 1 → −1 2 → 5 3 → 11 4 → 17

Shapes

You will learn how to:

- Recognise that if two 2D shapes are congruent, corresponding sides and angles are equal.
- Classify quadrilaterals according to their properties, including diagonal properties.
- Recognise that the longest side of a right-angled triangle is called the hypotenuse.
- Identify alternate angles and corresponding angles.

Starting point

Do you remember …?

- the conventions for labelling points, sides and angles of shapes?
  For example, in a triangle *ABC*, what are the labels for the two sides that form angle *ABC*?

- the terms parallel lines and perpendicular lines?
  For example, what is the name for lines that meet at right angles?

- the names of special triangles and quadrilaterals?
  For example, what types of quadrilaterals have four equal sides?

- how to find a missing angle in a triangle or a quadrilateral?
  For example, if two of the angles in a triangle are 100° and 30°, what is the third angle?

This will be helpful when you:

- solve problems that involve finding the sizes of angles in diagrams showing parallel lines, triangles and quadrilaterals
- find the lengths of sides in right-angled triangles.

Hook

Here is a tangram puzzle.

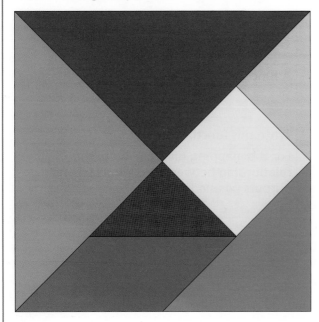

Cut a copy of the tangram into the 7 separate pieces.

Task 1: Arrange the 7 pieces to make 2 squares that are exactly the same size.

Task 2: Use the square piece and 4 triangles to make a parallelogram.

Task 3: Use some or all of the pieces to make other types of quadrilateral.

Right-angled triangles and congruent shapes

Key terms

The **hypotenuse** is the longest side in a **right-angled triangle**. It is the side opposite the right angle.

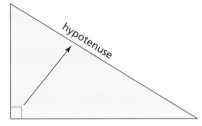

Two shapes are called **congruent** if they have exactly the same shape and size. In congruent shapes, corresponding sides and angles are equal.

Worked example 1

Here are two congruent triangles.

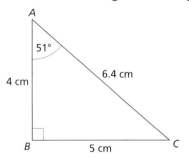

Not to scale

a) Which side in triangle *ABC* is the hypotenuse?

b) Write down the length of side *PR*.

c) Find the size of angle *RPQ*.

a) *AC* is the hypotenuse.	The hypotenuse is the side opposite the right angle.	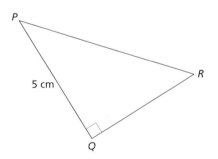

b) PR = 6.4 cm	PR is the hypotenuse in triangle PRQ. As the triangles are congruent, it must have the same length as the hypotenuse in triangle ABC.	
c) Angle $RPQ = 39°$	Corresponding angles in congruent triangles are equal. Angle RPQ is the angle that is between the hypotenuse and the 5 cm side. This corresponds to angle ACB, which is 39° (because the angles in a triangle add to 180°).	

Exercise 1

1 Write down the length of the hypotenuse in the right-angled triangles with sides of length:

   a) 18 cm, 24 cm and 30 cm   **b)** 29 cm, 20 cm and 21 cm   **c)** 11 cm, 61 cm and 60 cm.

2 Which side in each right-angled triangle is the hypotenuse?

  a) 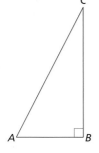   **b)** 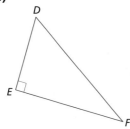   **c)**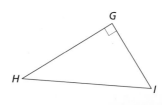

3 The diagram shows some triangles drawn on a dotted grid.

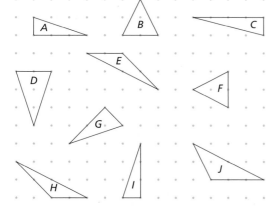

> **Tip**
>
> Remember that the word hypotenuse is only used in connection with right-angled triangles.

Find three pairs of congruent triangles.

4 The diagram shows a hexagon divided into 17 triangles.

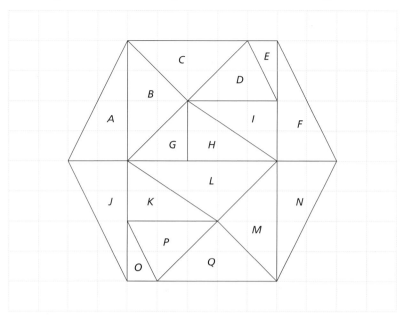

a) Write down the letters of all the triangles that are congruent to triangle C.

b) Which triangle is congruent to triangle D?

c) Which two triangles are congruent to triangle H?

5 These two triangles are congruent.

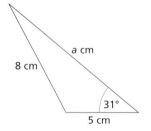

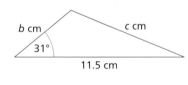

Not to scale

Write down the values of a, b and c.

6 Triangle ABC is congruent to triangle LMN.

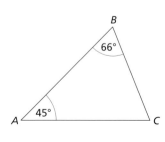

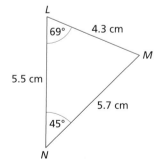

Not to scale

Find:

a) angle LMN

b) the length of BC

c) the length of AB.

7 Which of the following triangles is congruent to triangle *T*?

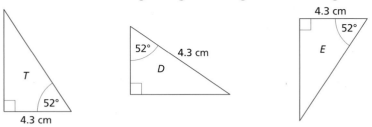

Discuss

Explain why the other triangles in Question 7 are not congruent to *T*.

Not to scale

Tip

Remember that the angles in any quadrilateral add up to 360°.

8 The two quadrilaterals are congruent.

Write down:

a) the length of *CD*

b) the length of *WX*

c) the length of *YZ*

d) the size of angle *XWZ*

e) the size of angle *BCD*.

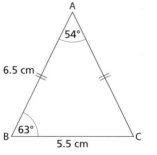

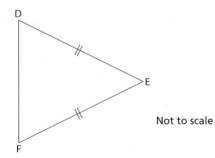

Not to scale

9 Here are two congruent isosceles triangles.

Write down:

a) the length of *DF*

b) the length of *DE*

c) the size of angle *FDE*

d) the size of angle *DEF*.

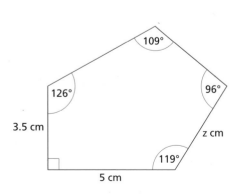

Not to scale

10 The two pentagons are congruent.

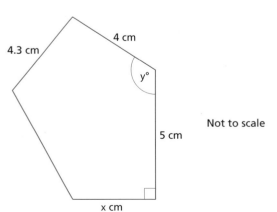

Not to scale

Find the values of *x*, *y* and *z*.

11 Channa says these two triangles are congruent.

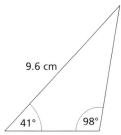

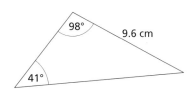

Not to scale

Is Channa correct? Explain your answer.

12 Here is a description of a quadrilateral:

Two sides measure 3 cm and two sides measure 7 cm.

Noor says that all quadrilaterals matching this description must be congruent. Draw diagrams to show that Noor is wrong.

13 Here are descriptions of two right-angled triangles, R and S.

Triangle R	Triangle S
The hypotenuse measures 10 cm. One of the other sides measures 6 cm.	One side measures 10 cm. Two of the angles are 25° and 65°.

By drawing accurate diagrams, decide whether triangles R and S could be congruent to each other.

Quadrilaterals

Key terms

The **diagonals** of a quadrilateral are the lines that connect one vertex of a quadrilateral to the opposite vertex.

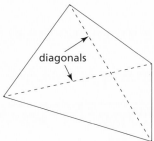

The diagonals of a quadrilateral **bisect** each other if one diagonal cuts the other exactly in half.

Properties of quadrilaterals

A **square** has four equal sides and angles. Opposite sides are parallel.

The diagonals of a square are equal in length, are perpendicular and bisect each other.

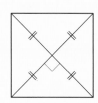

A **rectangle** has four equal angles. Opposite sides are parallel and equal in length.

The diagonals of a rectangle are equal in length and bisect each other.

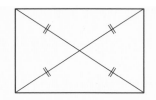

A **rhombus** has four equal sides. Opposite sides are parallel and opposite angles are equal.

The diagonals of a rhombus are perpendicular and bisect each other.

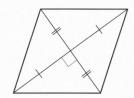

In a **parallelogram**, opposite sides are parallel and equal in length. Opposite angles are equal.

The diagonals of a parallelogram bisect each other.

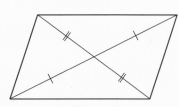

A **trapezium** has one pair of parallel lines.

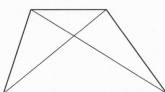

In an **isosceles trapezium**, the two non-parallel sides are equal in length. The diagonals in an isosceles trapezium are equal in length.

A **kite** has two pairs of equal, adjacent sides. One pair of opposite angles are equal.

The diagonals of a kite are perpendicular. One of the diagonals bisects the other.

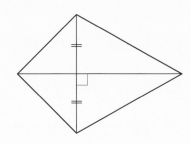

Worked example 2

a) Abdul thinks of a quadrilateral. It has rotational symmetry and diagonals that are perpendicular.

 What types of quadrilateral could Abdul be thinking of?

b) Write down one property about the diagonals of a rectangle that parallelograms do not generally have.

a) Square or rhombus	The types of quadrilateral with rotational symmetry are: Square Rectangle Rhombus Parallelogram Of these, the diagonals are perpendicular only in a square or a rhombus.	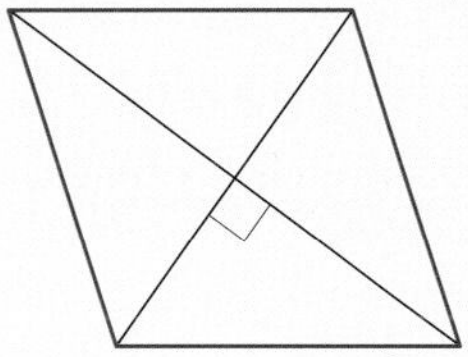 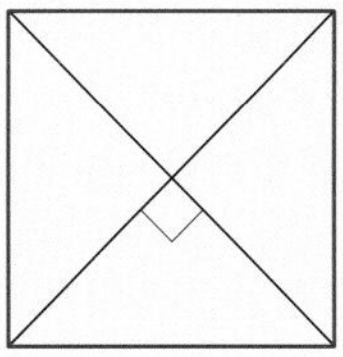
b) The diagonals of a rectangle are the same length.	The diagonals of a rectangle bisect each other and are equal in length. One diagonal of a parallelogram is longer than the other.	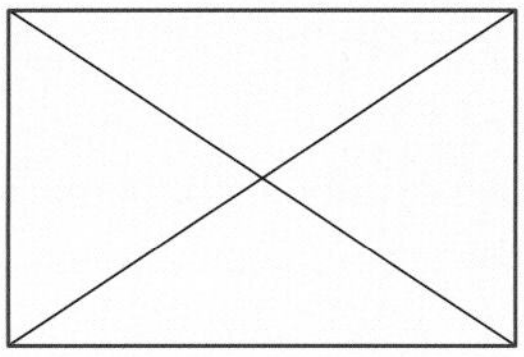 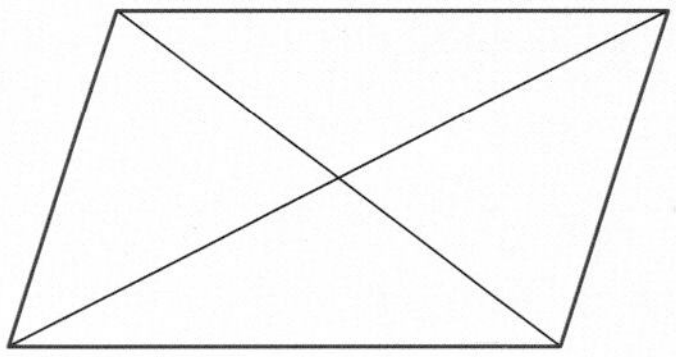

Did you know?

If the opposite angles of a quadrilateral add up to 180°, then it is possible to draw a circle that passes through all four of the vertices.

Exercise 2

1 Here are some properties relating to quadrilaterals.

Property A	Property B	Property C
Two pairs of equal length sides	At least one line of symmetry	Diagonals that are equal in length

Write down which of these properties, if any, the following quadrilaterals have.

a) kite   b) rectangle   c) trapezium

d) parallelogram   e) rhombus

2 Write down all the types of quadrilateral with the following property:

Each diagonal bisects the other.

Tip

There are 4 types of quadrilateral to find in Question 2.

3 Draw a quadrilateral with exactly one line of symmetry and diagonals that are equal in length.

4 Write down a property about the diagonals of a square that is not shared by all rectangles.

5 Copy and complete these quadrilaterals so that they have the property given.

a)

4 equal sides

b)

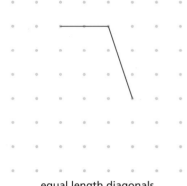

equal length diagonals

6 Copy this table.

	Diagonals are perpendicular	Diagonals are not perpendicular
Rotational symmetry		
No rotational symmetry		

Write the name of one type of quadrilateral in each cell in the table.

7 Clive describes a type of quadrilateral:

'One diagonal is longer than the other.

It has two lines of symmetry.'

Write down the name of the quadrilateral.

8 Maria draws a quadrilateral with angles of 50°, 70°, 80° and 160°.

She says, 'My quadrilateral is a kite.'

Explain how you can tell that she is wrong.

9 The diagram shows two sides of a quadrilateral.

A teacher asks her class to complete the quadrilateral to make a shape with diagonals that are perpendicular.

Max says that it can't be done. Is he correct? Explain your answer.

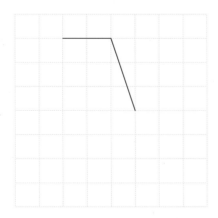

10 Explain why a rhombus is a special type of kite.

Alternate and corresponding angles

When a transversal crosses two (or more) parallel lines it forms sets of equal angles.

Alternate angles appear on opposite sides of the transversal:

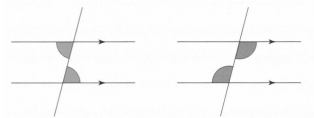

Alternate angles are **equal**.

Corresponding angles appear on the same side of the transversal:

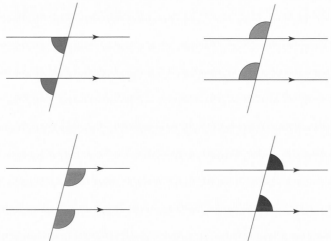

Corresponding angles are also equal.

Worked example 3

a) What name is given to the two shaded angles?

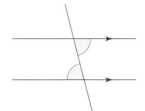

b) Find the sizes of angles *x* and *y*.

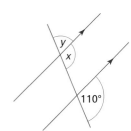

a) The angles are alternate angles.	The shaded angles form a Z-shape. They are on opposite sides of the transversal so are alternate angles.	
b) $x = 110°$ $y = 70°$	The angle marked x is corresponding to the 110° angle (the angles form a F-shape). The angles marked x and y form a straight line so add to 180°. So $y = 180 - 110 = 70°$.	

Exercise 3

The diagrams in Questions 5–11 are not to scale.

1 **a)** Draw each of these diagrams using dynamic geometry software. Measure each angle.

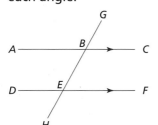 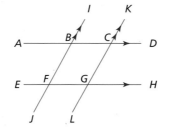

b) For each diagram write down two pairs of alternate angles and two pairs of corresponding angles.

Tip

If you don't have access to dynamic geometry software, draw each diagram on paper and measure the angles using a protractor.

2 Write down whether the marked angles are alternate angles or corresponding angles.

a) 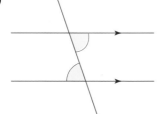   **b)** 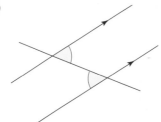   **c)**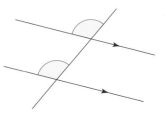

d)

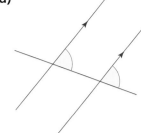

e)

f)

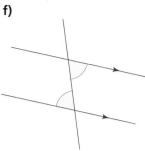

g)

h)

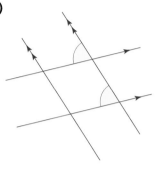

3 Which of these diagrams show corresponding angles?

Diagram 1

Diagram 2

Diagram 3

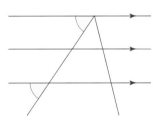

4 Which of the diagrams show alternate angles?

Diagram 1

Diagram 2

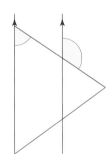

Diagram 3

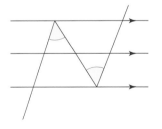

5 Find the size of each angle marked with a letter.

a)

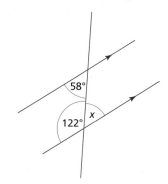

b)

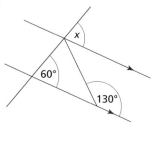

c)

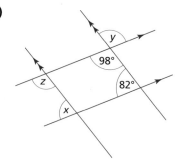

d)

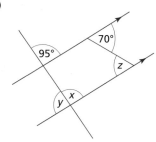

e)

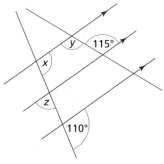

6 Here is a diagram involving parallel lines.

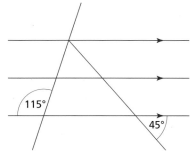

> **Think about**
>
> In the diagram in Question 7 Angles *CBE* and *FEB* are known as co-interior angles. What is the relationship between them?

Copy the diagram and mark on all the angles equal to 115° and all the angles equal to 45°.

7 The diagram is formed from two sets of parallel lines.
Say whether each statement is true or false.

a) Angles *CAG* and *FDG* are corresponding angles

b) Angle *HBC* = angle *BED*

c) Angles *BED* and *EDG* are alternate angles

d) Angle *BED* = 55°

e) Angles *ADF* and *ABE* are corresponding angles

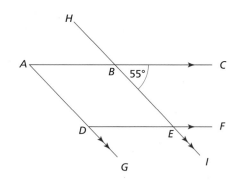

8 Find the size of each lettered angle. For each answer, say whether you are using corresponding angles or alternate angles.

a)

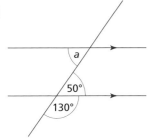

b)

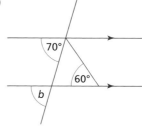

c)

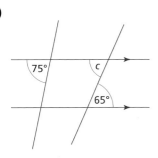

d)

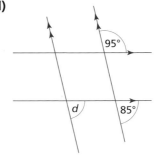

9 The diagram shows angles marked *a* to *k*.
Write down the letter of the angle that is:

a) alternate to *g*

b) corresponding to *b*

c) corresponding to *a*

d) alternate to *h*

e) corresponding to *j*.

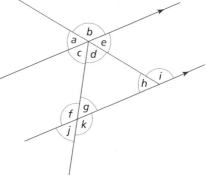

10 Are the lines *AB* and *CD* parallel? Explain your answer.

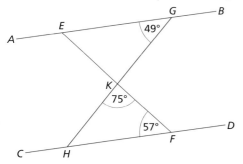

11 The diagram shows two right-angled triangles, *ABC* and *BCD*.
Copy the diagram and fill in the sizes of all the marked angles.

Vocabulary feature question

Complete the text using words from the box.

corresponding	alternate	equal
parallel	transversal	

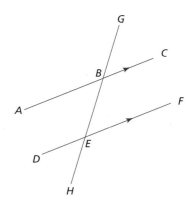

The lines *AC* and *DF* are _____ lines. They are crossed

by the line *GH* which is called a _____ . Angles *ABH* and

DEH are known as _____ angles. Angles *ABH* and *GEF*

are known as _____ angles. Corresponding angles and

alternate angles are _____ .

End of chapter reflection

You should know that ...	You should be able to ...	Such as ...
The hypotenuse is the longest side of a right-angled triangle.	Identify which of the sides in a right-angled triangle is the hypotenuse.	Write down the length of the hypotenuse in this triangle. 5 cm, 13 cm, 12 cm
Corresponding sides and angles are equal in congruent shapes.	Find side lengths and angles in congruent shapes by identifying corresponding sides.	If the two quadrilaterals are congruent, find the length of *AB* and the size of angle *ADC*. 5.6 cm, 3 cm, 50°, 3.2 cm, 3 cm, A, B, C, D
The diagonals of a quadrilateral join a vertex to its opposite vertex.	Identify a quadrilateral from some of its properties.	What type of quadrilateral has all these properties? the two diagonals bisect each other one diagonal is longer than the other the diagonals are not perpendicular

When a transversal crosses a pair of parallel lines, corresponding angles and alternate angles are equal.	Spot corresponding and alternate angles.	Which angle (*a*, *b*, *c* or *d*) is the corresponding angle to the angle marked yellow?

Midpoints

You will learn how to:

- Find the midpoint of the line segment *AB*, given the coordinates of points *A* and *B*.

Starting point

Do you remember …?

- how to give the coordinates of a point on a grid?
  For example, can you write the coordinates of points *A* and *B*?

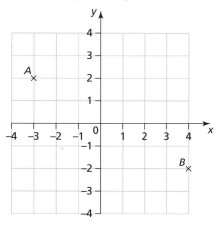

- how to add and subtract negative integers?
  For example, can you find the difference between 9 and −3?

- how to find the mean value of two numbers?
  For example, can you find the mean of 8 and −2?

This will also be helpful when you:

- find the perpendicular bisector of a line segment.

Hook

Here is a triangle *ABC*.

Copy the diagram onto squared paper.

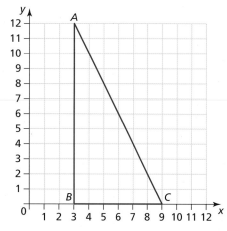

Use a ruler to mark the points *P*, *Q* and *R* onto your diagram, where:

> *P* is on the side *AB*, halfway between *A* and *B*
>
> *Q* is on the side *BC*, halfway between *B* and *C*
>
> *R* is on the side *AC*, halfway between *A* and *C*.

Draw the lines *AQ* and *BR*. These lines are both called medians of the triangle and the point where they meet is called the centroid. What are the coordinates of the centroid?

Draw the third median line *CP*. What do you notice about all three median lines?

Midpoint of a line segment

Key terms

A **line segment** is a section of a line. It has two end points.

The **midpoint** of a line segment is the point on it that is the same distance from both end points. It is halfway along the line segment.

Worked example 1

A and *B* are the points with coordinates (−2, 5) and (4, 2).

Find the coordinates of the midpoint of the line segment *AB*.

$\frac{-2+4}{2} = \frac{2}{2} = 1$ $\frac{5+2}{2} = \frac{7}{2} = 3.5$ So the coordinates of the midpoint are (1, 3.5).	Find the mean of the *x* coordinates of *A* and *B*. Then find the mean of the *y* coordinates.	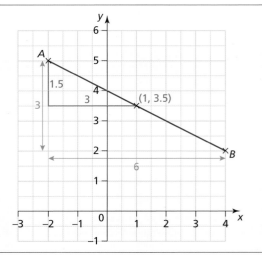

1 Write down the coordinates of the midpoint of each line segment *AB*.

a)

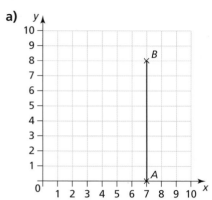

b)

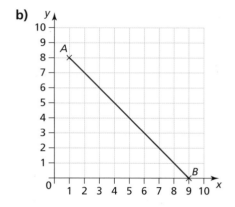

c)

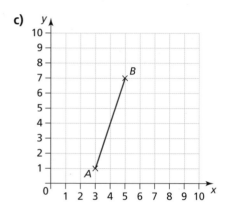

d)

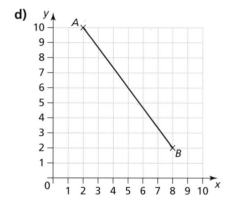

2 Write down the coordinates of the midpoint of the line segment joining each pair of points.

a) *A* and *B*

b) *A* and *C*

c) *B* and *C*

d) *B* and *E*

e) *A* and *D*

f) *C* and *E*

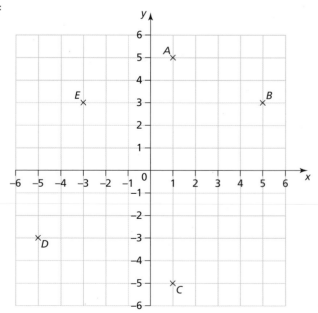

3 Find the midpoint of the line segment joining each pair of points.

a) (0, 6) and (8, 4)   b) (9, 2) and (1, 12)   c) (7, 5) and (2, 13)

d) (3, 2) and (10, 7)   e) (–1, 6) and (9, –10)   f) (9, –4) and (12, 16)

g) (13, 5) and (31, 17)   h) (4, –2) and (–5, –6)   i) (13, 25) and (–7, –7)

j) (–11, 1) and (3, 10)

4 *ABCD* is a kite with coordinates *A*(3, 7), *B*(7, 10), *C*(13, 2) and *D*(3, 2).

a) Find the coordinates of the midpoint of the diagonal *AC*.

b) Find the coordinates of the midpoint of the diagonal *BD*.

5 *P* has coordinates (11, 17). *Q* has coordinates (3, 1). *R* is the midpoint of the line segment *PQ*.

a) Find the coordinates of *R*.

b) Find the coordinates of *S*, the midpoint of *PR*.

c) Find the coordinates of *T*, the midpoint of *RQ*.

d) Show that the midpoint of *ST* is *R*.

> **Think about**
>
> Try changing the coordinates of *P* and *Q*. Are the coordinates of the midpoint of *ST* always the same as the coordinates of *R*? Can you draw a diagram to explain why?

6 A triangle has coordinates *A*(–1, 3), *B*(5, 11) and *C*(5, 3).

a) Plot triangle *ABC* on a set of axes.

b) *C* is the midpoint of a line segment *AD*. Find the coordinates of *D*.

c) What type of triangle is triangle *ABD*?

7 Find the missing coordinates from each row in this table.

	Coordinates of *A*	Coordinates of *B*	Coordinates of midpoint of *AB*
a)		(7, 8)	(6, 5)
b)		(–4, 23)	(0, 18)
c)	(8, 3)		(4, 4.5)
d)		(7, 11)	(5, 7)
e)	(–3, 17)		(1, 22)
f)	(6, –5)		(8.5, 1)

> **Tip**
>
> In Question 7, sketch a diagram and think about the differences in the *x* coordinates and the differences in the *y* coordinates.

8 The points *L* and *M* have coordinates *L*(*a*, *c*) and *M*(*b*, *d*). The values of *a*, *b*, *c* and *d* are all square numbers and *a* < *b* and *c* < *d*.

The coordinates of the midpoint of *LM* are (20, 25).

Find the values of *a*, *b*, *c* and *d*.

9 Use dynamic geometry software to draw a triangle *ABC*.

Find the midpoints of the three sides and label them *P*, *Q* and *R*.

The lines connecting the midpoints divide triangle *ABC* into four triangles.

How are these four triangles related? Investigate for a range of different starting triangles.

10 *ABCD* is a parallelogram.

The coordinates of vertices *A* and *B* are *A*(−3, −7) and *B*(−5, −1).

The coordinates of the midpoint of each diagonal are (0, 0).

Find the midpoint of side *CD*.

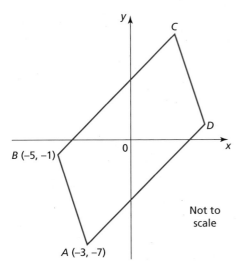

Not to scale

> **Discuss**
>
> If the midpoint of two points is (0, 0), how are the coordinates of the two points related?

11 *A* and *B* are points with coordinates (3*d*, −*d*) and (−5*d*, 5*d*).

a) *C* is the midpoint of *AB*. Find in terms of *d* the coordinates of *C*.

b) The coordinates of *C* are (−6, 12). Find the coordinates of *A*.

End of chapter reflection

You should know that …	You should be able to …	Such as …
The midpoint of a line segment is the point on it that is halfway between the two endpoints. The coordinates of the midpoint can be found from the mean of the coordinates of the endpoints.	Find the coordinates of the midpoint of a line segment.	*A* is the point (8, −5). *B* is the point (14, 3). Find the coordinates of the midpoint of *AB*.

Unit 1C
Handling data and measures

What it's all about?

- Measurement and scale drawing
- Collecting and displaying data
- Calculating measures of spread and average
- Probability

You will learn about:

- Drawing diagrams to scale
- Using different units of measurement
- Types of data
- Methods for collecting data
- Summarising data in frequency tables
- When to use different types of average and spread
- Finding the probability of outcomes.

You will build your skills in:

- understanding and using measurement systems
- using mathematical representations in 2 dimensions
- solving problems involving units and measures of average
- comparing approaches for collecting data.

Scale drawing and measures

You will learn how to:
- Interpret and make simple scale drawings.
- Choose suitable units of measurement to estimate, measure, calculate and solve problems involving mass, length, area, volume and capacity.

Starting point

Do you remember …?

- how to use ratio notation?

  For example, a paint is made by mixing red and yellow paint in the ratio 1 : 4. I use 2 litres of red paint. How much yellow paint do I use?

- how to convert between metric units of length, mass and capacity?

  For example, how many metres in a km or how many cm in a km?

- how to use square units such as m² and cm² for area?

- how to choose units of measurement to estimate, measure, calculate and solve problems?

This will also be helpful when you:

- use maps in real life.

Hook

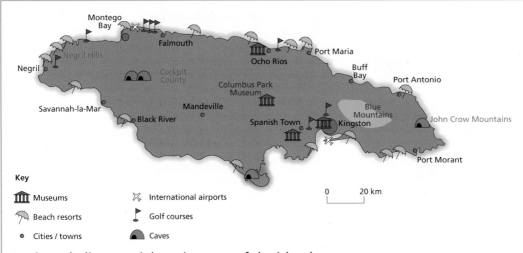

Key

🏛 Museums   ✕ International airports

🏖 Beach resorts   ⚑ Golf courses

• Cities / towns   🕳 Caves

Design a helicopter sightseeing tour of the island.

- Your trip must start and finish from an international airport.
- You must visit at least 1 beach and 1 golf course.
- Your trip must fly over the Blue Mountains.
- You can travel a maximum of 350 km.

Scale drawing

A map or object that is drawn **to scale** has each dimension in proportion to the original.

Drawings of very large objects are a **reduction** of their actual size.

This car is drawn so that 1 cm represents $\frac{1}{2}$ metre in real life.

The scale is 1 cm : $\frac{1}{2}$ m.

We can write this without units as 1 : 50.

Drawings of very small objects are an **enlargement** of their actual size.

Sometimes we draw things bigger than real life. Here is a drawing of an ant.

The drawing of the ant is 5 times bigger than in real life. The scale is 5 : 1.

Key terms

To scale means in proportion so that each length on the drawing or model is in proportion with the same length in real life.

A **map scale** tells us the relationship or ratio between a length on a map or drawing, and the length in real life, for example 1 cm on the map represents 5 km, or 1 : 500 000.

A **plan** is a drawing or sketch of an object or place as it would be seen from above, also called a birds-eye view.

Worked example 1

a) The scale of a map is 1 : 25 000. A road on this map measures 3.5 cm. What is the length of the road in metres?

b) This drawing of a door has a scale of 1 : 40. What is the real height and width of the door? Give your answers in metres.

a) 3.5 cm × 25 000 = 87 500 cm 87 500 ÷ 100 = 875 The length of the road is 875 m.	1 : 25 000 means that 1 unit on the map represents 25 000 units in real life. Multiply the length on the map by the scale. The map measurement was in centimetres, so the actual length is also in centimetres. Convert to metres using the conversion 1 m = 100 cm.

b) The height of the door in the sketch is 5 cm, and the width is 2 cm. 5 cm × 40 = 200 cm = 2 m 2 cm × 40 = 80 cm The real height is 2 m and the real width is 80 cm or 0.8 m.	First measure the lengths on the sketch. Use the scale to find the real life dimensions. Convert to the correct unit for the answer.

Exercise 1   1–7

1 Jack makes a scale drawing of a building. In real life the building is 7 m high, and in the drawing it is 14 cm. Work out the scale.

2 On a scale drawing 1 centimetre represents 8 centimetres in real life.

Calculate the real-life distance represented by:

a) 7 cm   b) 4.5 cm   c) 25 cm   d) 4 cm.

3 This trapezium is drawn to a scale of 1 small square equals 4 cm.

Draw the trapezium actual size.

Think about

Compare the angles inside the scale drawing of the shape and the actual size. Are they the same or different?

4 This rectangle is drawn to a scale of 1 : 3.

Draw the rectangle actual size.

Think about

Find the area of the scale drawing. Find the area of the rectangle in real life. Is the ratio also 1 : 3?

5 The floor plan of a school library is drawn with a scale of 1 cm : 40 cm.

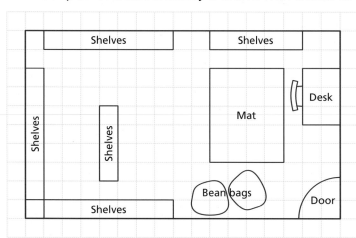

a) Work out the length and width of the desk.

b) Work out the length and width of the mat.

c) How many metres of the walls are covered by shelves?

d) The library wants four new computer workstations. Each workstation is 80 cm by 120 cm. Redesign the library to fit the new computer workstations.

Tip

Don't forget to leave space for a chair!

6 Victor has four plan drawings. The scales are:

1 : 50   1 : 10 000   1 : 10   1 : 100 million.

Match each scale to the map it fits best.

a) world map   **b)** a map of town

c) map of a school   **d)** a design for a model volcano

Explain your answers.

7 Sy draws a scale drawing of a playpark. The diameter of a roundabout is 1 cm on the drawing. It is 5 m in real life. What is the scale of the drawing?

Tip

Think about the units.

8 Write the scale for these maps. Give you answers without units.

a) 1 cm on the map is equal to 0.5 m in real life

b) 2 cm on the map is equal to 2 m in real life

c) 5 cm on the map is equal to 25 m in real life

9 Match the scale to the real-life measurement.

1 : 10	1 cm represents 10 cm
1 : 100	1 cm represents 100 m
1 : 1000	1 cm represents 1 m
1 : 10 000	1 cm represents 10 m

10 Joanne draws a scale drawing of a sports club. The scale is 1 : 500.

Work out the real-life length of:

a) the tennis court, which is 4.8 cm on the sketch the drawing. Give your answer in metres.

b) the shower, which is 1.7 mm on the sketch. Give your answer in centimetres.

11 Tim finds a crab on the beach that is 18 cm wide and 15 cm high. He draws a scale drawing of it using a scale of 1 : 3. What is the height and width of his drawing?

12 Mike is 1.6 m tall. This drawing shows him standing next to his house.

a) Work out the scale of the drawing.

b) Work out the height of his house.

1.6 m

?

13 Explore the area you live in on a digital map. How does the map show the scale? Why is it different to a paper map?

Units of measurement

Key terms

The **metric system** is a decimal system of measuring, using metres, litres and grams as the basic units for length, capacity and mass.

A **tonne** is a unit we use for measuring very heavy masses. 1 tonne = 1000 kg

A **hectare** is equal to 10 000 square metres.

A **cubic unit** is a unit of volume. It expresses a cube with a given length, width and depth. For example, 1 m³ is a cube of 1 × 1 × 1 m in dimensions.

	Metric units	
Length	millimetres (mm), centimetres (cm), metres (m), kilometres (km) 10 mm = 1 cm 100 cm = 1 m 1000 m = 1 km	Length $\times$ 1000 $\quad$ $\times$ 100 $\quad$ $\times$ 10 km $\quad$ m $\quad$ cm $\quad$ mm $\div$ 1000 $\quad$ $\div$ 100 $\quad$ $\div$ 10
Mass	grams (g), kilograms (kg), tonnes (t) 1000 g = 1 kg 1000 kg = 1 t	Mass $\times$ 1000 $\quad$ $\times$ 1000 $\quad$ $\times$ 1000 t $\quad$ kg $\quad$ g $\quad$ mg $\div$ 1000 $\quad$ $\div$ 1000 $\quad$ $\div$ 1000
Capacity	millilitres (ml), litres (l), kilolitres (kl) cubic metres (m³) 1000 ml = 1 l 1000 l = 1 kl or 1 cubic metre	Capacity $\times$ 1000 $\quad$ $\times$ 1000 kl $\quad$ l $\quad$ ml $\div$ 1000 $\quad$ $\div$ 1000
Area	mm², cm², m² and km²	Area $\times$ 1000² $\quad$ $\times$ 100² $\quad$ $\times$ 10² km² $\quad$ m² $\quad$ cm² $\quad$ mm² $\div$ 1000² $\quad$ $\div$ 100² $\quad$ $\div$ 10²
Volume	1 ml = 1 cm³	Volume $\times$ 1000³ $\quad$ $\times$ 100³ $\quad$ $\times$ 10³ km³ $\quad$ m³ $\quad$ cm³ $\quad$ mm³ $\div$ 1000³ $\quad$ $\div$ 100³ $\quad$ $\div$ 10³

Worked example 2

Mila is painting some boxes. She needs 320 ml for each box. She buys 5 litres of paint. How many whole boxes can she paint? How much paint will she have left over?

Give units with your answer.

5 litres ÷ 320 ml 5000 ÷ 320	The number of boxes she can paint is the number of times 320 millilitres goes into 5 litres.
	The volumes used in the calculation are given in different units. Convert them into the same units. Use 1 litre = 1000 ml.
= 15.625 boxes	She can cover 15 whole boxes.
	She has 0.625 of a tin of paint left over.
0.625 × 320	A tin of paint is 320 ml.
= 200	There is 200 ml left in the last tin.
She can paint 15 boxes and have 200 ml left over.	Give units with your answer.
	Check your answer!
	15 × 320 + 200 = 5000

Exercise 2   1–12

1. Which unit would be most suitable for measuring each item – mm, cm, m or km?
   a) distance between countries
   b) distance between neighbours' houses
   c) thickness of a ruler
   d) length of a ruler
   e) height of a bedside lamp
   f) height of a building

2. Which unit would be most suitable for measuring the mass of each item – grams, kilograms or tonnes?
   a) bus
   b) chair
   c) teacup
   d) large bag of potatoes
   e) pencil
   f) box of books

3. Which unit would be the most suitable for measuring the capacity of each item – ml, l, or kl?
   a) teapot
   b) reservoir
   c) washing machine

4. Convert:
   a) 25 m = ___ cm
   b) 0.095 cm = ___ m
   c) 0.1 cm = ___ m
   d) 4.5 kg = ___ g
   e) 900 g = ___ kg
   f) 55 g = ___ kg
   g) 0.5 t = ___ kg
   h) 140 kg = ___ t
   i) 25 g = ___ kg
   j) 5 litres = ___ ml
   k) 0.7 litres = ___ ml
   l) 8347 ml = ___ l

5. a) A water tank has a capacity of 2.5 litres.
      The water tank is $\frac{3}{4}$ full. How many litres of water are in the tank?
   b) Give your answer to part a) in mixed units (litres and millilitres)

6 A parking lot has dimensions 52.5 m by 20 m.

There are 4 rows of parking.

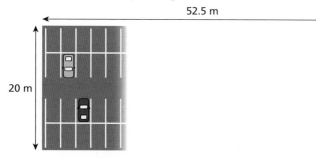

52.5 m

20 m

Each parking space is 2.5 metres wide.

How many parking spaces are in the parking lot in total.

7 Mary needs 8 m² of fabric.

Store A sells the fabric in a roll with a width of 50 cm.
The cost is $2.75 per metre.

Store B sells fabric in a roll with a width of 0.75 m.
The cost is $4.05 per metre.

Calculate the difference in price for 8 square metres.

8 Makito is wallpapering a room with dimensions 2.4 m by 4.5 m. The room has a height of 1.6 m.

A roll of wallpaper is 0.5 m wide and 15 m long.

How many rolls of wall paper will he need?

Ignore any windows and doors.

9 A health service needs to collect 15 000 units of blood per week to meet demand. 1 unit is 450 ml.

How many litres of blood does this health service need per week?

10 A container has dimensions 40 cm by 50 cm by 25 cm. It is full of water.

Dean fills his glass with half a litre of water from the container. How much water is left in the container?

11 1 mm of rainfall equals 1 litre of water over an area of 1 square metre.

A news station reported that 25 ml of rainfall fell in the past 24 hours.

The school playground has an area of 18 m².

How many litres of water fell in total on the school playground in these 24 hours?

> **Tip**
> Convert the number of litres used into cubic metres.
> 1 cubic metre = 1000 litres

End of chapter reflection

You should know that ...	You should be able to ...	Such as ...
A scale is expressed as a ratio. It tells what a given length on a plan represents in real life.	Interpret map scales. Express given scales as ratios. Work out what a length on a scale drawing represents in real life. Draw simple scale drawings.	What does 1 : 1 000 000 000 mean? 1 cm on the map represents 15 km in real life. What is the scale? In a 1 : 10 plan, what does 1 cm on the plan represent? Draw a scale plan of your bedroom.
Measurement are always given with units.	Select the most appropriate units to work with. Convert between metric units. Solve multistep problems using different units of measurement.	What would you use to measure the mass of a bulldozer – g, kg or t? How many millilitres are in 8.52 litres? A sandpit has dimensions of 2 metres by 1.5 m. The sandpit contains 1350 litres of sand. How deep is the sand?

Data collection

You will learn how to:

- Identify and collect data to answer a question; select the method of collection, sample size and degree of accuracy needed for measurements.
- Recognise the difference between discrete and continuous data.
- Construct and use:
  - frequency tables with given equal class intervals to gather continuous data
  - two-way tables to record discrete data.

Starting point

Do you remember …?

- how to design a questionnaire for a survey?
- how to complete a frequency table using a tally?

This will be helpful when you:

- learn how to calculate probabilities using a two-way table.

Hook

Estimate the number of students in your school who bring packed lunches.

First try to answer the following questions.

- How many students on your table bring packed lunches?
- How many students in your class bring packed lunches?
- How many students are there in the school? (Ask your teacher.)

Use this information to make your estimate.

Decide whether your results will be similar for other schools in the country.

Collecting data

Key terms

The **sample size** is the number of people you decide to survey from the total population.

The **degree of accuracy** is when you decide whether to round your measurements to the nearest whole number or to 1 or 2 decimal places, etc.

Worked example 1

A school has 1000 students and they want to investigate the average time that the students spend travelling to school.

The school decides to ask 10 pupils in year 7 to give their journey time to school to the nearest half hour.

Comment on the sample size and the degree of accuracy chosen for the journey times.

Selecting 10 students is too small a sample size to gain a variety of results.	The more students you survey, the more reliable your results will be. In this instance it may be more appropriate to ask about 100 students.
A selection of students from all year groups should be used, not just students from year 7.	This will take into account any differences in travelling times between younger and older students.
Rounding to the nearest minute would be more appropriate.	Always think about a sensible degree of accuracy. Rounding to the nearest half hour would lead to some very inaccurate responses. If you were measuring the time taken to run 200 m, you would round to the nearest second or even one tenth of a second.

Worked example 2

A company wants to build a shopping centre in a town. They want to find out whether the people who live in the area would use the shopping centre and which shops they would like to be in it.

The researcher is trying to decide whether to:

conduct face-to-face interviews

or

post out a questionnaire.

Comment on the advantages and disadvantages of each of the approaches.

Advantages of interviews The researcher can clarify the questions if people are unclear. Disadvantages of interviews People may not be as honest during a face to face interview. It may be time consuming to interview lots of people. It will cost more to employ people to conduct the interviews.	The researcher can think about: • Time – how long will it take to collect the data? • Cost – how expensive will it be to collect the data? • Honesty – will people be more or less likely to tell the truth using each method? • Number of responses – will people answer the questions?

Advantages of a postal questionnaire	
The researcher can send the questionnaire to a lot of people.	
People can take their time when completing the questionnaire.	
People are more likely to be honest.	
Disadvantages of a postal questionnaire	
People may not complete it or forget to hand it in.	
You cannot explain the questions to the person answering the questionnaire.	

Think about

Are there any other advantages or disadvantages that you can think of for worked example 2?

Exercise 1

1 Lucia wants to find out the average height of students in her class. Choose the accuracy of the measurement she should use from the options below and give a reason for this choice.
- nearest metre
- nearest 10 centimetres
- nearest centimetre
- nearest millimetre

2 Andrei and Cathy want to find out how many people would be interested in coming to a film club at school.

Andrei says, 'We should ask a sample of 20 people from our classes.'

Cathy says, 'We should ask a sample of 100 people in the school canteen.'

Comment on which approach would be better and give a reason for your answer.

3 Write down whether each of these topics can best be answered by using questionnaires or research.

Frequency of volcanic eruptions in Iceland

Average amount of pocket money students in your school receive

Number of people who own a bike in your local neighbourhood

Amount of plastic in the world's oceans

4 Valentina wants to find out the views of people in her town about plans to re-open an old cinema. She decides to send out 1000 questionnaires to people in the town.

Write down whether each statement about the questionnaires is true or false.

It will be less time consuming than doing face to face interviews.

She will definitely get all of the questionnaires back.

The answers will be more accurate than if she does face to face interviews because she can explain the questions if there is any confusion.

5 Filip wants to investigate the following research question:

Do snakes live longer in the wild or in captivity?

a) Which two of the following would it be most useful to collect data about?

A	B	C	D
Age of the snake	Colour of the snake	Where the snake lives	Name of the snake

b) How would it be best for Ethan to collect his data?

Write down two.

Buy a pet snake and see how long it lives.

Look up information on the internet about the lifespan of different species of snake.

Conduct interviews with friends and family to ask their opinion.

Contact several experienced snake handlers and conduct telephone interviews.

6 Andrei wants to know how many hours a week people spend exercising.

He asks 30 people at his local running club.

Give one disadvantage of this approach.

7 Jeremy has been asked to investigate the ages of people who use the library. He stands in the library between 10 a.m. and 11 a.m. on a Wednesday and he takes a tally of the ages of the people who come in during that period.

Give two disadvantages of this method.

8 Some students are asked to compare the amount of homework that children in Europe and North America receive each week.

They are given some data on several countries from the two continents.

Write down all the true statements.

The data they are using is reliable.

It will still take a long time to collect the data.

It would be impossible to collect the data themselves.

They will not know how reliable the data is.

9 A first-aid trainer wants to find out how useful people thought his training was. Which one of the following two methods should he use?

Interview people face to face before they leave

or

Give them a questionnaire to fill out at the end

Give a reason for your answer.

10 Mathias wants to find out how often people from his town go to the cinema. He decides to interview people for his survey.

Suggest a time and a place where Geoff could conduct the survey.

Give a reason for your answer.

11 A college has 2000 students and 100 staff. The college wants to find out what students and staff think about the new timetable. Write down a plan for data collection. Ensure that you include all of the details.

Discrete and continuous data

Key terms

Discrete data can be counted and will have an exact value such as: number of books read, number of female staff, etc.

Continuous data needs to be measured and has to be rounded to a suitable degree of accuracy such as: height, mass and speed.

Worked example 3

Jim is going to compare some flowers in his local park. He is going to be comparing:

- the number of petals
- the height of the flower
- the colour of the petals
- the name of the flower
- the diameter of the stem.

Categorise these types of data under the headings: non-numerical data, discrete data and continuous data.

Non-numerical data The name of the flower The colour of the petals	The name and the colour of the flower cannot be counted or measured.
Discrete data The number of petals	The data collected here can be counted and the results will be given as whole numbers.
Continuous data The height of the flower The diameter of the stem	The height and diameter are measurements and will be rounded to perhaps 1 or 2 decimal places.

Discuss

Decide if each of the following are examples of discrete or continuous data.

Area   Number of people who live in a country   Speed

Exercise 2

1. Tim is collecting information about some of the albums of his favourite bands. Decide if each of the following types of data are discrete or continuous.

   a) The number of tracks on an album

   b) The total running time of each album

   c) The length of the song names on the albums

2. Sofia is measuring the height of sunflowers in her garden.

   Is the height of the sunflowers discrete data or continuous data?

3. Humna is collecting data about the voluntary work that some of her friends and family do. Decide if each of the following variables is non-numerical, discrete or continuous data.

   - Time spent per week doing voluntary work
   - Age (in years)
   - Number of volunteers in their organisation
   - Gender (male or female)
   - Type of voluntary work undertaken

4 A football coach is analysing his players' fitness and performance in the run up to the next season. He wants to collect the following data from each player.

Write down whether each variable is continuous data or discrete data.

Heart rate (beats per minute)

Height

Mass

Age (in years)

Time taken to run 100m sprint

Number of goals scored in training

5 Robin wants to investigate people's shopping habits. He decides to send out a questionnaire to a sample of people in his home town.

List two examples of discrete data he could collect and two examples of continuous data he could collect.

6 Sally says that age is discrete data. Jordan says that age is continuous data. Explain how Sally and Jordan can both be correct.

Frequency tables and two-way tables

Key terms

Class intervals are used to group continuous data in a frequency table. You can use class intervals with equal widths or class intervals with unequal widths.

Two-way tables allow you to organise data for two different variables using columns and rows.

Worked example 4

These are the lengths of 18 fish caught in a cove in Europe.

6.7 cm	12.8 cm	5.9 cm	1.5 cm	3.6 cm	6.59 cm
4.25 cm	8.3 cm	9.0 cm	7.1 cm	11.2 cm	10.8 cm
15.05 cm	17.3 cm	6.2 cm	9.1 cm	13.2 cm	15.0 cm

a) Construct and complete a frequency table for this data using equal class intervals.

b) How many fish were greater than 9 cm in length?

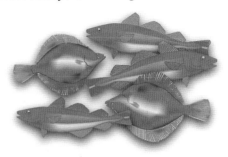

a)

Length(*l*) in cm	Tally	Frequency
$0 < l \le 3$		
$3 < l \le 6$		
$6 < l \le 9$		
$9 < l \le 12$		
$12 < l \le 15$		
$15 < l \le 18$		

We want the class intervals to be equal width and to cover the whole range of lengths in our data.

In this case using intervals of 3 cm gives us a reasonable number of classes.

Length (*l*) in cm	Tally	Frequency
$0 < l \le 3$	I	
$3 < l \le 6$	III	
$6 < l \le 9$	ⅢI I	
$9 < l \le 12$	III	
$12 < l \le 15$	III	
$15 < l \le 18$	II	

Input the data using tally marks.

9.0 cm is in the $6 < l \le 9$ interval since there is a 'less than or equal to' sign next to the 9.

Length (*l*) in cm	Tally	Frequency
$0 < l \le 3$	I	1
$3 < l \le 6$	III	3
$6 < l \le 9$	ⅢI I	6
$9 < l \le 12$	III	3
$12 < l \le 15$	III	3
$15 < l \le 18$	II	2

The third column is used to write down the total frequency for each class interval.

b) 3 + 3 + 2 = 8
   8 fish

In order to work out the number of fish that are greater than 9 cm in length, add the totals for the last three rows.

Tip

Check to see if the total frequency matches the amount of data that you started with.

Worked example 5

A farmer keeps 18 sheep in a field. They are either white or black.

He has:

- 9 male sheep
- 10 black sheep
- 5 white female sheep.

Construct and complete a two-way table to show this information.

	White	Black	Total
Male			
Female			
Total			18

The two-way table needs to show whether the sheep are male or female and whether the sheep are black or white. We can use one row for male and one row for female. We can use one column for white sheep and one column for black sheep.

We need a total column and a total row, with the overall total in the bottom right corner.

	White	Black	Total
Male			9
Female	5		
Total		10	18

You can then input the data that is given in the question.

Total white sheep = overall total − total black sheep
$$= 18 - 10$$
$$= 8$$

Total female sheep = overall total − total male sheep
$$= 18 - 9$$
$$= 9$$

Use the totals to complete the missing cells. Start with working out the total number of white sheep and the total number of female sheep.

	White	Black	Total
Male			9
Female	5		9
Total	8	10	18

Number of male white sheep = number of white sheep
                            − number of female white sheep
                          = 8 − 5
                          = 3

Number of female black sheep = number of female sheep
                              − number of female white sheep
                            = 9 − 5
                            = 4

Now we can work out the number of male white sheep and the number of female black sheep.

	White	Black	Total
Male	3		9
Female	5	4	9
Total	8	10	18

Number of male black sheep
= number of black sheep − number of female black sheep
= 10 − 4
= 6

Now we can work out the number of male black sheep.

	White	Black	Total
Male	3	6	9
Female	5	4	9
Total	8	10	18

Finally, check carefully that all of the columns and rows add up to the correct totals.

3 + 6 = 9   5 + 4 = 9   9 + 9 = 18
3 + 5 = 8   6 + 4 = 10   8 + 10 = 18

So our table is correct.

Exercise 3

1 These are the heights of 12 trees in an orchard.

3.5 m	2.9 m	5.1 m	7.9 m	6.0 m	9.1 m
5.5 m	1.2 m	4.5 m	8.3 m	7.7 m	6.3 m

a) Copy and complete the frequency table for this data.

Height (h) in m	Tally	Frequency
$0 < h \leq 2$		
$2 < h \leq 4$		
$4 < h \leq 6$		
$6 < h \leq 8$		
$8 < h \leq 10$		

b) How many trees are 4 m or less in height?

2 Look at the frequency table.

a) Write down the missing class interval.

b) Write down the missing value in the frequency column.

Mass (*m*) in grams	Frequency
$0 < m \leq 5$	4
$5 < m \leq 10$	7
	6
$15 < m \leq 20$	8
$20 < m \leq 25$	
$25 < m \leq 30$	11
Total	41

3 The diameter, in millimetres of 14 tomatoes are:

41 mm	49 mm	62 mm	46 mm	58 mm	61 mm
55 mm	58 mm	54 mm	60 mm	59 mm	56 mm
57 mm	56 mm				

a) Copy and complete the frequency table for this data using equal class intervals.

Diameter (*d*) In mm	Tally	Frequency
$40 < d \leq 45$		
$45 < d \leq 50$		
$50 < d \leq 55$		
$55 < d \leq 60$		
$60 < d \leq 65$		

b) How many tomatoes had a diameter of more than 50 mm?

4 The frequency table shows the speed, in km/h, of some cars as they pass a school between 2.55 p.m. and 3.00 p.m. The school is in a 40 km/h zone.

a) How many cars were recorded?

b) How many cars were travelling at less than 30 km/h?

c) How many cars drove above the speed limit?

d) Joe says that $\frac{1}{4}$ of the cars drove above the speed limit.

Is Joe Correct? Give a reason for your answer.

Speed (*s*), in km/h	Frequency
$0 < s \leq 10$	1
$10 < s \leq 20$	5
$20 < s \leq 30$	3
$30 < s \leq 40$	10
$40 < s \leq 50$	5
$50 < s \leq 60$	4

Think about

If $5 < x \leq 10$

What is the biggest value *x* could be?

What is the smallest value *x* could be?

Did you know?

You may be given a two-way table without the totals for the rows and columns. You may need to work these out for yourself in order to better understand the data.

5 The two-way table gives information about the gender and ages of the members of a running club.

Age (years)	11–20	21–30	31–40		51–60	60+
Male	5	3	12	14	3	2
Female	7	2	15	11	5	3

a) What is the missing age range in the table?

b) How many members of the running club are female?

c) How many members of the running club are male and have an age between 21 and 30 years old?

d) How many members of the running club are above 50 years in age?

6 28 musicians are taking a practical exam.

The two-way table gives information about the instruments that the musicians have decided to use for their practical exam.

	Male	Female	Total
Voice	1	3	
Piano	2		
Guitar		1	6
Clarinet		2	2
Percussion	4		5
Saxophone	1	3	
Total			

a) Complete the two-way table.

b) How many students decided to play the piano?

7 On a bus there are 38 students from two different schools:
Heartshead High and Staley Farm College.
7 of the 18 pupils who go to Heartshead High are male.
There are 8 female students who go to Staley Farm College.
In total, how many students on the bus are male?

End of chapter reflection

You should know that ...	You should be able to ...	Such as ...

There are different ways of collecting data such as questionnaires, face to face interviews or by recording numerical measures.	Identify which information needs to be collected.
	
	Decide which method of data collection is appropriate and comment on the different approaches.
		James is going to investigate whether adults eat more or less chocolate than teenagers.
		
		Which one of the following would be most relevant?
		  • height
		  • age
		  • gender
		Give the advantages and disadvantages of:
		  • face to face interviews
		  • postal Questionnaires.

A larger sample size gives more reliable results. The degree of accuracy is how accurately you are going to record your measurements.	Choose an appropriate sample size for the population you are investigating. Use an appropriate degree of accuracy for the measurements you are recording.	Explain why a sample of 10 from a population of 1000 may be an inappropriate size. Draw a ring around a suitable degree of accuracy for measuring the length of cars in metres. Nearest whole metre 1 decimal place 3 decimal places
There are different types of data such as non-numerical, continuous and discrete.	Identify data that is continuous and data that is discrete.	Which of the following variables are continuous? height, number of siblings, mass, number of press ups
Equal class intervals may be used to organise continuous data into a frequency table.	Construct and complete a frequency table using equal class intervals.	Complete the following table using equal class intervals.

Time (t) in minutes	Frequency
$0 \leq t \leq 10$	3
$10 \leq t \leq 20$	5
$20 \leq t \leq 30$	
	6
Total	18

You should know that ...	You should be able to ...	Such as ...
Two-way tables are used to organise data with two sets of categories.	Complete and interpret the information in a two-way table.	

	Child	Adult
Male	5	3
Female	7	2

How many adults are in the survey?

How many children are female?

How many people are in the survey altogether?

Averages and spread

You will learn how to:

- Calculate statistics for sets of discrete and continuous data; recognise when to use the range, mean, median and mode and, for grouped data, the modal class.

Starting point

Do you remember …?

- how to find the mean, mode and range from a frequency table?

  For example, look at the frequency table showing the age of cars in a secondhand car dealership.

Age, in years	Frequency
1	4
2	7
3	3
4	5

  What is the modal and the mean age of the cars?

  What is the range of the ages of the cars?

- how to find the median from a list of results?

  For example, find the median for this set of data:

  4, 7, 3, 9, 2, 6, 5, 4

This will be helpful when you:

- learn to select which average to use when comparing two data sets.

Hook

This is a game for two players and will test your reaction time.

Hold a ruler vertically above your opponent's hand. Drop the ruler without saying anything. Your opponent must then catch the ruler as quickly as possible and record the length at which they caught it. Repeat the experiment 10 times each.

The winner is the one with the best average.

Will you use the mean, median or mode?

Did the winner have the most consistent results?

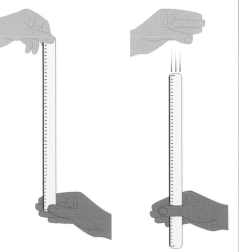

Mean, median, mode and range

Worked example 1

Decide whether the mode, median, mean or range should be used to answer the following questions.

a) Find the most common colour of European snakes.

b) Find the average mass of the planets in the solar system.

c) Find which athlete throws the most consistent distances with a javelin.

d) Find the average salary of 10 workers, 9 of which are manual labourers and 1 is the managing director.

a) The data is non-numerical. The only average you can use for non-numerical data is the mode.	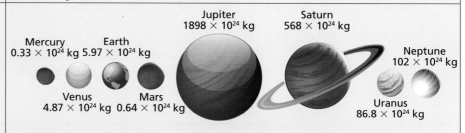 Mode = green
b) Use the mean to take into account the mass of all 8 planets to find the average.	Jupiter 1898 × 10²⁴ kg — Saturn 568 × 10²⁴ kg — Mercury 0.33 × 10²⁴ kg — Earth 5.97 × 10²⁴ kg — Neptune 102 × 10²⁴ kg — Venus 4.87 × 10²⁴ kg — Mars 0.64 × 10²⁴ kg — Uranus 86.8 × 10²⁴ kg You could also use the median in this instance. **Think about** Calculate both the mean and median mass of the planets in the solar system. What is the difference between them?
c) You are looking at how spread out the distances of each javelin throw are for each athlete. Use the range. The athlete with the smallest range is the most consistent.	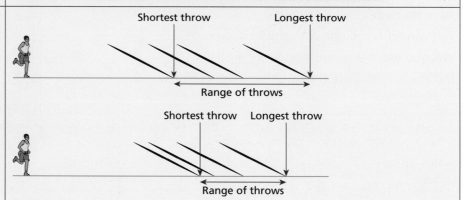

d) The median may be the best average to use as the managing director could earn a significant amount more than the manual labourers.

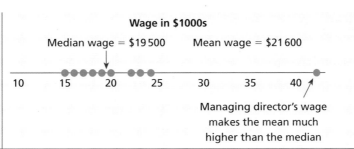

Wage in $1000s

Median wage = $19 500   Mean wage = $21 600

Managing director's wage makes the mean much higher than the median

Discuss

Why might someone need to calculate an average in their job?

Think of three different jobs which would require people to find averages.

Worked example 2

Jake has six old coins in his collection. The mean average diameter of his coins is 3.5 cm.

The diameters of five of his coins are: 2.4 cm, 4.9 cm, 3.1 cm, 5.1 cm and 2.9 cm.

Find the diameter of the missing coin.

3.5 × 6 = 21 cm	Find the total diameter of all 6 coins by multiplying the mean by 6.
21 − (2.4 + 4.9 + 3.1 + 5.1 + 2.9) = 2.6 The missing coin has a diameter of 2.6 cm.	Subtract the total diameter of the other 5 coins from total you have just found.

2.4	4.9	3.1	5.1	2.9	?
21					
3.5	3.5	3.5	3.5	3.5	3.5

Think about

Can you think of 3 different numbers which have the same mean and median?

Exercise 1   2, 4, 6 and 8

1 James measured the rainfall in his garden every day over a two-week period in August. Here are his results to the nearest tenth of a centimetre.

1.5 cm	3.9 cm	0.0 cm	0.7 cm	0.0 cm
5.9 cm	2.4 cm	3.4 cm	4.7 cm	0.0 cm
2.1 cm	4.5 cm	1.7 mm	3.1 cm	

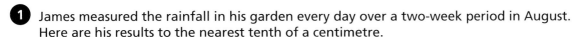

Find the:

a) mode   **b)** median   **c)** mean   **d)** range.

2 The table shows the area of the gardens of the houses on an estate.

Area of garden, in m²	Frequency
$0 < l \le 10$	13
$10 < l \le 20$	17
$20 < l \le 30$	18
$30 < l \le 40$	16
$40 < l \le 50$	8
$50 < l \le 60$	3

Key term

The **modal class** is the name given to the category or class of data that contains the highest frequency.

Write down the modal class interval for this data.

3 Aaliyah asks eight of her friends how much pocket money they receive each week.

They say:

$5 $7.50 $6 $8 $3.50 $7 $4.50 $8.50

Aaliyah's mum says that she will give her the average amount of pocket money that her friends receive.

Do you think Aaliyah will use the mean or the median average?

Give a reason for your answer and state any figures which you calculate.

4 Write down whether the mode, median or mean should be calculated in each circumstance.

Rian wants to find the average test score on a maths exam.

Jane wants to find out the average eye colour of her classmates.

Mamadu took part in a gymnastics competition. He wants to know whether he came in the top half of all of the athletes who took part.

Did you know?

Life expectancy in the UK is calculated using the mean. However, using the median would give a figure of about 2–3 years higher and using the mode would give a figure of about 6 years higher.

5 There are 50 fish tanks in a reptile shop. The table shows the numbers of fish in the tanks.

Number of fish	Frequency
18	15
19	9
20	3
21	4
22	13
23	6

a) Find the mean number of fish in the tanks.

b) Find the median number of fish in the tanks.

c) Casey says, 'The range is 12.' Show that Casey is incorrect.

6 Look at the number cards. Each card has a number, but one of the numbers is hidden.

Find the missing number if the four cards have:

a) a median of 10.5   b) a mean of 13.5   c) a range of 12.

7 Eight swimmers take part in a sponsored swim for charity. The following figures show how much money they each raised.

£26   £87   £52   £106.50   £23.25   £47.52   £134.80   £10.50

The local paper is going to publish the average amount of money raised by the swimmers. Should the paper use the mean or the median average?

Give a reason for your answer and show your calculations.

8 The table shows the number of potholes on some roads in a town centre.

Number of potholes	5	6	7	8	9
Frequency	5	8	6	3	5

Hasnain is asked to work out the mean number of potholes per road.
This is his working out:

5 + 8 + 6 + 3 + 5 = 27

Mean = $\frac{27}{5}$

Mean = 5.4 potholes per road.

a) Explain why Hasnain's working out is incorrect.

b) Write down some clear instructions that Hasnain could use to correctly calculate the mean.

9 Peter missed a maths lesson and so copied down the example shown from his friend's exercise book.

When Peter got home he realised that he had copied down one number incorrectly in the frequency column.

Given that the total of 25 and the mean of 1.88 are both correct, find the error.

You must show all of your working out.

> **Tip**
>
> First calculate the total number of pets in the class using the two values which you know are correct.

Number of pets of students in the class

Number of pets	Frequency
0	4
1	7
2	6
3	3
4	3
5	1
Total	25

Mean number of pets = 1.88

End of chapter reflection

You should know that …	You should be able to …	Such as …
The mode, median and mean are all averages.	Calculate the mean, median and mode from a continuous data set.	Find the mean and median from this data set: 2.3 cm, 5.9 cm, 7.8 cm. 2.5 cm, 6.3 cm, 9.2 cm
	Solve problems which involve averages and range.	Six cards have a mean of 3.2. What is the value of the unknown number? 4 2 3 4 2 ?
Sometimes it's more useful to use one average over another. The mean takes into account every piece of data, whereas the median is the value of the middle piece of data. The mode can be used for non-numerical data. The range is a measure of spread.	Select which average is the most appropriate to use in a given situation.	State whether the mean, median, mode or range should be used in each investigation. • Finding the average eye colour. • Finding the average height. • Finding the most consistent goal scorer.
The modal class interval is the group with the highest frequency in a grouped frequency table.	Find the modal class interval from a grouped frequency table.	Write down the modal class interval for this table.

Mass, in grams	Frequency
$0 < w \leq 5$	4
$5 < w \leq 10$	6
$10 < w \leq 15$	7
$15 < w \leq 20$	6

Probability

You will learn how to:
- Use the fact that if the probability of an event occurring is p, then the probability of it not occurring is $1 - p$.
- Find probabilities based on equally likely outcomes in practical contexts.

Starting point

Do you remember ...?

- the language of probability (likely, unlikely, certain, impossible)?

  For example, it is _____ that I will be at school tomorrow.

- the probability scale from 0 to 1 where 0 means that an outcome is impossible and 1 means that an outcome is certain?

  For example, what is the probability that tomorrow is Sunday?

- how to find probabilities based on equally likely outcomes in simple contexts?

  For example, if a number is picked at random from the numbers 1, 2, 3, 4, 5 and 6, what is the probability that the number chosen is a 3?

- the notation P() to mean the probability of the outcome in the bracket?

  For example, P(3) means the probability of getting a 3.

- the word 'fair' to mean that a dice or spinner is equally likely to land on any side or face?

Hook

Work in pairs with a set of 10 identical size and colour cards with a different number from 1 to 10 written on each card. You can either make the cards or your teacher will give them to you.

Place the cards face down and mix them up.
Now pick a card.

What is the probability that the card has the number 8 on it?

What is the probability that the card has a multiple of 5 on it?

Can you think of two questions which both have the answer $\frac{5}{10}$ or $\frac{1}{2}$?

Write down some probability questions of your own about picking a card from your 10 cards. Try to find questions with different answers.

Probability of events not happening

The probability of picking a multiple of 4 from the cards numbered 1 to 10 in the Hook is $\frac{2}{10}$ because the numbers 4 and 8 are the only two multiples of 4.

You could also write this as 0.2 or 20%.

If you were asked for the probability of picking a number that is NOT a multiple of 4 then any of the numbers 1, 2, 3, 5, 6, 7, 9 and 10 would work so the probability is $\frac{8}{10}$ or 0.8 or 80%.

If the probability of a particular outcome of an event happening is p, then the probability of that outcome not happening is $1-p$.

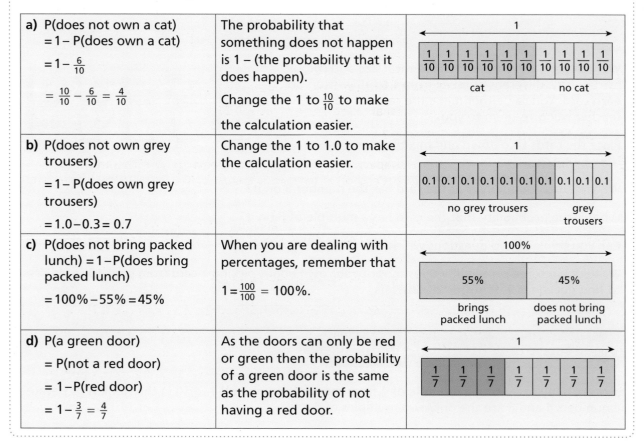

Worked example 1

a) The probability that a student chosen at random from class 7C owns a cat is $\frac{6}{10}$.

   What is the probability that a student chosen at random from class 7C does NOT own a cat?

b) The probability that a student chosen at random from class 7C owns a pair of grey trousers is 0.3.

   What is the probability that a student chosen at random from class 7C does NOT own a pair of grey trousers?

c) The probability that a student chosen at random from class 7C brings a packed lunch to school every day is 55%.

   What is the probability that a student chosen at random from class 7C does NOT bring a packed lunch to school every day?

d) All of the apartments in a block have either a green door or a red door. If the probability of an apartment chosen at random having a red door is $\frac{3}{7}$, what is the probability that an apartment chosen at random has a green door?

a) P(does not own a cat) $= 1 - $ P(does own a cat) $= 1 - \frac{6}{10}$ $= \frac{10}{10} - \frac{6}{10} = \frac{4}{10}$	The probability that something does not happen is 1 – (the probability that it does happen). Change the 1 to $\frac{10}{10}$ to make the calculation easier.	
b) P(does not own grey trousers) $= 1 - $ P(does own grey trousers) $= 1.0 - 0.3 = 0.7$	Change the 1 to 1.0 to make the calculation easier.	
c) P(does not bring packed lunch) $= 1 - $ P(does bring packed lunch) $= 100\% - 55\% = 45\%$	When you are dealing with percentages, remember that $1 = \frac{100}{100} = 100\%$.	
d) P(a green door) $= $ P(not a red door) $= 1 - $ P(red door) $= 1 - \frac{3}{7} = \frac{4}{7}$	As the doors can only be red or green then the probability of a green door is the same as the probability of not having a red door.	

Exercise 1

1 The probability that the school bus arrives on time on any Friday is $\frac{1}{3}$. What is the probability that the school bus will not arrive on time next Friday?

2 The probability of a student chosen at random from class 8a owning a dog is $\frac{5}{9}$. What is the probability of a pupil chosen at random from class 8a not owning a dog?

3 Jana picks a sweet at random from a box of sweets, of identical shape and size, that are all either orange or lemon sweets. If the probability that she picks an orange sweet is 0.2, what is the probability that the sweet she chooses is a lemon sweet?

4 In Marco's sock drawer there are only black socks and red socks. If Marco picks a sock at random, the probability that the sock will be black is 0.63. What is the probability that Marco picks out a red sock?

5 The probability that a member of Marika's class gets the bus to school is 53%. What is the probability that a member of Marika's class, chosen at random, does not get the bus to school?

6 This table shows the probability that it will rain on each day of a given week. Copy and complete the table.

Event	Monday	Tuesday	Wednesday	Thursday	Friday
P(rain)	0.5	0.88	0.95	0.72	0.15
P(no rain)					

7 There are 100 sweets, of identical shape and size, in a box.

The probability that a sweet chosen at random is not red is 0.35.

How many red sweets are in the jar?

8 There are 80 sweets, of identical shape and size, in a jar. The sweets are all either mints or toffees. The probability that a sweet chosen at random is a mint is 40%. How many toffees are in the jar?

9 A bag holds a number of counters, of identical shape and size, which are either red, yellow or blue. The probability that a counter chosen at random is red is 0.2. The probability that a counter chosen at random is yellow is 0.35.

What is the probability that a counter chosen at random is blue?

10 The probability that the school bus will be late on a morning when it is raining is 0.75.

Hanna says that this means that the probability that the bus will be late on a morning when it is not raining is 0.25.

Explain, with reasons, why Hanna is not correct and write a correct statement from the information given.

Equally likely outcomes

Key terms

Outcomes that have the same probability are **equally likely**.

When outcomes of an event are equally likely, you can use this formula to find the probability:

$$\text{probability of an outcome} = \frac{\text{number of favourable events}}{\text{total number of possible outcomes}}.$$

Worked example 2

60 students were asked which of three colours they preferred. The results are shown in the table.

	Blue	**Red**	**Purple**
Boys	12	8	8
Girls	8	16	8

a) What is the probability that a student, chosen at random, is a boy who prefers blue? Write your answer as a fraction, a decimal and a percentage.

b) What is the probability that a student chosen at random preferred blue? Write your answer as a fraction.

c) What is the probability that a student chosen at random is a boy? Write your answer as a fraction.

a) P(boy who prefers blue) $= \frac{12}{60} = \frac{1}{5}$ $\frac{1}{5} = 0.2 = 20\%$	Number of boys who prefer blue = 12 Total number of students = 60 To find the probability, divide the number that satisfy the condition (boy who prefers blue) by the total number of students $= \frac{12}{60}$. To simplify the fraction divide both the top and bottom of the fraction by 12.	
b) P(student who prefers blue) $= \frac{12 + 8}{60} = \frac{20}{60} = \frac{1}{3}$	Total number of students who prefer blue = 12 + 8 = 20. Divide this by the total number of students to find the probability.	
c) P(student is a boy) $= \frac{12 + 8 + 8}{60} = \frac{28}{60} = \frac{7}{15}$	The number of boys is 12 + 8 + 8 = 28 Divide this by the total number of students to find the probability. To simplify the fraction, divide the top and bottom by 4.	

1 Melanie has 10 counters, each labelled with a letter and a colour.

If Melanie chooses one counter at random, what is the probability that she chooses:

a) a counter with the letter A

b) a counter with the letter C or D

c) a blue counter

d) a pink or yellow counter?

Write your answers as fractions.

2 Write your answers to question 1 as decimals and percentages.

3 A bowl of fruit contains 8 red apples, 5 green apples and 7 oranges. If I pick a fruit at random, what is the probability that I pick:

a) a red apple   b) a green apple   c) an orange   d) an apple?

4 Joran has 20 T-shirts. They are in different colours, some are plain and some have a pattern. The table below shows how many of each type there are.

	Blue	Black	White
Plain T-shirt	3	5	4
Patterned T-shirt	3	2	3

Joran picks a T-shirt at random. What is the probability that the T-shirt is:

a) plain blue   b) patterned white   c) black   d) plain black or plain white

e) black or white?

Write your answers as fractions.

5 a) Copy and complete the table to show the different types of counter in the diagram opposite.

	Blue	Pink	Yellow
A	4		2
B			
C		1	
D	0		

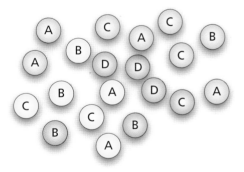

b) A counter is picked at random from the counters shown. What is the probability that:

i) the counter is yellow

ii) the counter has the letter C

iii) the counter is either yellow or shows the letter A?

c) Copy and complete this sentence.

The probability that the counter chosen is _____ is 0.4.

d) How many different ways could you complete the sentence below?

The probability that the counter chosen is _____ is 0.3.

6 The chocolates in a box are all either white, milk or dark chocolate and some of the chocolates are wrapped. The table shows the number of each type.

Wrapped	
Milk	8
White	3
Dark	5

Not wrapped	
Milk	3
White	4
Dark	2

A chocolate is selected at random. Complete these sentences correctly.

The probability that the chocolate chosen is a:

a) wrapped milk chocolate is _____%.

b) dark chocolate and not wrapped is _____%.

c) white chocolate is _____%.

d) _____ is 16%.

e) _____ or _____ is 48%.

End of chapter reflection

You should know that …	You should be able to …	Such as …
If the probability that an event occurs is p, then the probability that it does not occur is $1 - p$.	Calculate the probability that an event does not occur when you are given the probability of the event occurring.	If there is a 23% probability of rain tomorrow, what is the probability that it does not rain?
When an event has equally likely outcomes, you can use this formula to calculate probability: probability of an event $= \dfrac{\text{number of favourable outcomes}}{\text{number of possible outcomes}}$.	Calculate the probability of a favourable outcome given all the possible outcomes of the event.	If you pick a letter at random from the English alphabet written in capital letters, what is the probability of picking: **a)** the letter Q **b)** one of the vowels (A, E, I, O or U) **c)** a letter that is not a vowel.

Unit 2A

Number and calculation

What it's all about?

- Factors and multiples
- Calculations involving fractions and percentages
- Comparing quantities using fractions, decimals and percentages
- Mental methods for calculation and solving problems
- Calculations involving decimals

You will learn about:

- finding and using the prime factorisation of a number
- powers and roots
- written methods for calculating with fractions and decimals
- increasing and decreasing a number by a percentage
- using equivalences between fractions, decimals and percentages
- calculating mentally with fractions, decimals and percentages
- solving proportion problems using mental methods

You will build your skills in:

- calculating accurately using appropriate mental and written methods
- handling fractions, decimals and percentages
- solving word problems

Types of number

You will learn how to:
- Identify and use multiples, factors, common factors, highest common factors, lowest common multiples and primes; write a number in terms of its prime factors, e.g. $500 = 2^2 \times 5^3$.
- Recall squares to 20×20, cubes to $5 \times 5 \times 5$, and corresponding roots.

Starting point

Do you remember ...?

- how to find multiples and factors?

  For example, can you find a multiple of 6? Can you find a factor of 6?

- how to find prime numbers?

  For example, is 1 a prime number? Is 2 a prime number?

- how to use indices?

  For example, $8 \times 8 = 8^2$.

This will also be helpful when you:

- simplify ratios.
- write a fraction in its simplest form by cancelling common factors.
- cancel common factors before multiplying and dividing fractions.

Hook

The numbers on the grey diagonal have a product of 192. The numbers on the purple diagonal have a product of 210. What could the numbers be if they are all greater than 2 but less than 10?

Can you find more than one solution?

What factors do the numbers 192 and 210 have in common?

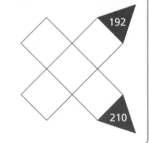

Key terms

The **highest common factor** or **HCF** is the highest number that divides exactly into two or more numbers. For example, the common factors of 12 and 18 are 1, 2, 3 and 6. The **HCF** of 12 and 18 is 6.

The **lowest common multiple** or **LCM** is the lowest multiple of two or more integers. For example, common multiples of 12 and 18 are 36, 72, 108. The **LCM** of 12 and 18 is 36.

The factors of a number that are prime numbers are called **prime factors**. The process of expressing a number as a product of its prime factors is called **prime factorisation**. For example $500 = 2 \times 2 \times 5 \times 5 \times 5$ or $500 = 2^2 \times 5^3$.

The LCM is used when a teacher orders textbooks and workbooks. Students need to have one copy of each book. The books may come in packs of different quantities, for example, 25 books in a pack of textbooks and 20 books in pack of workbooks. To find the minimum number of each pack that must be bought for the books to be paired, the teacher must work out the LCM of the number of books in each pack (the LCM of 25 and 20 is 100).

The HCF is used by a carpenter when he cuts two different lengths of wood into pieces of the same size. To find the greatest length that each piece of wood can be, the carpenter needs to find the HCF of the lengths of pieces of wood.

HCF, LCM and prime factorisation

Worked example 1

Find the HCF and LCM of 40 and 88.

Write 40 and 88 as a product of its prime factors.	Start by writing a factor tree for each number.	Factor tree for 40
$40 = 2 \times 2 \times 2 \times 5$ $88 = 2 \times 2 \times 2 \times 11$	Write each number as a product of its prime factors.	Factor tree for 88
The HCF of 40 and 88 is 8. The LCM of 40 and 88 is 440.	The HCF is the product of the common prime factors. HCF = $2 \times 2 \times 2 = 8$ The LCM is the product of the common prime factors 2, 2, 2 and any other prime factors, in this case 5 and 11. LCM = $2 \times 2 \times 2 \times 5 \times 11 = 440$ You can also use a Venn diagram to find the HCF and LCM. The HCF is the product of the numbers in the intersection. The LCM is the product of all the numbers in the diagram.	$40 = 2 \times 2 \times 2 \times 5$ $88 = 2 \times 2 \times 2 \times 11$

Discuss

Why do you think **LCM** is called 'Lowest' and **HCF** is called 'Highest'?

Worked example 2

a) Find the factors of 48.

b) Write as a product of its prime factors: **i)** 120 **ii)** 48.

a) The factors of 48 are 1, 2, 3, 4, 6, 8, 12, 16, 24 and 48.	Find a pair of numbers that multiply to make 48. Check 2, 3, 4, 5... to see if it is a factor. 48 is not divisible by 5 and 7 so they are not factors of 48. Stop when you reach a number that is already on the list. $1 \times 48 = 48$ $4 \times 12 = 48$ $2 \times 24 = 48$ $6 \times 8 = 48$ $3 \times 16 = 48$	48 1 and 48 6 and 8 2 and 24 4 and 12 3 and 16

b) i) Write down all the prime factors of 120.
 	
$120 = 2 \times 2 \times 2 \times 3 \times 5$
 	
$120 = 2^3 \times 3 \times 5$
	Set out your calculation using a factor tree.
	
	Draw branches of two numbers that multiply to make 120, e.g. 2 and 60.
	
	Repeat for 60, 30 and 15.
	
	When the end number is prime, stop. Circle all the prime factors.
	
	Write the numbers in terms of its prime factors.
	
	This can also be written using power notation.
		120
		2 60
		  2 30
		    2 15
		      3 5

b) ii) Write down all the prime factors of 48.
 	
$48 = 2 \times 2 \times 2 \times 2 \times 3$
 	
$48 = 2^4 \times 3$
	Set out your calculation using a factor tree.
	
	Draw branches of two numbers that multiply to make 48.
	
	Repeat for 24, 12 and 6. Circle all the prime factors.
	
	Write the numbers in terms of its prime factors.
	
	Write the number using power notation.
		48
		2 24
		  2 12
		    2 6
		      2 3

1 Which of these are prime numbers?

    a) 31　　　　　　**b)** 33　　　　　　**c)** 43　　　　　**d)** 47

    e) 51　　　　　　**f)** 53　　　　　　**g)** 77　　　　　**h)** 79

2 List all the factors of each number.

    a) 60　　　　　　**b)** 84　　　　　　**c)** 100

    d) 110　　　　　**e)** 165　　　　　**f)** 196

3 **a)** Which of these numbers are multiples of 21?

       7　21　44　61　84　99　101　105　121

    b) Which of these numbers are multiples of 35?

       35　50　55　70　110　135　140　175　200　205

    c) Which of these numbers are multiples of 44?

       11　22　33　44　80　88　122　132　144　188

4 True or false? Explain your answer.

    a) 6 is a factor of the number $2 \times 3 \times 3$

    b) 10 is a factor of the number $2 \times 3 \times 3$

    c) 12 is a factor of the number $2 \times 3 \times 4$

    d) 12 is a factor of the number $2 \times 2 \times 4$

    e) 30 is a factor of 3×5

    f) 40 is a factor of the number $2 \times 5 \times 2$

    g) $42 = 2 \times 3 \times 6 \times 7$

    h) $50 = 5 \times 10 \times 2 \times 5$

    i) $121 = 10 \times 1 \times 11$

5 Each number is written as the product of its prime factors.

    a) $2 \times 5 \times 5 \times 7$　　　　　　**b)** $2 \times 2 \times 3 \times 3 \times 3$

    List all the factors of each number.

6 Amy says that if you subtract 1 from any multiple of 6, you always get a prime number. Give an example to show that Amy is wrong.

7 Write each number as the product of its prime factors.

    a) 50　　　　　　**b)** 72　　　　　　**c)** 92　　　　　**d)** 105

    e) 108　　　　　**f)** 120　　　　　**g)** 125　　　　**h)** 148

    i) 160　　　　　**j)** 171　　　　　**k)** 177　　　　**l)** 198

8 Write down the number that is represented by:

    a) $2^2 \times 7$　　　　　**b)** $2^2 \times 3 \times 5$　　　　**c)** 5×7^2

    d) $2^3 \times 3^2$　　　　**e)** $2 \times 5^3 \times 7$　　　　**f)** $2^4 \times 3 \times 11$

9 Use the prime factorisation of each number to calculate the HCF and LCM.

a) $50 = 2 \times 5 \times 5$
$70 = 2 \times 5 \times 7$

b) $66 = 2 \times 3 \times 11$
$110 = 2 \times 5 \times 11$

c) $90 = 2 \times 3 \times 3 \times 5$
$117 = 3 \times 3 \times 13$

d) $121 = 11 \times 11$
$132 = 2 \times 2 \times 3 \times 11$

e) $65 = 5 \times 13$
$130 = 2 \times 5 \times 13$

f) $104 = 2 \times 2 \times 2 \times 13$
$135 = 3 \times 3 \times 3 \times 5$

10 Find the HCF and LCM of:

a) 32 and 24   b) 50 and 60   c) 54 and 45   d) 70 and 55

e) 72 and 80   f) 165 and 145   g) 18, 24 and 30   h) 30, 45 and 75

11 Two numbers have HCF = 5 and LCM = 60.

a) Ellie thinks that one of the numbers is 15. What is the other number?

b) Jake thinks that there is another set of numbers that have HCF 5 and LCM 60. What could that be?

> **Tip**
>
> Use a Venn diagram. Where would the HCF be in the Venn diagram?

Squares, cubes and roots

Worked example 3

Work out: a) $7^2 + 5^3$ **b)** $\sqrt{3^2 + 4^2}$ **c)** $\sqrt[3]{11^2 + 2^2}$

> **Tip**
>
> Don't forget to use BIDMAS.

a) $7^2 = 49$ $5^3 = 125$ $7^2 + 5^3 = 174$	First calculate 7^2, then calculate 5^3. Add the answers. $7^2 = 7 \times 7 = 49$ $5^3 = 5 \times 5 \times 5 = 125$ $49 + 125 = 174$
b) $3^2 + 4^2 = 25$ $\sqrt{3^2 + 4^2} = 5$ or $\sqrt{3^2 + 4^2} = -5$ **Tip** Think of $\sqrt{}$ $\sqrt[3]{}$ as brackets. Complete the calculations inside the root first.	First calculate 3^2, then calculate 4^2. Add the answers. $3^2 = 3 \times 3 = 9$ $4^2 = 4 \times 4 = 16$ $9 + 16 = 25$ $\sqrt{25} = 5$ or -5 as $5^2 = 25$ and $(-5)^2 = 25$.
c) $11^2 + 2^2 = 125$ $\sqrt[3]{11^2 + 2^2} = 5$	Start by finding the value of the sum inside the cube root. $11^2 = 11 \times 11 = 121$ $2^2 = 2 \times 2 = 4$ $121 + 4 = 125$ $\sqrt[3]{11^2 + 2^2} = \sqrt[3]{125} = 5$

1 Write down the value of:

a) 12^2 b) 16^2 c) 18^2 d) 19^2

e) $17^2 - 1^2$ f) $16^2 + 5^2$ g) $18^2 + 7^2$ h) $14^2 - 6^2$

2 Write down the value of:

a) $\sqrt{144}$ b) $\sqrt{196}$ c) $\sqrt{256}$ d) $\sqrt{324}$

e) $\sqrt{289}$ f) $\sqrt{121}$ g) $\sqrt{6^2 + 8^2}$ h) $\sqrt{9^2 + 12^2}$

3 Find the value of:

a) 1^3 b) 3^3 c) 5^3 d) $3^3 + 2^2$

e) $4^3 - 3^3$ f) $3^3 + 2^3$ g) $3^3 - 2^3$ h) $5^3 + 4$

4 a) Which of these numbers is not a square number?

196   200   111   121   125   225   259   289   400   404

b) Which of these numbers is not a cube number?

1   8   9   15   25   27   33   64   69   100   109   125

5 Which answer is not an integer?

a) $\sqrt{144}$ b) $\sqrt{200}$ c) $\sqrt{111}$ d) $\sqrt{120}$

e) $\sqrt{225}$ f) $\sqrt{169}$ g) $\sqrt{400}$ h) $\sqrt{196}$

6 Which has the greater value?

a) $\sqrt[3]{27}$ or 4   b) $\sqrt[3]{8}$ or 3   c) $\sqrt[3]{1}$ or $\sqrt{1}$

d) $\sqrt[3]{64}$ or 3^2 e) $\sqrt[3]{125}$ or 2^3 f) $\sqrt[3]{27} + \sqrt[3]{8}$ or $\sqrt[3]{125}$

7 Calculate the value of each expressions.

a) $4^3 + 2^2$ b) $15^2 - 2^3$ c) $1^2 - 1^3$ d) $4^3 \div 2^3$

e) $\sqrt{10^2} + \sqrt{5^2}$ f) $\sqrt[3]{33 - 6}$ g) $\sqrt[3]{800 - 675}$ h) $\sqrt[3]{900 + 100}$

> **Tip**
>
> Add or subtract the numbers inside the root first.

8 Put the numbers in order starting with the smallest.

a) $\sqrt{50}$, 3^2, $\sqrt{20}$, $\sqrt{18 \times 2}$, $\sqrt{2^2 + 3^2}$ b) 3^3, $\sqrt[3]{100}$, $\sqrt[3]{8^2}$, 1^3, $\sqrt[3]{5^2 + 10^2}$

9 Jo says that:

$$\sqrt{100 + 25} = \sqrt{100} + \sqrt{25} \qquad \sqrt{100 + 25} = 10 + 5 = 15$$

Explain how you can check that Jo is wrong.

10 If ⬤ and ▢ are prime numbers and $\sqrt{⬤^2 - ▢}$ is a whole number, what could the values of ⬤ and ▢ be?

End of chapter reflection

You should know that ...	You should be able to ...	Such as ...
The **highest common factor** of two numbers **(HCF)** is the largest number that is a factor of them both. The **lowest common multiple (LCM)** of two numbers is the smallest number that they both divide into.	Find the HCF and LCM of two given numbers. Find the HCF and LCM by listing all the factors and/or using a Venn diagram.	Find the HCF and LCM of 80 and 128.
Any number greater than 1 can be written as a unique product of its **prime factors**. This is called the **prime factorisation** of the numbers.	Write a number as a product of its prime factors. Use a factor tree diagram to find all the prime factors of a number.	Write 100 as a product of its prime factors.
A **square number** is the product of a number multiplied by itself. A **cube number** is the product of a number multiplied by itself and then by itself again. A **square root** is a number that when multiplied by itself gives a result equal to the number given. A **cube root** is a number that when multiplied by itself, then multiplied again by itself, gives a result equal to the number given.	Recall square numbers to 20×20 and cube numbers to $5 \times 5 \times 5$.	Match the numbers that have the same value. 400, 13^3, 3, $\sqrt[3]{27}$, 169, 20^2

Fractions

You will learn how to:
- Add and subtract fractions and mixed numbers; calculate fractions of quantities (fraction answers); multiply and divide an integer by a fraction.
- Calculate and solve problems involving percentages of quantities and percentage increases or decreases; express one given number as a fraction or percentage of another.
- Use equivalent fractions, decimals and percentages to compare different quantities.

Starting point

Do you remember …?

- how to calculate fractions of a quantity?
  For example, find $\frac{1}{4}$ of 128.
- how to calculate % of a quantity?
  For example, find 20% of 80 kg.

This will also be helpful when you:

- learn how to add and subtract algebraic fractions
- solve problems involving reverse percentage. For example, I bought a jumper for £18 when it was reduced by 70% in a sale. What was the original price?

Hook

True or false?

Work in pairs. Choose a box and decide if the statement is true or false.
- If the statement is true, you win 3 points.
- If the statement is false, change one of the numbers so that the statement becomes true.
- A new correct statement wins you 2 points.
- The winner is the one that has the most points.

$\frac{1}{5}$ of 10 km $= \frac{1}{10}$ of 5 km	1% of 100 m = 100% of 1 m	40% of \$60 = 60% of \$40
20% of \$80 = 80% of \$20	$\frac{1}{4}$ of 8 kg $= \frac{1}{8}$ of 4 kg	20% of 40 $= \frac{1}{4}$ of 20

Key terms

In a **proper fraction** the numerator is less than the denominator. For example, $\frac{7}{11}$.

In an **improper fraction** the numerator is greater than the denominator. For example, $\frac{17}{11}$.
A **mixed number** is a combination of a whole number and a proper fraction used to represent a quantity with a value greater than 1. For example, $3\frac{1}{4}$.

We can use fractions (and whole numbers) to increase or decrease a value. You can also use a **multiplier** to increase or decrease a number. For example, multiplying 20 by 1.2 will increase it by 20%. 1.2 is called the **multiplier**.

Fractions, decimals and percentages are equivalent if they have the same value. A percentage represents the number of parts per hundred. For example, 21% means 21 parts per 100 or 0.21.

> Did you know?
>
> **Numerator** stems from the Latin *numerare* meaning 'to count'. It (counts) tells us how many equal parts of a whole we have.
>
> **Denominator** stems from the Latin *denominare* meaning 'to name'. It tells us (names) how many equal parts our whole is divided into.

Adding and subtracting mixed numbers

Worked example 1

Work out:

a) $\frac{3}{4} + \frac{3}{5}$

b) $\frac{4}{5} - \frac{2}{3}$

a) $\frac{3}{4} + \frac{3}{5}$	Make the denominators the same by changing the denominators to their lowest common multiple (LCM). 20 is the LCM of 4 and 5.	
$= \frac{15}{20} + \frac{12}{20}$	Change $\frac{3}{4}$ to $\frac{15}{20}$ by multiplying the numerator and denominator by 5. Change $\frac{3}{5}$ to $\frac{12}{20}$ by multiplying the numerator and denominator by 4.	
$= \frac{27}{20}$ or $1\frac{7}{20}$	The answer is an improper fraction so write this as a mixed number.	
b) $\frac{4}{5} - \frac{2}{3}$	Write the fractions over a common denominator. You can use 15 because 15 is the LCM of 5 and 3.	

$= \frac{12}{15} - \frac{10}{15}$	Change $\frac{4}{5}$ to $\frac{12}{15}$ by multiplying the numerator and denominator by 3.	
	Change $\frac{2}{3}$ to $\frac{10}{15}$ by multiplying the numerator and denominator by 5.	
	Now the denominators are the same, subtract the fractions.	
$= \frac{2}{15}$		

Worked example 2

Work out:

a) $1\frac{1}{2} + 1\frac{1}{3}$

b) $2\frac{1}{4} - 1\frac{5}{8}$

a) $1\frac{1}{2} + 1\frac{1}{3}$ $= 1 + \frac{1}{2} + 1 + \frac{1}{3}$	$1\frac{1}{2}$ and $1\frac{1}{3}$ are made of a whole number and a fractional part.	
$\frac{1}{2} + \frac{1}{3}$ $= \frac{3}{6} + \frac{2}{6}$ $= \frac{5}{6}$	Add the fractional parts first. Start by writing the fractions over a common denominator.	
$\frac{5}{6} + 1 + 1$ $= 2\frac{5}{6}$	Add on the whole number parts.	
b) $2\frac{1}{4} - 1\frac{5}{8}$	Sometimes it is easier to convert the mixed numbers to improper fractions.	

$2\frac{1}{4} = 1 + 1 + \frac{1}{4}$

$= \frac{4}{4} + \frac{4}{4} + \frac{1}{4}$

$= \frac{9}{4}$

Write $2\frac{1}{4}$ as an improper fraction.

$1\frac{5}{8} = 1 + \frac{5}{8}$

$= \frac{8}{8} + \frac{5}{8}$

$= \frac{13}{8}$

Write $1\frac{5}{8}$ as an improper fraction.

$2\frac{1}{4} - 1\frac{5}{8}$

$= \frac{9}{4} - \frac{13}{8}$

$= \frac{18}{8} - \frac{13}{8}$

Write the fractions over a common denominator.

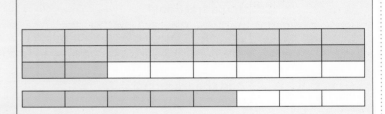

$= \frac{5}{8}$

Subtract the fractions.

Think about

Which subtraction calculations is it most useful to convert mixed numbers into improper fractions for?

Exercise 1 1–7

1 Work out:

a) $\frac{1}{2} + \frac{3}{8}$

b) $\frac{8}{9} + \frac{5}{6}$

c) $\frac{7}{10} + \frac{5}{6}$

d) $\frac{5}{7} - \frac{2}{5}$

e) $\frac{7}{8} + \frac{1}{3}$

f) $\frac{7}{11} - \frac{2}{7}$

g) $\frac{3}{8} + \frac{3}{5}$

h) $\frac{11}{12} - \frac{5}{8}$

2 Each pair of blocks adds to give the block above them. Use addition and subtraction to find the missing fractions.

a)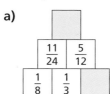

b)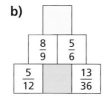

c)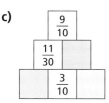

3 Work out these calculations. Give your answers in their simplest form.

a) $1\frac{1}{2} + \frac{7}{12}$ b) $1\frac{7}{10} - \frac{3}{5}$ c) $1\frac{5}{6} - \frac{2}{3}$ d) $\frac{7}{9} + 1\frac{5}{6}$

e) $1\frac{4}{5} - \frac{3}{4}$ f) $1\frac{1}{9} + 1\frac{2}{3}$ g) $1\frac{1}{2} - 1\frac{1}{4}$ h) $2\frac{3}{20} + 1\frac{1}{10}$

i) $2\frac{1}{15} - 1\frac{2}{3}$ j) $1\frac{3}{5} + 2\frac{2}{3}$

4 Work out these calculations. Show your workings clearly.

a) $1\frac{1}{2} - \frac{3}{4}$ b) $1\frac{4}{5} - \frac{3}{10}$ c) $2\frac{1}{6} - \frac{2}{3}$ d) $2\frac{1}{9} + \frac{5}{6}$

e) $1\frac{1}{4} - \frac{5}{6}$ f) $2\frac{4}{9} - 1\frac{2}{3}$ g) $2\frac{1}{2} - 1\frac{3}{8}$ h) $2\frac{8}{15} - 1\frac{4}{5}$

i) $2\frac{4}{5} - 1\frac{3}{4}$ j) $3\frac{1}{7} - 2\frac{4}{5}$

5 Here is a list of fractions and mixed numbers.

$1\frac{4}{5}$ $\frac{3}{4}$ $2\frac{1}{2}$ $\frac{5}{6}$ $3\frac{1}{7}$ $\frac{3}{8}$

Choose from the list:

a) two fractions that have the highest sum. What is the sum?

b) two fractions that have the lowest difference.

> **Tip**
>
> Add the fractions to find their sum. Subtract them to calculate their difference.

6 Use the digits 2, 3, 4, 5, 6 and 7 each exactly once to make this calculation true.

 $= 5\frac{1}{12}$

7 Work out:

a) $1\frac{1}{8} + 3\frac{5}{16} + 2\frac{1}{4}$ b) $1\frac{1}{5} + 1\frac{3}{20} + 2\frac{1}{2}$ c) $2\frac{8}{9} - 1\frac{3}{6} + 1\frac{13}{36}$ d) $3\frac{9}{10} - 1\frac{1}{3} - 1\frac{1}{5}$

Multiplying and dividing an integer by a fraction

Worked example 3

a) i) $2 \times \frac{2}{5}$ ii) $\frac{2}{3}$ of 2 kg

b) $4 \div \frac{1}{3}$

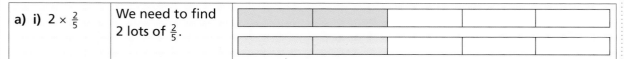

a) i) $2 \times \frac{2}{5}$	We need to find 2 lots of $\frac{2}{5}$.	

$= \frac{2 \times 2}{5}$ $= \frac{4}{5}$	Multiply the numerator of the fraction by 2.	
ii) $\frac{2}{3}$ of 2 kg	We need to find $\frac{2}{3}$ of each kilogram.	
$= \frac{2}{3} \times 2$	Multiply the numerator of the fraction by 2.	
$= \frac{2 \times 2}{3} = \frac{4}{3}$ $= 1\frac{1}{3}$ kg	Change the answer from an improper fraction to a mixed number.	
b) $4 \div \frac{1}{3}$ $= 4 \times \frac{3}{1}$ $= \frac{12}{1}$ $= 12$	Invert the fraction and change division into multiplication.	Divide each of the 4 units into three thirds. 12

Exercise 2   1–5

1 Work out the following calculations. Give your answers as mixed numbers.

   a) $\frac{3}{4} \times 21$ kg   **b)** $\frac{4}{5} \times 33$ km   **c)** $41 \times \frac{2}{3}$ **d)** $12 \times \frac{2}{9}$

   e) $13 \times \frac{5}{6}$ **f)** $\frac{2}{3} \times 10$ kg   **g)** $3 \times 1\frac{3}{8}$ **h)** $8 \times 1\frac{4}{5}$

   i) $5 \times 1\frac{3}{4}$ **j)** $1\frac{1}{5} \times 12$ ml

2 Write the calculations in order from smallest answer to largest answer.

   a) $\frac{2}{3} \times 25$ **b)** $\frac{4}{5} \times 31$ **c)** $25 \times \frac{3}{4}$

   d) $12 \times 1\frac{1}{8}$ **e)** $18 \times 1\frac{1}{2}$ **f)** $2\frac{4}{5} \times 11$

3 Which of the numbers in this list is not an answer to the calculations in parts a) to c)?

   6   8   10   12   25   30   32.

   a) $20 \div \frac{4}{5}$ **b)** $10 \div 1\frac{1}{4}$ **c)** $36 \div \frac{6}{5}$

   d) Write division calculations for the other answers. How many can you find for each one?

124   Unit 2A: Number and calculation

4 Ben and Sophie use two different methods to calculate $10 \div 2\frac{1}{2}$.

Use both methods to calculate the following:

a) $21 \div 1\frac{3}{4}$ b) $44 \div 1\frac{3}{8}$

c) $24 \div 2\frac{2}{5}$

Which method do you prefer? Why?

Ben's method

$10 \div 2\frac{1}{2}$

$= 10 \div \frac{5}{2}$

$= 10 \times \frac{2}{5}$

$= 10 \div 5 \times 2$

$= 2 \times 2 = 4$

Sophie's method

$10 \div 2\frac{1}{2}$

$= 10 \div \frac{5}{2}$

$= \frac{10 \times 2}{5}$

$= \frac{20}{5}$

$= 4$

5 a) Sami divides an integer by a fraction. The answer is 10.

$$\boxed{} \div \frac{\boxed{}}{\boxed{}} = 10$$

Write down what the integer and the fraction could be. Now think of a different pair of answers.

b) Find the missing fraction.

$$3 \times \boxed{} \frac{\boxed{}}{\boxed{}} = 20 \div 2\frac{1}{2}$$

Increasing and decreasing a quantity by a percentage

Worked example 4

Calculate 2.5% of $120:

a) without a calculator

b) with a calculator.

a) 10% of $120	Start by finding 10% of the amount by dividing by 10.	100% $120
$= \$120 \div 10$		
$= \$12$		10% $12, 10% $12, 10% $12, 10% $12, 10% $12, 10% $12, 10% $12, 10% $12, 10% $12, 10% $12
2.5% of $120		10% $12
$= \$12 \div 4$	To find 2.5%, divide 10% by 4 or halve 10% twice.	2.5% $3
$= \$3$		
b) $2.5\% = 0.025$	Change 2.5% to a decimal.	
120×0.025		
$= \$3$	Multiply 120 by the decimal.	

Worked example 5

a) Increase 20 grams by 16% without using a calculator.

b) Decrease 260 metres by 21% using a calculator

a) 10% of 200 g = 20 g 1% of 200 g = 2 g 6% of 200 g = 6 × 2 = 12 g 16% of 200 g = 20 g + 12 g = 32 g 200 g + 32 g = 232 g	Find 10% and 1% first. To find 6%, multiply 1% by 6. To find 16%, add 10% and 6%. Add the increase on to the original amount.
b) 100% − 21% = 79% 79% = 0.79 260 m × 0.79 = 205.4 m	Calculate the multiplier by subtracting 21% from 100% and converting to a decimal. Multiply 260 m by the multiplier.

Exercise 3   1–3, 5, 10

1 Use an appropriate method to work out:

   a) 2% of 1200   **b)** 15% of 2000   **c)** 5% of 2300   **d)** 19% of 3000

   e) 45% of 3000   **f)** 35% of 5000   **g)** 40% of 8600   **h)** 9% of 2800

2 Increase:

   a) $3600 by 1%   **b)** 1600 ml by 2%   **c)** 160 m by 10%   **d)** 250 kg by 25%

3 Decrease:

   a) $5000 by 4%   **b)** 250 km by 5%   **c)** 180 m by 20%   **d)** 300 g by 25%

4 Use a calculator to find:

   a) 13% of 350 kg   **b)** 45% of $82   **c)** 6% of 19 cm   **d)** 67% of 3200 km

   e) 3% of 820 kg   **f)** 99% of 104 km   **g)** 8% of 1200 ml   **h)** 12% of $2900

5 Find the value of the multiplier in each case.

   a) Increase by 12%   **b)** Increase by 3%   **c)** Decrease by 26%   **d)** Decrease by 36%

   e) Increase by 45%   **f)** Decrease by 48%   **g)** Increase by 72%   **h)** Decrease by 83%

6 Use a calculator to:

   a) increase $3680 by 38%   **b)** increase 38.5 km by 49%

   c) increase 298 kg by 35%   **d)** increase 876 litres by 8%

7 Use a calculator to:

   a) decrease 3560 kg by 7%   **b)** decrease 485 m by 38%

   c) decrease 178.5 cm by 48%   **d)** decrease $67.50 by 32%

8 Which calculation in each pair has the larger answer?

a) Increase $60 by 20% or decrease $65 by 20%

b) Increase 420 kg by 35% or increase 400 kg by 40%

c) Increase 560 kg by 35% or decrease 900 kg by 15%

d) Increase 875 g by 24% or decrease 1 kg by 16%

9 Rearrange these cards to make three correct calculations.

28%	$225	of	$175	=
Increase	$238	by 32%	$261	=
Decrease	$850	by 16%	$231	=

10 a) Jo increases $100 by 100%.

Here is her working.

100% + 100% = 200%

200% = 2

$100 × 2 = $200.

Is Jo correct? Explain your answer.

b) James wants to increase $4.20 by 6%. Here is his working.

1 + 0.6 = 1.6

$4.20 × 1.6 = $6.76

Is James correct? Explain your answer.

Think about

If you increase a number by 10%, then decrease the answer by 10%, do you get back to the original number?

One number as a fraction or percentage of another

Worked example 6

a) Write 48 cm as a fraction of 0.76 m.

b) 96 out of 200 students are girls. Write this as a percentage.

c) Use a calculator to work out what percentage $351 is of $1800.

| a) 0.76 m = 76 cm $\frac{48}{76}$ | Start by changing 0.76 m into cm. Form the fraction. | |
| $\frac{48}{76} = \frac{12}{19}$ | Simplify the fraction by dividing both numerator and denominator by 4. | |

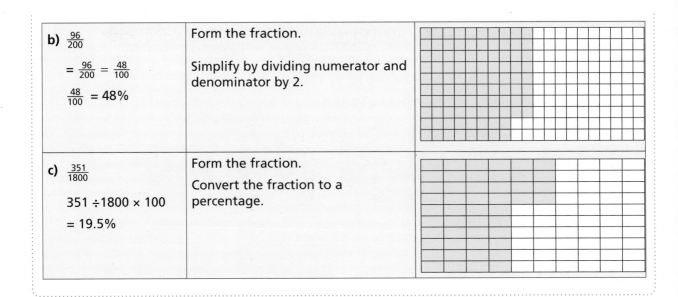

b) $\frac{96}{200}$

$= \frac{96}{200} = \frac{48}{100}$

$\frac{48}{100} = 48\%$

Form the fraction.

Simplify by dividing numerator and denominator by 2.

c) $\frac{351}{1800}$

$351 \div 1800 \times 100$

$= 19.5\%$

Form the fraction.

Convert the fraction to a percentage.

Exercise 4   1–4

1 Write the following as a fraction and as a percentage. Write the fractions in their simplest form.

a) 18 out of 20 **b)** 36 out of 60 **c)** 27 out of 45

d) 12 out of 150 **e)** 14 out of 40 **f)** 78 out of 120

2 Express each of the following as a percentage.

a) $6 of $20 **b)** 12 minutes of 1 hour **c)** 212 kg of 848 kg

d) 39 weeks of a year **e)** 48 minutes of 2 hours **f)** 15 seconds of 1 minute

3 Jake makes these calculations:

If $\frac{1}{4} = 25\%$, then $\frac{1}{8} = 50\%$ and $\frac{3}{8} = 150\%$.

Amy thinks this is wrong because $\frac{3}{8}$ is less than 1, so the answer should be less than 100%.

Who is right? What is the correct percentage equivalent to $\frac{3}{8}$?

4 Write each proportion as a percentage.

a) 37 bikes out of 148 bikes **b)** 127 apples out of 635 apples **c)** 3 boys out of 300 boys

d) 11 pencils out of 220 pencils **e)** 67 cups out of 201 cups **f)** 39 trees out of 156 trees

g) 40 minutes out of 2 hours **h)** 86 cm out of 3.44 m

5 Use >, < or = to make these statements true.

a) $\frac{3}{16}$ of $40 ☐ $\frac{7}{32}$ of $40 **b)** $\frac{7}{15}$ of 750 ml ☐ 70% of 500 ml

c) $\frac{3}{4} \times 160$ kg ☐ $\frac{1}{4}$ of 480 kg **d)** 0.45×120 km ☐ $\frac{4}{9} \times 120$ km

e) $\frac{9}{50} \times 300$ litres ☐ 0.18×307 litres **f)** $20\% \times \$80$ ☐ $1.2 \times \$40$

g) $1.25 \times \$88$ ☐ $\frac{1}{8} \times \$1500$ **h)** $2\frac{1}{4} \times 32$ g ☐ 2.14 ☐ 2.14×32 g

6 If ● and ■ are different integers less than 10 and $\frac{●}{■} > 60\%$, what could the values of ● and ■ be? Can you find a different answer?

Comparing quantities using fractions, decimals and percentages

Worked example 7

Which of these proportions is greater?

a) 18.5% or $\frac{7}{20}$ **b)** 60% or $\frac{2}{5}$ **c)** 0.31 or $\frac{1}{3}$

> **Tip**
>
> You can compare two or more proportions by converting them to:
> - fractions with a common denominator
> - decimals
> - percentages.

a) $\frac{7}{20} = \frac{35}{100}$ Compare by converting $\frac{7}{20}$ to a percentage.

$= 35\%$ To change $\frac{7}{20}$ to a percentage, multiply the numerator and denominator by 5.

$18.5\% < 35\%$ Compare the percentages.
$18.5\% < \frac{7}{20}$

b) $60\% = \frac{60}{100}$ Change 60% to a fraction.

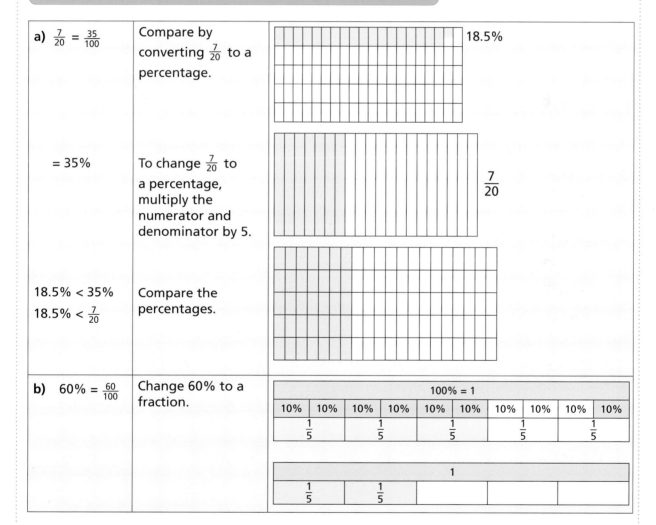

$\frac{60}{100} = \frac{3}{5}$ $\frac{3}{5} > \frac{2}{5}$ $60\% > \frac{2}{5}$	Simplify the fraction by dividing the numerator and denominator by 20. Compare the fractions.	$\frac{1}{5}$	$\frac{1}{5}$	$\frac{1}{5}$		
		$\frac{1}{5}$	$\frac{1}{5}$			

c) $\frac{1}{3} = 0.3$

$0.\dot{3} > 0.31$

Write $\frac{1}{3}$ as a decimal. Compare the decimals.

0.31

0   0.10 0.20 0.30 0.40 0.50 0.60 0.70 0.80 0.90 1.00

$\frac{1}{3}$	$\frac{1}{3}$	$\frac{1}{3}$

Exercise 5   1–2, 4

1 Which proportion in each pair is greater?

  a) 59% $\frac{3}{5}$ **b)** 0.44 $\frac{11}{20}$ **c)** $\frac{9}{25}$ 36.6%   **d)** 0. 77 $\frac{3}{4}$

2 Write each set in order starting with the smallest.

  a) $\frac{3}{12}$ 0.24   24.9% $\frac{1}{5}$

  b) 0.6 $\frac{2}{3}$ 61%   0.605

  c) 0.88 $\frac{48}{60}$ 81%   39 out of 50

3 These are Tom's results in his mocks.

Maths	English	Science
$\frac{139}{160}$	82.5%	40 out of 50

In which of the mocks did he achieve the best result?

4 Ben exercised for 1 hour. He ran for 39 minutes and stretched for the rest.

'I ran 39% of the time!' he said.

Is Ben correct? Explain your answer.

5 The proportions below are in order starting with the smallest value.

Use each of the digits 2, 3, 4, 5 exactly once to complete the statement.

  4 ☐ % $\frac{☐}{7}$ 0.4 ☐   4 ☐ %

End of chapter reflection

You should know that ...	You should be able to ...	Such as ...
To **add or subtract fractions,** first convert to equivalent fractions with the same denominator, and then add or subtract the numerators. To **add mixed numbers,** add the fractional part and the integer part separately, then combine. To **subtract mixed numbers,** it is sometimes easier to convert both numbers to improper fractions before subtracting them.	Add and subtract fractions with different denominators. Add and subtract two mixed numbers. Give your answer as an improper fraction. Give your answer as a mixed number.	$\frac{3}{7} + \frac{2}{9}$ $1\frac{3}{8} + 1\frac{1}{5}$ $2\frac{1}{2} - 1\frac{8}{9}$
To **multiply a fraction by an integer,** multiply the numerator by the integer. If it is a mixed number, convert to an improper fraction first. **When dividing an integer by a fraction,** invert the fraction and then multiply.	Multiply a fraction by an integer. Divide an integer by a fraction.	$\frac{3}{7} \times 9$ $7 \div \frac{3}{5}$
To **increase or decrease** a number by a percentage, use a **multiplier.** To find the multiplier, add or subtract the % increase or decrease to 100%, then change the answer to a decimal.	Increase or decrease a quantity by a given percentage.	Increase 200 g by 15%.
To **express one number as a percentage of another,** write the numbers as fractions first, then multiply by 100.	Write a number as fraction of another number. Simplify the fraction. Multiply by 100.	Write 120 cm as a percentage of 150 cm.
To compare two or more proportions, you can convert them to fractions with a common denominator, or you can convert all of them to decimals or percentages.	Compare proportions by converting them to fractions with the same denominator or percentages or decimals.	Which of these proportions is the greatest? 16.5% 0.16 $\frac{3}{20}$

Using known facts

You will learn how to:

- Use known facts and place value to multiply and divide simple decimals, e.g. 0.07 × 9, 2.4 ÷ 3.
- Use known facts and place value to calculate simple fractions and percentages of quantities.

Starting point

Do you remember …?

- your multiplication facts up to 10 × 10?

  For example, write down 8 × 9, 7 × 7, and 6 × 8.

- how to use the multiplication facts you know to make other multiplication and division facts?

  For example, 8 × 9 = 72, write down 8 × 90, 72 ÷ 8, $\frac{1}{8}$ of 72.

This will also be helpful when you:

- calculate averages

  For example, there was a total of 8.4 cm of rain in one week, find the average amount of rain for one day in this week.

- cancel common factors before multiplying and dividing fractions.

Hook

You should know that 4 × 5 = 20.

Did you know that we can use this fact to work out 4.5 × 4.5? (*4.5 is exactly halfway between 4 and 5.*)

To work out 4.5 × 4.5, work out 4 × 5 first, then add 0.25.

4.5 × 4.5 = 4 × 5 + 0.25

Look at the picture on the right. Can you see why it works?

Using the method shown above, work out:

a) 7.5 × 7.5 **b)** 8.5² **c)** 99.5 × 99.5

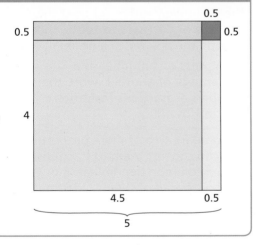

Did you know?

Number facts are used when buying and selling in the food spices market.

For example, if the shopkeeper knows what $7 × 8 is, he can use this to work out how much 0.8 kg at $7 per kg or 0.08 kg at $7 per kg will be, when selling food spices.

At the end of the day, if he reduces the prices of certain items, for example by 30% or 45%, he can use his knowledge of finding 1%, or 10% to work out how much he can sell his items for.

Key terms

A **multiple** of a number is the result of multiplying it by a whole number.
A **digit** is a numeral used to show a number or a part of a number. 439 is a 3-digit number with digits 4, 3 and 9.

The **place value grid** (below) shows the value of each digit in a number.

1 000 000	100 000	10 000	1000	100	10	1	•	0.1	0.01	0.001
millions	hundred thousands	ten thousands	thousands	hundreds	tens	units	decimal point	tenths	hundredths	thousandths
							•			

Multiplying and dividing decimals by whole numbers

Worked example 1

a) Given that 7 × 9 = 63, write down the value of:

   i) 7 × 0.9   **ii)** 7 × 0.09.

b) Given the fact that 8 × 3 = 24, write down the value of: **i)** 2.4 ÷ 3 **ii)** 0.024 × 3.

a i) 7 × 0.9 = 6.3	Seven groups of 9 make 63 so seven groups of 9 tenths make 63 tenths or 6.3	63 = 9 9 9 9 9 9 9 6.3 = 0.9 0.9 0.9 0.9 0.9 0.9 0.9
ii) 7 × 0.09 = 0.63	and seven groups of 9 hundredths make 63 hundredths.	0.63 = 0.09 0.09 0.09 0.09 0.09 0.09 0.09
b i) 2.4 ÷ 3 = 0.8	8 × 3 = 24 so 24 ÷ 3 = 8.	24 → 8
ii) 0.024 ÷ 3 = 0.008	If we divide 24 tenths or 2.4 by 3, the answer is 8 tenths or 0.8. If we divide 24 thousandths or 0.024 by 3, the answer is 8 thousandths or 0.008.	2.4 → 0.8 0.024 → 0.08

Exercise 1   1–13

1 Calculate:

   a) 0.08 × 7   **b)** 9 × 0.06   **c)** 0.006 × 6   **d)** 0.007 × 8

   e) 0.56 ÷ 8   **f)** 0.49 ÷ 7   **g)** 0.036 ÷ 2   **h)** 0.027 ÷ 3

2 What is the product of:

a) 0.07 and 8   b) 0.004 and 6   c) 0.008 and 5   d) 0.0003 and 9?

3 What is the quotient of:

a) 0.36 and 3   b) 0.024 and 8   c) 0.018 and 9   d) 0.0033 and 11?

4 Which of these is the odd one out? Explain your answer.

a) 0.081 ÷ 9   b) 0.03 × 3   c) 0.036 ÷ 4   d) 0.001 × 9

5 Amy and Tom calculate 0.005 × 6. Amy thinks the answer is 0.03. Tom thinks the answer is 0.0030. Which one is correct? Explain your answer.

6 If ■ × ◆ = 0.072, ■ is a decimal number and ◆ is an integer less than 13, list all the values that ■ and ◆ could be.

> **Tip**
>
> Use your times table knowledge, together with divisibility tests.

7 Write the missing numbers.

a) 3 × ☐ = 0.06   b) ☐ ÷ 7 = 0.004   c) 6 × ☐ = 0.024   d) 0.0016 ÷ 8 = ☐

e) 0.009 × ☐ = 0.045   f) 0.035 ÷ ☐ = 0.005   g) ☐ × 8 = 0.04   h) ☐ ÷ 4 = 0.0008

8 Write whether these statements are true or false. If a statement is false, write down the correct answer.

a) 0.003 × 4 = 0.0012   b) 0.0006 × 5 = 0.00030   c) 4 × 0.011 = 0.044

d) 0.0012 × 5 = 0.006   e) 0.042 ÷ 7 = 0.060   f) 0.02 ÷ 4 = 0.005

g) 0.028 ÷ 7 = 0.004   h) 0.0004 ÷ 8 = 0.005

> **Think about**
>
> Is 0.02 ÷ 5 = 0.0020 ÷ 5?

9 Copy and complete the table below.

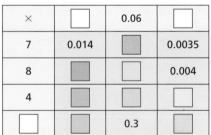

×	☐	0.06	☐
7	0.014	▨	0.0035
8	▨	☐	0.004
4	▨	☐	☐
☐	▨	0.3	▨

10 Find the missing numbers.

a) 0.03 + 0.03 + 0.03 + 0.03 × 5 = ☐ × 0.03 = ☐

b) 13 × 0.0005 − 0.0005 × 6 = ☐ × 0.05 = ☐

11 Ben has one roll of string that is 1.44 m long. He cuts it into two equal parts. He then cuts the first half into 12 equal pieces and the second half is cut into 3 equal pieces. Which pieces are longer? How much longer?

12 a) 1 m of wire has mass 0.08 kg. Write down the mass of 9 m of this wire.

b) 9 m of a different type of wire has mass 0.63 kg. Write down the mass of 1 m of the wire.

Discuss

Jake says that when multiplying 0.006 by 4, he works out $6 \times 4 = 24$, then he counts the number of places that are to the right of the decimal point of the number he is multiplying (in this example there are 3 digits after the decimal point in 0.006). He then moves the decimal point from right to left the same number of decimal places in his answer.

$$0.\underline{006} \times 4 = \underline{24}$$
$$0.\underline{006} \times 4 = 0.\underline{024}$$

Why does Jake's method work? Is it always correct? Does it work for 0.006×5?

13 Alex thinks that $0.012 \div 2 = 0.06$. He is wrong. Explain why.

Calculating fractions and percentages of quantities

Worked example 2

a) Work out: **i)** $\frac{5}{9}$ of 72 **ii)** $\frac{1}{9}$ of 72 000

b) Work out: **i)** 3% of 900 **ii)** 85% of 900

	We know that $8 \times 9 = 72$.	
a) i) $\frac{1}{9}$ of $72 = 72 \div 9 = 8$	We can use this fact to work out $\frac{1}{9}$ of 72.	
$\frac{5}{9}$ of $72 = 5 \times 8 = 40$	We can then find $\frac{5}{9}$ of 72 by multiplying $\frac{1}{9}$ of 72 by 5.	
ii) $\frac{1}{9}$ of $72 = 8$	$\frac{1}{9}$ of 72 is 8.	
$\frac{1}{9}$ of 72 000 =	To get from 72 to 72 000 we multiply by 1000.	
$\frac{1}{9} \times 72 \times 1000 =$	We also multiply the answer by 1000.	
$8 \times 1000 =$		
8000		

Chapter 15: Using known facts **135**

b) i) 1% of $900 =$ $900 \div 100 = 9$	You can find 1% of 900 and use this to work out 3% of 900.	100% 900 / 1% 9
3% of $900 =$ $3 \times 9 = 27$	To find 3%, multiply 1% by 3.	100% 900 / 1% 9 1% 9 1% 9
ii)	To find 85%, you add 80% and 5%.	
$10\% = 90$	You can find 10% of 900 by dividing by 10.	100% 900 / 10% 90 (×10)
80% of $900 =$ $8 \times 90 = \mathbf{720}$	To find 80%, multiply 10% by 8.	100% 900 / 10% 90 (×10)
$10\% = 90,$ $5\% =$ $90 \div 2 = \mathbf{45}$	To find 5%, halve the 10% that you have found.	100% 900 / 10% 90 ... 5% 45 5% 45 10% 90
$85\% =$ $80\% + 5\% =$ $720 + 45 = 765$	You can find 85% by adding 80% and 5%.	

Exercise 2   1–8

1 Write down the value of:

a) $\frac{1}{8}$ of 3200   b) $\frac{1}{9}$ of 5400   c) $\frac{1}{7}$ of 21 000   d) $\frac{1}{11}$ of 12 100

e) $\frac{5}{8}$ of 32   f) $\frac{7}{9}$ of 54   g) $\frac{6}{7}$ of 21   h) $\frac{8}{11}$ of 121

2 Find the value of:

a) 2% of 70   b) 8% of 900   c) 5% of 400   d) 10% of 68

e) 10% of 500   f) 5% of 700   g) 2% of 4000   h) 20% of 4000

3 Look at these calculations.

If the answer is wrong, write down the correct answer.

a) 30% of $80 = 24$ b) 7% of $800 = 560$ c) 5% of $500 = 5$ d) 35% of $120 = 14$

e) $\frac{5}{9}$ of $2700 = 1500$ f) $\frac{5}{9}$ of $45 = 81$ g) $\frac{2}{11} \times 8800 = 1600$ h) $\frac{11}{12}$ of $60 = 66$

4 Which answers are not whole numbers?

a) $\frac{4}{11}$ of 22   b) 3% of 700   c) $\frac{1}{12}$ of 60   d) 5% of 2300

e) 25% of 120   f) $\frac{5}{8}$ of 240   g) 10% of 35   h) 5% of 250

5 In each pair, which has the greater value?

   a) $\frac{1}{8}$ of \$400 or 10% of \$200   **b)** 5% of 400 kg or 90% of 80 kg

   c) 50% of 6.8 litres or $\frac{2}{5}$ of 10 litres   **d)** 60% of 80 cm or $\frac{1}{7}$ of 3.5 m

> **Tip**
>
> Remember 1 kg = 1000 g, 1 km = 1000 m and 1 m = 100 cm.

6 Write each set of numbers in order starting with the smallest.

   a) 1% of 3800 km, $\frac{3}{4}$ of 204 km, 25% of 120 km, 3% of 700 km, $\frac{3}{5}$ of 600 km

   b) $\frac{2}{9}$ of 63 kg, 9% of 200 kg, 25% of 120 kg, $\frac{2}{5}$ of 350 kg, $\frac{6}{7}$ of 490 kg

7 **a)** Joe uses the fact that 90% of \$400 = \$360 to work out

        9% of \$40 = \$36.

     Can you explain why Joe is wrong?

   b) Alice uses the fact that 27 × 11 = 287 to work out

        $\frac{1}{33}$ of 287 = 81.

     Explain why Alice is wrong. Write the correct answer.

8 Find the missing numbers.

   a) 2% of 400 m = $\frac{1}{5}$ of ☐ m   **b)** 25% of 8 kg = $\frac{1}{☐}$ of 4 kg

   c) 0.9 × 4 = ☐ × 0.6   **d)** 0.4 × ☐ = 0.8 × 3

End of chapter reflection

You should know that ...	You should be able to ...	Such as ...
You can use known facts and place value to multiply decimals by whole numbers mentally.	Use your times tables and place values to work out calculations.	3 × 9 = 27 Write down the value of 0.003 × 9.
You can use known facts and place value to divide decimals by whole numbers mentally.		36 ÷ 3 = 12 Write down the value of 0.036 ÷ 3.
You can use times table facts and place value to find fractions of other numbers (multiples to the original number) and other fractions of the same number.	Work out fractions of an amount by using unit fractions and place value.	If 8 × 4 = 32, what is **a)** $\frac{1}{8}$ of 3200 **b)** $\frac{5}{8}$ of 32?
Percentages of an amount can be found by using known facts and place value.	Work out percentages of an amount by combining percentages that are easy to find, e.g. 10%, 5%, 1%.	Work out: **a)** 3% of 4000 **b)** 5% of 4000.

Solving word problems mentally

You will learn how to:
* Solve simple word problems including direct proportion problems.

Starting point

Do you remember ...?

* how to find the value of 1 unit?

  For example, if 6 pencils cost 60¢, 1 pencil costs 10¢.

* how to solve a scaling problem?

  For example, if 6 identical cupcakes cost $3, then 3 cupcakes will cost $1.50 and 12 cupcakes will cost $6.

* how to multiply and divide numbers mentally?

  For example, calculate 2.6 × 4 and 144 ÷ 6.

* how to convert between basic metric units?

  For example, how many cm are in 2 m.

This will also be helpful when you:

* draw and interpret graphs in real-life contexts.

  For example, drawing travel graphs and exploring how distance changes if the speed or time travelled changes.

* explore the relationship between the circumference of a circle and its radius.

  For example, what happens to the circumference of a circle if the radius doubles in length?

* derive and use simple formulae.

  For example, to convert degrees Celsius (°C) to degrees Fahrenheit (°F).

Hook

Driven to school by a robot!

Some scientists believe that children born today may never drive a car! They predict that cars will drive themselves automatically. Imagine being driven to school by a robot in a flying car, a driveless pod or hyperloop (very fast train).

* Imagine that in 2050 10 flying cars can take 20 children to school. How many flying cars can take 10 children to school? How many would you need for 40 children?

* Image that 10 driverless pods can carry 40 children. How many children can travel in 5 driverless pods? How many pods would you need to take 400 children to school?

> **Tip**
>
> How many children can travel in one flying car?

Two values are in **direct proportion** when they increase or decrease in the same ratio. When you multiply or divide one of the variables by a certain number, you have to multiply or divide the other variable by the same number. For example, if one of the values doubles, so does the other value.

Discuss

Which of these examples is in direct proportion?

- The amount of items you buy in the supermarket and their cost.

- The number of builders building a wall and the time that it takes to build the wall.

Direct proportion problems

Worked example 1

6 kg of apples costs $9.

a) Calculate the cost of 2 kg of apples.

b) How many kg of apples can you buy with $12?

a) 6 kg ÷ 2 kg = 3 $9 ÷ 3 = $3	Use a bar model. The new amount of 2 kg is 3 times less than the original amount of 6 kg. The price will be 3 times less also.	
b) 2 kg of apples cost $3. $12 ÷ $3 = 4 2 kg × 4 = 8 kg	Represent the information in a diagram. We have 4 times more money, so we can buy 4 times more apples.	

1 10 sheets of paper weigh 68 g. Calculate the mass of:

  a) 5 sheets of paper   **b)** 20 sheets of paper

  c) 100 sheets of paper   **d)** 300 sheets of paper.

2 20 balloons cost $4. Calculate the cost of:

  a) 10 balloons   **b)** 2 balloons   **c)** 40 balloons   **d)** 120 balloons.

  e) How many balloons can you buy with $12?

  f) How many balloons can you buy with $18?

> **Tip**
>
> $1 = 100 cents

3 True or false? If 4 m of shelving weighs 6 kg:

  a) 16 m of shelving weighs 16 kg   **b)** 40 m of shelving weighs 60 kg

  c) 14 m of shelving weighs 20 kg   **d)** 10 m of shelving weighs 14 kg.

4 Joe is paid $55 for 10 hours' work in the supermarket. To calculate how much he gets paid for 2 hours, he does the following calculations.

    $ 55 = 10 hours

    $110 = 20 hours

    $11 = 2 hours

  a) Is he correct?

  b) Use two different methods to calculate how much Joe will be paid for:

    i) 3 hours of work   **ii)** 25 hours of work.

5 Which of these calculations is the odd one out?

  a) 5 cakes for $4 or 15 cakes for $12   **b)** 12 cupcakes for $9 or 4 for cupcakes for $3

  c) 7 lollies for $8 or 35 lollies for $40   **d)** 3 biscuits for $1.50 or 12 biscuits for $6

6 The height of 6 identical bricks is 72 cm.

Which method of finding the height of 18 of these bricks is not right? Correct it.

  a) Find the height of 1 brick, then multiply the answer by 18.

  b) Multiply 72 cm by 3.

  c) Find the height of 2 bricks, then multiply the answer by 9

  d) Find the height of 3 bricks, then multiply the answer by 3.

> **Tip**
>
> Use bar models to see how the height of the bricks changes as the number of bricks changes.

7 The length of a shadow of an object at noon is directly proportional to the height of the object. A tree of height 6 m has a shadow of length 1.8 m at noon. Which of the values of the shadows below can't be correct?

  a) Object of height 2 m has a shadow of 1.2 m

  b) Object of height 15 m has a shadow of 6 m

  c) Object of height 1.5 m has a shadow of 45 cm

  d) Object of height 1.8 m has a shadow of 0.6 m

8 In general, a child's height increases by 6 centimetres per year from the age of 2 until the age of 12.

Milli's sister is 2 years old and 86 cm tall. To predict her height at the age of 10 years old, Milli does the following calculations:

Increase in height until the age of 10 = 6 cm × 10 = 60 cm

Predicted height at 10 years old = 87 cm + 60 cm = 147 cm

Milli's brother Owen does this working:

Age when born = 86 cm ÷ 2 = 43 cm

Increase in height = 6 cm × 10 = 60 cm

Predicted height at 10 years old = 43 cm + 60 cm = 103 cm

What is the predicted height at 10 years old for Milli's sister? Explain your answer.

9 Amy is trying to determine the mass of the sweets in her jar based on their quantity.

Number of sweets	10	40	400
Mass	42 g	168 g	

She finds the answer in three different ways.

Method 1	Method 2	Method 3
42 ÷ 10 = 4.2	400 ÷ 10 = 40	400 ÷ 40 = 10
4.2 × 400 = g	42 × 40 = g	168 × 10 = g

a) Explain the steps in her working.

b) What do her solutions have in common?

10 Is the following statement always, sometimes or never true? Give examples to justify your answer.

"If Pems is in direct proportion with Rads and Pems increases by 1 unit, then Rads increases by 1 unit. If Pems decreases by 2 units, then Rads decreases by 2 units."

End of chapter reflection

You should know that ...	You should be able to ...	Such as ...
Two values are in direct proportion when they increase or decrease in the same ratio.	Mentally solve simple problems, including direct proportion problems.	If 6 cinema tickets cost $66, calculate the cost of: a) 2 cinema tickets b) 12 cinema tickets.

Decimals

You will learn how to:
- Consolidate adding and subtracting integers and decimals, including numbers with differing numbers of decimal places.
- Divide integers and decimals by a single-digit number, continuing the division to a specified number of decimal places, e.g. 68 ÷ 7.

Starting point

Do you remember ...?

- how to add and subtract numbers mentally?
  For example, add 567 and 261.
- how to add and subtract integers and decimals, including numbers with differing numbers of decimal places?
  For example, add 25.3 and 1.62.
- how to multiply and divide numbers mentally?
  For example, calculate 36 × 4 and 126 ÷ 6.
- how to multiply a whole number by a single-digit number using a written method?
  For example, multiply 587 by 9.
- how to multiply and divide decimals with one and/or two places by single digit number?
  For example, 14.9 × 7? 6.25 ÷ 5?

This will also be helpful when you:

- learn to find the perimeter of different shapes. For example, find the perimeter of a parallelogram with sides of 5.09 cm and 8.9 cm.
- find the length of the sides from the area of a shape. For example, find the height of a triangle if its area is 58.16 cm² and its base is 8 cm.

Hook

Hidden Codes

A	B	C	D	E	F	G	H	I	J	K	L	M
11.75	117.5	4.02	42	290100	29100	8.6	0.3	0.1	0.21	83.5	9	0.987
N	**O**	**P**	**Q**	**R**	**S**	**T**	**U**	**V**	**W**	**X**	**Y**	**Z**
5190	51900	0.006	0.337	0.377	0.85	8.5	67	0.9	2.11	0.6	8	9.1356

a) Complete these calculations using a mental or written strategy. Write the answers in a copy of the table below.

1) 0.28 + 0.097
2) 289 137 + 963
3) 8 − 5.89
4) 5.1 ÷ 6
5) 129 000 − 123 810
6) 47 ÷ 4

Answers

1)	2)	3)	4)	5)	6)

- Look at the word KITTEN written backwards. Make addition, subtraction or division questions for each of the 6 letters. The values of each letter are given in the 'Hidden Codes' box.

N	E	T	T	I	K

- Hide the letters and write the questions instead of them. Give your code to a friend. Can they find the hidden word?

- Did you use a mental or written strategy to solve the questions?

Addition and subtraction

Worked example 1

Calculate 15.879 + 0.9574.

15 . 879
+ 0 . 9574
———————
15 . 8790
+ 0 . 9574
———————

Start by setting out your calculation in columns with the decimal points in line.

It's useful to fill any gaps with 0s to act as **placeholders.**

Tens	Units	•	Tenths	100ths	1000ths	10000ths
10	1 1		0.1 0.1 0.1	0.01 0.01 0.01	0.001 0.001 0.001	
	1 1	•	0.1 0.1 0.1	0.01 0.01 0.01	0.001 0.001 0.001	
	1		0.1 0.1	0.01	0.001 0.001 0.001	
			0.1 0.1 0.1	0.01 0.01 0.01	0.001 0.001 0.001	0.0001 0.0001 0.0001
		•	0.1 0.1 0.1	0.01 0.01	0.001 0.001 0.001	0.0001
			0.1 0.1 0.1		0.001	

15 . 8790
+ 0 . 9574
———————
4

Start adding from the column on the right.

Add the ten-thousandths.

Tens	Units	•	Tenths	100ths	1000ths	10000ths
10	1 1		0.1 0.1 0.1	0.01 0.01 0.01	0.001 0.001 0.001	
	1 1	•	0.1 0.1 0.1	0.01 0.01 0.01	0.001 0.001 0.001	
	1		0.1 0.1	0.01	0.001 0.001 0.001	
			0.1 0.1 0.1	0.01 0.01 0.01	0.001 0.001 0.001	0.0001 0.0001 0.0001
		•	0.1 0.1 0.1	0.01 0.01	0.001 0.001 0.001	0.0001
			0.1 0.1 0.1		0.001	

Tens	Units	•	Tenths	100ths	1000ths	10000ths
						0.0001 0.0001 0.0001
		•				0.0001

$1\,5\,.\,8\,7\,9\,0$
$+\ \ 0\,.\,9\,5\,7\,4$
$\underline{\hspace{4em}6\,4}$
1

Now add the thousandths.

Exchange ten of the thousandths for 1 hundredth.

Tens	Units	•	Tenths	100ths	1000ths	10000ths
		•			0.001 0.001 0.001 0.001 0.001 0.001 0.001 0.001 0.001	
		•			0.001 0.001 0.001 0.001 0.001 0.001 0.001	0.0001 0.0001 0.0001 0.0001 0.0001

Tens	Units	•	Tenths	100ths	1000ths	10000ths
		•			0.001 0.001 0.001 0.001 0.001 0.001	0.0001 0.0001 0.0001 0.0001

0.01

$1\,5\,.\,8\,7\,9\,0$
$+\ \ 0\,.\,9\,5\,7\,4$
$\underline{\hspace{3em}3\,6\,4}$
1

You can now add the hundredths.

Exchange 10 hundredths for 1 tenth.

Tens	Units	•	Tenths	100ths	1000ths	10000ths
		•		0.01 0.01 0.01 0.01 0.01 0.01 0.01		
		•		0.01 0.01 0.01 0.01 0.01	0.001 0.001 0.001 0.001 0.001 0.001	0.0001 0.0001 0.0001 0.0001

0.01

Tens	Units	•	Tenths	100ths	1000ths	10000ths
		•		0.01 0.01 0.01	0.001 0.001 0.001 0.001 0.001 0.001	0.0001 0.0001 0.0001 0.0001

0.1

$1\,5\,.\,8\,7\,9\,0$
$+\ \ 0\,.\,9\,5\,7\,4$
$\underline{\hspace{2em}8\,3\,6\,4}$
1

Add the tenths.

Exchange 10 tenths for 1 unit.

Tens	Units	•	Tenths	100ths	1000ths	10000ths
		•	0.1 0.1 0.1 0.1 0.1 0.1 0.1 0.1			
		•	0.1 0.1 0.1 0.1 0.1 0.1 0.1 0.1 0.1	0.01 0.01 0.01	0.001 0.001 0.001 0.001 0.001 0.001	0.0001 0.0001 0.0001 0.0001

0.1

Tens	Units	•	Tenths	100ths	1000ths	10000ths
		•	0.1 0.1 0.1 0.1 0.1 0.1 0.1 0.1	0.01 0.01 0.01	0.001 0.001 0.001 0.001 0.001 0.001	0.0001 0.0001 0.0001 0.0001

1

15.8790 + 0.9574 6.8364	Add the units.

Tens	Units	•	Tenths	100ths	1000ths	10 000ths
	1 1					
	1 1	•				
	1					

Tens	Units	•	Tenths	100ths	1000ths	10 000ths
			0.1 0.1 0.1	0.01 0.01 0.01	0.001 0.001 0.001	0.0001 0.0001 0.0001
		•	0.1 0.1 0.1		0.001 0.001 0.001	0.0001
			0.1 0.1			

1

Tens	Units	•	Tenths	100ths	1000ths	10 000ths
	1 1		0.1 0.1 0.1	0.01 0.01 0.01	0.001 0.001 0.001	0.0001 0.0001 0.0001
	1 1	•	0.1 0.1 0.1		0.001 0.001 0.001	0.0001
	1 1		0.1 0.1			

15.8790 + 0.9574 16.8364	Finally add the tens.

Tens	Units	•	Tenths	100ths	1000ths	10 000ths
10						
		•				

Tens	Units	•	Tenths	100ths	1000ths	10 000ths
	1 1		0.1 0.1 0.1	0.01 0.01 0.01	0.001 0.001 0.001	0.0001 0.0001 0.0001
	1 1	•	0.1 0.1 0.1		0.001 0.001 0.001	0.0001
	1 1		0.1 0.1			

Tens	Units	•	Tenths	100ths	1000ths	10 000ths
10	1 1		0.1 0.1 0.1	0.01 0.01 0.01	0.001 0.001 0.001	0.0001 0.0001 0.0001
	1 1	•	0.1 0.1 0.1		0.001 0.001 0.001	0.0001
	1 1		0.1 0.1			

Worked example 2

Calculate 2 600 734 − 27 689.

2 600 734 − 27 689	Start by setting out your calculation in columns so that units line up under units, tens under tens and so on.

1 000 000s	100 000s	10 000s	1000s	100s	Tens	Units
1 000 000 1 000 000	100 000 100 000 100 000			100 100 100	10 10 10	1 1 1
	100 000 100 000 100 000			100 100 100		1
				100		

1 000 000s	100 000s	10 000s	1000s	100s	Tens	Units
		10 000 10 000	1000 1000 1000	100 100 100	10 10 10	1 1 1
			1000 1000 1000	100 100 100	10 10 10	1 1 1
			1000		10 10	1 1 1

2 600 73⁴ (²¹) − 27 689 5	Start by subtracting the units. Exchange 1 ten for 10 units. Subtract 9 units from the 14 units.

1 000 000s	100 000s	10 000s	1000s	100s	Tens	Units
1 000 000 1 000 000	100 000 100 000 100 000			100 100 100	10 10	1 1 1
	100 000 100 000 100 000			100 100 100		1 1 1
				100		1 1 1
						1 1 1
						1 1

1 000 000s	100 000s	10 000s	1000s	100s	Tens	Units
		10 000 10 000	1000 1000 1000	100 100 100	10 10 10	1 1 1
			1000 1000 1000	100 100 100	10 10 10	1 1 1
			1000		10 10	1 1 1

10 000s	10 000s	10 000s	1000s	100s	Tens	10 000s
						1 1 1
						1 1

$\overset{6}{}\overset{12}{7}\overset{1}{3}4$	Now subtract the tens.
2 6 0 0 7 3 4	Exchange 1 hundred
− 2 7 6 8 9	for 10 tens.
4 5	

1000 000s	100 000s	10 000s	1000s	100s	Tens	Units

10 000s	10 000s	10 000s	1000s	100s	Tens	10 000s

$2\ 6\ 0\ 0\ \overset{6}{7}\ \overset{12}{3}\ 4$
−   2 7 6 8 9
0 4 5

Subtract 6 hundred from the remaining 6 hundred.

1000 000s	100 000s	10 000s	1000s	100s	Tens	Units

10 000s	10 000s	10 000s	1000s	100s	Tens	10 000s

$2\ 6\ 0\ 0\ \overset{5\ 19}{7}\ \overset{6\ 12}{3}\ \overset{1}{4}$
−   2 7 6 8 9
3 0 4 5

Subtract the thousands.

Exchange 1 hundred thousand for ten thousands.

Then exchange 1 ten thousand for 10 thousands.

Subtract 7 thousands from 10 thousands

1000 000s	100 000s	10 000s	1000s	100s	Tens	Units

10 000s	10 000s	10 000s	1000s	100s	Tens	10 000s

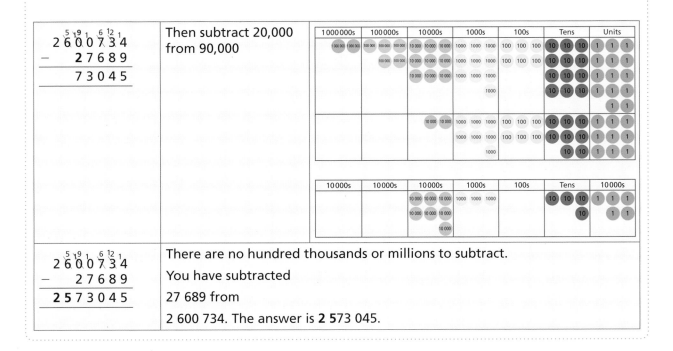

There are no hundred thousands or millions to subtract.

You have subtracted

27 689 from

2 600 734. The answer is **2 573 045**.

1 Calculate:

a) 13 356 + 10 544
b) 26 389 + 824
c) 18 235 – 11 618
d) 76 203 – 37 614
e) 763 567 + 768 465
f) 587 954 + 187 101 – 257 709

2 Calculate:

a) 56 909 + 43 275
b) 918 763 – 907 563
c) 107 834 + 824 329
d) 952 761 – 941 562
e) 624 295 + 58 705
f) 845 880 – 162 879

3 Use a written method to find the answers to these calculations.

a) 26.93 + 23.6
b) 105.67 – 57.38
c) 5.6 + 8.617
d) 87.8 + 56.25
e) 26.74 – 8.508
f) 7.197 + 13. 8235

4 Use a written method to find the answers to these calculations.

a) 9.65 + 5.123 + 23.8
b) 0.6325 + 1.789 + 0.8675
c) 65.65 + 23.6 – 8.617
d) 17.8 – 4.89 + 5.257
e) 6.74 – (0.508 + 6.97)
f) 7.107 – 6.567 – 2.981

5 Each block of the pyramid is completed by adding the 2 numbers below.

Use a written strategy to find the missing numbers.

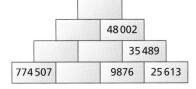
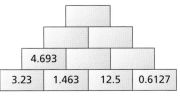

6 The calculations below are incorrect. Explain the mistake that has been made and find the correct answer.

a)
$$
\begin{array}{r}
2\,7\,5\,.\,\overset{8}{9}\,\overset{1}{4} \\
-\ \ 3\,4\,.\,5\,7 \\
\hline
4\,9\,.\,3\,7
\end{array}
$$

b)
$$
\begin{array}{r}
2\,0\,4\,.\,6\,5 \\
+\ \ 3\,9\,.\,3\,7 \\
\hline
2\,4\,3\,1\,0\,2
\end{array}
$$

7 a) Use the digits 0, 1, 2, 3, 4, 5, 6, 7, 8 once only to make this calculation true.

$$
\begin{array}{r}
\ \ \square\,.\,\square\,\square \\
-\ \square\,.\,\square\,\square \\
\hline
\ \ \square\,.\,\square\,\square
\end{array}
$$

b) Now find a different calculation.

$$
\begin{array}{r}
\ \ \square\,.\,\square\,\square \\
-\ \square\,.\,\square\,\square \\
\hline
\ \ \square\,.\,\square\,\square
\end{array}
$$

8 Tom bought some books for the school library. He spent $5.98 more on Geography books than on History books and $6.87 more on Mathematics books than on Science books. Work out the missing values in the table.

	($)
Art	26.90
Geography	
History	12.99
Mathematics	34.75
Science	
Total	

Think about

How can you check whether your answer is reasonable? For example, what would you estimate the answer to 26.90 + 12.99 + 34.75 be? Use a written method to check your calculations.

9 Wendy has bamboo plants in her garden. Last month one plant was 1.59 m tall. This month the plant has grown by 48 cm.

a) How tall is the plant now?

b) How much more does it need to grow to be 2.1 m tall?

10 The table shows the population of the world in 1950 and 1990.

a) Complete the missing values.

b) By how many millions did the population of the world increase from 1950 to 1990?

Regions of the world	Population in millions in 1950	Population in millions in 1990
Africa	222	642
Asia		3402
Europe	393	
Latin America	166	448
North America	166	276
Oceania	13	26
World	**2518**	**5292**

11 Search the internet to find the latest figures for the population of the world by regions/continents as in the table above. Make a spreadsheet using Excel and compare the change in population from 1990 to the results you found.

Dividing whole numbers and decimals by a whole number

Worked example 3

a) Work out 92 ÷ 7. Give your answer correct to one decimal place.

b) Work out 1.39 ÷ 6. Give your answer correct to one decimal place.

Tip

When you divide an integer or a whole number by a single digit number, it may not divide exactly. When continuing the division to a given number of decimal places, always work out the answer to one more decimal place than you are asked to, then round the answer to the required degree of accuracy.

---

a)

$7\overline{)9\ 2\ .\ 0\ 0}$

Set out your calculation.

You are asked to work out the answer to one decimal place, so you need to work out the answer to 2 decimal places first. Write 92 as 92.00.

Tens	Units	•	Tenths	100ths

$\begin{array}{r} 1 \\ 7\overline{)9\ {}^{2}2\ .\ 0\ 0} \end{array}$

Start by dividing or grouping the 9 tens into groups of 7.

Exchange the remaining tens for 20 units, making 22 units.

Tens	Units	•	Tenths	100ths

$\begin{array}{r} 1\ \ \ 3 \\ 7\overline{)9\ {}^{2}2\ .\ {}^{1}0\ 0} \end{array}$

Divide the 22 units into groups of 7s.

Exchange the remaining 1 unit for 10 tenths.

Tens	Units	•	Tenths	100ths

13.1 7$\overline{)9\ ^22.\ ^10\ ^30}$	Divide or group the tenths into 7s. Exchange the remaining 3 tenths for 30 hundredths.	Tens / Units / Tenths / 100ths place value chart
1 3 . 1 4 7$\overline{)9\ ^22.\ ^10\ ^30}$	Divide the 30 hundredths into groups of 7s. You can make 4 groups of 7s with 2 remaining.	Tens / Units / Tenths / 100ths place value chart
13.14 (2 d.p.) **13.1 (1 d.p.)**	Your answer is one ten, three units, 1 tenth and 4 hundredths or 13.14. The answer is 13.1 correct to one decimal place.	10 · 1 1 1 · 0.1 · 0.01 0.01 0.01 0.01
b) 6$\overline{)1.39}$	Set out your calculation. You are asked to work out the answer to 1 decimal place, so you need to work out the answer to 2 decimal places first.	Units / Tenths / 100ths place value chart
0 6$\overline{)1.^13\ 9}$	Start by dividing or grouping the 1 unit into 6s. You can make 0 groups of 6s. Exchange the 1 unit for 10 tenths. You now have 13 tenths.	Units / Tenths / 100ths place value chart

$\begin{array}{r} 0.2 \\ 6\overline{)1.{}^13\,{}^19} \end{array}$	Divide or group the 13 tenths into 6s. You can make 2 groups with 1 tenth remaining. Exchange the 1 tenths for 10 hundredths.	Units • Tenths 100ths (place value chart showing tenths grouped and hundredths)
$\begin{array}{r} 0.23 \\ 6\overline{)1.{}^13\,{}^19} \end{array}$	Finally, divide or group the hundredths into 6s. You can make 3 groups with 1 hundredth remaining. You can stop here.	Units • Tenths 100ths (place value chart)
0.23 (2 d.p.) **0.2 (1 d.p.)**	You have 0 units, 2 tenths and 3 hundredths or 0.23. The answer correct to 1 decimal place is 0.2.	(0.1 0.1 0.01 0.01 0.01)

Exercise 2 1–5

1 Find the exact answer to each division.
- **a)** 1782 ÷ 6
- **b)** 2703 ÷ 3
- **c)** 185 ÷ 8
- **d)** 191.2 ÷ 5
- **e)** 18.72 ÷ 9
- **f)** 16.723 ÷ 7

2 Work out these divisions. Give your answers, to one decimal place.
- **a)** 79 ÷ 3
- **b)** 366 ÷ 9
- **c)** 5213 ÷ 6
- **d)** 0.8 ÷ 3
- **e)** 0.85 ÷7
- **f)** 2.3 ÷ 8

3 Work out the answers to two decimal places.
- **a)** 2 ÷ 9
- **b)** 7.6 ÷ 6
- **c)** 10.7 ÷ 7
- **d)** 0.82 ÷ 3
- **e)** 6.513 ÷ 8
- **f)** 29.078 ÷ 5

4 Work out the answers to each of these divisions. Round each answer to the accuracy stated.
- **a)** 3.529 ÷ 7 (1 decimal place)
- **b)** 12.87 ÷ 5 (2 decimal places)
- **c)** 22.058 ÷ 9 (1 decimal place)
- **d)** 3.65 ÷ 7 (3 decimal places)
- **e)** 13.569 ÷ 8 (3 decimal places)
- **f)** 0.0089 ÷ 8 (3 decimal place)

5 The calculation below is incorrect. Explain what the error is and find the correct answer.

$$1 \cdot 712$$

$$5\overline{)5.3^3 5^1 6 0}$$

6 **a)** If $2.3 \div \bullet = \blacksquare$, and $\bullet$ is a single-digit number, what is the smallest and the biggest value that $\blacksquare$ could be? Round your answer to 2 d.p.

   b) What other values could you have used instead of 2.3 to achieve the same result as the value of $\blacksquare$ you found?

End of chapter reflection

You should know that ...	You should be able to ...	Such as ...
When decimals are added or subtracted, the calculations are set out in columns. so that the decimal points are in line.	Add and subtract decimals including numbers with differing numbers of decimal places.	0.8976 + 0.768 0.1234 – 0.0978
Zeros may act as placeholders. When adding or subtracting integers and decimals, always start from the column on the right.	Add and subtract integers.	2 345 187 + 567 234
When an integer or decimal is divided by a single-digit number, you can continue the division to a specified number of decimal places.	Divide a whole number by a single-digit number. Divide a decimal number by a single-digit number.	$9 \div 8$ $14.19 \div 6$
When continuing the division to a specific number of places, make sure you work out the answer to one decimal place more than you are asked for, then round your answer to the appropriate degree of accuracy.	Divide a whole number or decimal continuing the division to 1, 2 or 3 decimal places.	Calculate $58 \div 7$. Give your answer to 3 d.p. Calculate $2.33 \div 8$. Give your answer to 2 d.p.

2B

Unit 2B

Algebra and geometry

What it's all about?

- Constructing and using formulae
- Drawing straight line graphs
- Nets of 3D solids
- Geometrical constructions
- Symmetry and transformations

You will learn about:

- finding a formula to describe a situation
- substituting into a formula
- plotting straight line graphs
- drawing nets of different solids
- constructing the perpendicular bisector of a line segment and the bisector of an angle
- finding all the symmetries of a 2D shape
- finding the image of a shape under one or more transformations.

You will build your skills in:

- representing situations mathematically
- substituting accurately by applying the order of operations
- drawing accurate graphs, diagrams and constructions
- solving problems involving shape and space

Formulae

You will learn how to:
- Derive and use simple formulae, e.g. to convert degrees Celsius (°C) to degrees Fahrenheit (°F).
- Substitute positive and negative integers into formulae, linear expressions and expressions involving small powers, e.g. $3x^2 + 4$ or $2x^3$, including examples that lead to an equation to solve.

Starting point

Do you remember …?

- how to use the four operations with negative numbers?
  For example, calculate $-4 \times 5 = -20$ and $-8 + -3 = -11$
- what a term, an expression and an equation are?
- how to substitute positive integers into expressions?
  For example, write an expression for the perimeter of an equilateral triangle with side length x.
  Use your expression to find the perimeter when $x = 6$.
- the correct order of operations for calculating with numbers and algebra?
  For example, calculate $4 + 2 \times 8$.
- how to solve an equation?
  For example, solve $3x + 1 = 16$.

This will also be helpful when you:

- use formulae in mathematics and other subjects.
- learn how to substitute any number into expressions and formulae.

Hook

This is a game for two or more players.
You will need:
- two sets of number cards labelled −10 to 10.
- two dice.

How to play

Choose six cards at random from the set of number cards.

Roll both dice to generate two numbers.

You can use the numbers generated as either negative or positive.

You could add, subtract, multiply or divide the two numbers.

Use your dice to make one of the numbers shown on your cards then turn over the card.

If you are unable to make any of the numbers on your cards, you must pass.

The winner is the person to turn over all of their cards.

Think about

Ash and a friend are playing the game in the Hook section.

Ash has the cards –8, –4, –1, 0, 2 and 5.

Ash rolls a 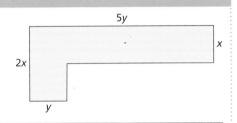 and a

Ash decides to use the two dice to make –8. (–3 – 5 = –8)

What other numbers could he make?

Constructing and using formulae

Key terms

A **variable** is a letter that represents an unknown number or value.

A **formula** is a mathematical relationship between two or more variables expressed algebraically.

A formula does not mean anything unless you say what your variables represent.

Worked example 1

a) Write down a formula to calculate the perimeter P of this shape.

b) Use your formula to calculate the perimeter of the shape when $x = 4$ cm and $y = 2$ cm.

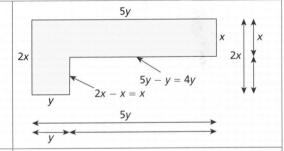

a) $P = 2x + y + x + 4y$ $+ x + 5y$ $P = 4x + 10y$	First calculate the missing lengths in terms of x and y. Then add together the lengths of each side of the shape to find the perimeter. Write your answer as simply as possible.	
b) $P = 4x + 10y$ $P = 4 \times 4 + 10 \times 2$ $P = 16 + 20$ cm $P = 36$ cm	Replace the x in the formula with 4 and the y in the formula with 2 to find the perimeter. Remember to include units when needed.	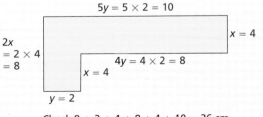

Think about

Can you think of any formulae that you have seen or met before? Write them down.

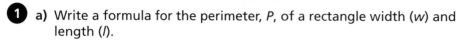
1 a) Write a formula for the perimeter, P, of a rectangle width (w) and length (l).

b) Use your formula to calculate the perimeter of a rectangle with width 8 cm and length 6 cm.

> **Discuss**
>
> How else can you write the formula for the perimeter of the rectangle?

2 a) Write a formula for the perimeter, P, of this shape.

b) Use your formula to calculate the perimeter when $a = 3$ and $b = 2$.

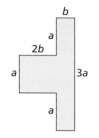

3 a) Write a formula for the perimeter, P, of this shape.

b) Use your formula to calculate the perimeter when $c = 5$ and $d = 4$.

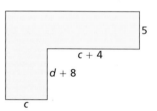

4 To convert a temperature given in degrees Celsius (°C) to degrees Fahrenheit (°F) you need to multiply the temperature in °C by 1.8 and then add 32.

a) Which of these formulae can be used to convert temperatures given in degrees Celsius (°C), C, to degrees Fahrenheit (°F), F?

$F = 1.8 + 32C$ $F = \frac{9}{5}C + 32$ $F = \frac{9C + 32}{5}$

$F = 1.8C + 32$ $F = 1.8(C + 32)$ $F = 32 + 1.8C$

b) Use your formula to convert the following temperatures from °C into °F:

i) 0°C   **ii)** 20°C   **iii)** 25°C   **iv)** 33°C

c) Oven temperatures can sometimes be given as a gas mark, sometimes in degrees Celsius and sometimes in degrees Fahrenheit.

Here is a table showing some oven temperatures. Use your formula from part a) to help you complete a copy of the table.

Gas Mark	Fahrenheit (°F)	Celsius (°C)
1	275	
2		150
3	325	
4		190

> **Did you know?**
>
> Fahrenheit is now only used in the USA, Belize and Jamaica. In the UK the unofficial benchmark summer temperature, however, is 100 degrees Fahrenheit but otherwise Celsius is used. Celsius is the standard for the rest of the world. However, in certain scientific fields such as astronomy, the Kelvin scale is used. Zero Kelvin is equivalent to −273.15°C (or −459.67°F).

5 In this rectangle the length is three times the width.

w is the width of the rectangle.

Bert says,

'The perimeter of the rectangle = $w + 3w + w + 3w = 8w$.'

Claire says,

'The perimeter of the rectangle = $w + w + 3 + w + w + 3 = 4w + 6$.'

a) Who do you agree with? Explain your answer.

b) For the person who has made a mistake, write a question for which their answer is correct.

6 A taxi driver charges a fixed fee of $3.50 plus 20¢ per kilometre.

a) Write a formula for the total cost C for a journey k kilometres long.

b) Use your formula to work out the cost of a 12 kilometre journey.

c) If a journey cost $8.50, how far would the taxi have travelled?

7 A phone company charges $15 per month, 5¢ for each text message and 2¢ per minute for phone calls.

a) Write a formula for the total bill (b), where (t) texts are sent and (c) minutes of calls are made.

b) Use your formula to work out the cost of a month where 25 text messages are sent and 10 minutes of phone calls are made.

c) Denise has just received her phone bill, but it has some missing information.

If Denise spent half an hour making phone calls, how many text messages did she send?

> **Tip**
>
> You should make sure that the fixed fee and the cost per kilometre are both in dollars or both in cents when writing your formula.

PHONE BILL	
Monthly charge	$15
Calls	$
Text messages	$
Total	**$18**

8 The sum of the angles in a polygon with n sides is given by the formula, sum of angles = $(n - 2) \times 180°$.

a) Find the sum of the angles in a heptagon (7 sides).

b) Find the sum of the angles in a polygon with 14 sides.

9 A formula is often used to calculate cooking times. For example, to cook a whole chicken takes 25 minutes per 500 g, plus an extra 25 minutes.

a) Write this information as a formula.

b) Enter your formula in a spreadsheet to create your own cooking time calculator and use this to calculate the cooking time for chickens of mass 2 kg and 4.2 kg.

To challenge yourself further, give your time in hours and minutes.

c) Research the formula used to calculate cooking times of other meats and create cooking time calculators.

> **Tip**
>
> Mass is commonly called weight in everyday language.
> You will need to convert kg to grams. Remember 1 kg = 1000 g.

Substitution

Worked example 2

If $p = 4$ and $q = -2$, find the value of:

a) $p + q$ **b)** $p - q$ **c)** q^2 **d)** $2p^2$ **e)** $4p - 2q^2$

a) $p + q =$ $4 + -2 = 2$	$p + q$ means add the value q to the value of p. So add -2 to 4 to give the value of $p + q$.
b) $p - q =$ $4 - -2 =$ $4 + 2 = 6$	$p - q$ means subtract the value of q from the value of p. So subtract -2 from 4 to give the value of $p - q$. Remember that subtracting a negative number is equivalent to addition.
c) $q^2 = q \times q$ $= -2 \times -2$ $= 4$	q^2 means multiply the value of q by the value of q. Multiplying a negative number by a negative number gives a positive number.
d) $2p^2 = 2 \times p^2$ $= 2 \times 4^2$ $= 2 \times 16$ $= 32$	p^2 means multiply the value of p by the value of p. $2p^2$ means multiply the value of p^2 by 2.
e) $4p - 2q^2 = 4p - 2 \times q^2$ $= 4p - 2 \times (-2)^2$ $= 4 \times 4 - 2 \times 4$ $= 16 - 8$ $= 8$	You need to remember the order of operations. First, find the value of q^2. Next, find the value of $4p$ by multiplying p by 4, and find the value of $2q^2$ by multiplying 2 by the value of q^2. Finally, subtract the value of $2q^2$ from $4p$.

Exercise 2   1–6

1 If $x = -6$, find the value of:

     a) $x - 10$ **b)** $15 - x$ **c)** $4x$ **d)** $3x + 5$ **e)** $5 - 4x$

2 If $x = -2$, find the value of:

     a) x^2 **b)** $3x^2$ **c)** $4 - x^2$

     d) $5 + 2x^2$ **e)** x^3

> **Tip**
>
> $x^3 = x \times x \times x$

Think about

If $x^2 = 16$, what are the possible values of x?

3 If $p = 2$ and $q = -3$, find the value of:

a) $p + q$ b) $p - q$ c) $2p - q$

d) $20 + 2q$ e) $5 - 3q$ f) q^2

g) $2p^2$ h) q^3 i) $p^2 - q^2$

j) $p^2 + q^2$ k) $p^3 - q^3$ l) $3p^3$

> **Tip**
>
> Ensure you use the correct order of operations (BIDMAS).

4 If $a = 6$, $b = -2$ and $c = -5$, find the value of:

a) $a + 2b$ b) $b + c$ c) $b - c$ d) $a + b + c$

e) $ab + c$ f) abc g) $2b^2$ h) $2b^2 + c$

i) $a^2 - b^2$ j) $b^3 + 5$ k) $b^3 - a$ l) $b^2 - 2c^2$

5 Here is a formula: $c = 4a + b$

Find the value of c if:

a) $a = 2$, $b = 5$ b) $a = -3$, $b = 2$ c) $a = 4$, $b = -6$ d) $a = -5$, $b = -4$

6 Here is a formula: $y = x^2 - 6$

Find the value of y if:

a) $x = 2$ b) $x = 9$ c) $x = -1$ d) $x = -4$

7 The freezing point of mercury is $-38.8°C$.

Fred and Tom convert this temperature into degrees Fahrenheit (°F).

Fred converts $-38.8°C$ into °F like this:

$1.8 \times -38.8 + 32 = 1.8 \times -6.8 = -12.24$ °F

Tom converts $-38.8°C$ into °F like this:

$1.8 \times -38.8 + 32 = -69.84 + 32 = -37.84$ °F

Explain who has made a mistake in their calculation. Discuss your answer with a partner.

8 Beryl has been given this formula:

$y = 3x^2 + 4$

Beryl has to find the value of y when $x = -4$.

She says,

'When $x = -4$, $y = 3 \times -4^2 + 4 = -12^2 + 4 = -144 + 4 = 140$'

Do you agree with Beryl? Explain your answer.

9 Write these expressions in ascending order (smallest to largest).

Use the values $x = 3$, $y = -2$ and $z = -1$.

xy^2 x^2y $2yz^2$ $3x^2 + y$ $2y^2 - z$

10 Decide if these statements are always true, sometimes true or never true. You must explain your answers.

a) x^2 is more than x.

b) $2x$ is more than x.

c) c^3 is more than x.

11 **Vocabulary feature question**

Complete the text using words from the box.

variables	expression	equation
substituting	variable	formula

A _____ is a mathematical relationship between two or more _____.

A _____ is a letter that represents a number that can take different values.

_____ is when you replace a letter with a number.

An _____ can be solved, an _____ cannot.

End of chapter reflection

You should know that ...	You should be able to ...	Such as ...
A variable is a letter that represents a number that can take different values.	Derive a formula to connect two variables.	Derive a formula for the area of a rectangle with width w and length l.
A formula represents a mathematical relationship between two or more variables.	Use a simple formula to find missing information.	The area A of a triangle with base b and height h is found using the formula $A = \frac{bh}{2}$. Find the area of a triangle with base 7 cm and height 4 cm.
Substitution is when you replace a variable with a known value.	Substitute positive and negative numbers into expressions and formulae.	If $A = 5p^2 - q$, calculate the value of A when $p = 3$ and $q = -9$.

Straight-line graphs

You will learn how to:

- Construct tables of values and use all four quadrants to plot the graphs of linear functions, where y is given explicitly in terms of x; recognise that equations of the form $y = mx + c$ correspond to straight-line graphs.

Starting point

Do you remember ...?

- how to plot a coordinate?

  For example, plot the point $(-2, 4)$.

- how to substitute into a formula?

  For example, substitute $x = -3$ into the formula $y = 2x + 1$.

- how to generate coordinate pairs that satisfy a linear equation?

  For example, copy and complete this table to give the coordinate pairs for $y = 2x + 1$ for $x = 0, 1, 2, 3$:

x	0	1	2	3
y				

- how to recognise straight-line graphs parallel to the x- or y-axis?

  For example, recognise the equations of the straight lines shown.

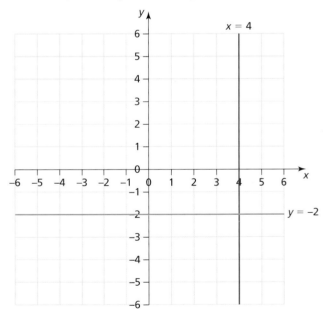

This will also be helpful when you:

- find the approximate solutions of a simple pair of simultaneous linear equations by finding the point of intersection of their graphs.

Hook

Coordinate Battleships

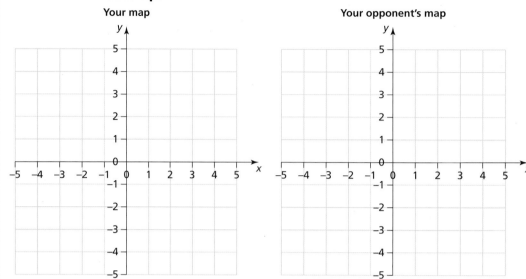

Your map

Your opponent's map

On your map, you need to use the grid lines to draw 7 boats.

You need two boats of: 1 square in length, 2 squares in length and 3 squares in length and one boat of: 4 squares in length as shown in the diagram.

Your boats must be either horizontal or vertical (not diagonal) and must be placed on the grid lines.

Now decide who is starting.

Try to guess where your opponent's boats are by guessing a coordinate.

If the coordinate that you choose hits one of your opponent's boats, mark this coordinate with a cross. If it does not hit a boat, mark this with a circle. Do this on the copy of the map marked opponent's map.

Your opponent now has their turn to guess where your boats are hidden.

To sink your opponent's boats, give the equation of the line that the boat is on. Keep playing until one player has sunk all of their opponent's boats.

Plotting graphs of linear functions

Key terms

A **coordinate** is a point specified by a pair of numbers (x, y).

A **linear function** is any function that graphs to a straight line.

Longitude and latitude are the most common use of coordinates.

Latitude is parallel to the equator and longitude is perpendicular to the equator. The earth is divided in two sections of Southern hemisphere and Northern hemisphere due to the presence of the equator.

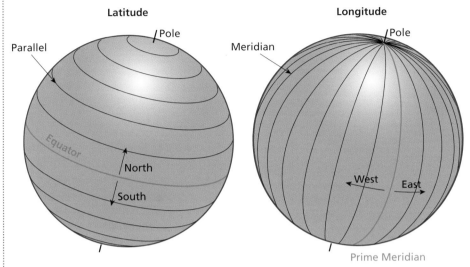

Latitude

Longitude

The latitude for Cambridge, UK is: 52.20534 and the longitude is: 0.121817.

Worked example 1

Here is the equation of a line: $y = 2x - 1$

a) Complete the table of values for values of x between –2 and 3.

b) Plot the graph for values of x between –2 and 3.

a)

x	–2	–1	0	1	2	3
y	–5	–3	–1	1	3	5

You need to use the values of x, and calculate the corresponding values of y.

When $x = -2$,
$y = 2 \times -2 - 1 = -5$
so (–2, –5) is a coordinate on this line.

When $x = -1$,
$y = 2 \times -1 - 1 = -3$
so (–1, –3) is a coordinate on this line.

When $x = 0$,
$y = 2 \times 0 - 1 = -1$
so (0, –1) is a coordinate on this line.

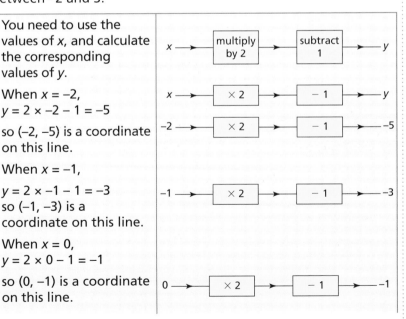

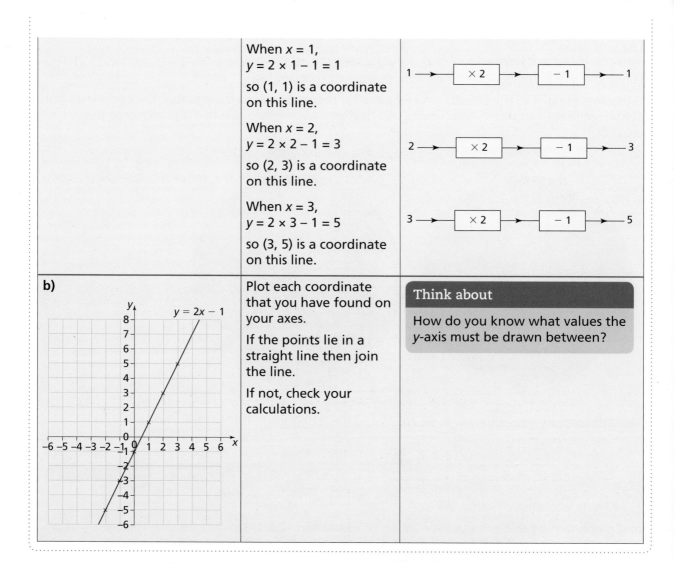

When $x = 1$,
$y = 2 \times 1 - 1 = 1$

so (1, 1) is a coordinate on this line.

When $x = 2$,
$y = 2 \times 2 - 1 = 3$

so (2, 3) is a coordinate on this line.

When $x = 3$,
$y = 2 \times 3 - 1 = 5$

so (3, 5) is a coordinate on this line.

b)

$y = 2x - 1$

Plot each coordinate that you have found on your axes.

If the points lie in a straight line then join the line.

If not, check your calculations.

Think about

How do you know what values the y-axis must be drawn between?

Discuss

What is the minimum number of coordinates you need in order to plot a line?

Exercise 1

1 **a)** Copy and complete this table of coordinates for the line $y = 3x$.

b) Draw an x-axis from −2 to 3 and a y-axis from −6 to 9. Use your table of coordinates to help you draw the line $y = 3x$.

x	−2	−1	0	1	2	3
y						

Discuss

Do you notice a pattern in the y-coordinates? Can you see a link between the pattern and the equation of the line?

2 a) Copy and complete this table of coordinates for the line $y = x$.

b) Draw an x-axis from –2 to 3 and a y-axis from –2 to 3. Use your table of coordinates to help you draw the line $y = x$.

x	–2	–1	0	1	2	3
y						

3 a) Copy and complete this table of coordinates for the line $y = x - 3$.

b) Draw an x-axis from –2 to 3 and a y-axis from –5 to 0. Use your table of coordinates to help you draw the line $y = x - 3$.

x	–2	–1	0	1	2	3
y						

4 a) Copy and complete this table of coordinates for the line $y = x + 5$.

b) Draw an x-axis from –2 to 3 and a y-axis from 3 to 8. Use your table of coordinates to help you draw the line $y = x + 5$.

x	–2	–1	0	1	2	3
y						

> **Discuss**
>
> Can you spot a link between the coordinates where $x = 0$ and the equation of the line?

For Questions 5 to 6, draw a table of values for each of the equations and then draw the graph for each equation on a separate set of axes.

x	–3	–2	–1	0	1	2	3
y							

5 a) $y = 3x + 1$ (Draw an x-axis from –3 to 3 and a y-axis from –8 to 10.)

b) $y = 4x - 3$ (Draw an x-axis from –3 to 3 and a y-axis from –15 to 9.)

c) $y = 2x + 3$ (Draw an x-axis from –3 to 3 and a y-axis from –3 to 9.)

6 a) $y = 2x - 5$ **b)** $y = 3x - 4$ **c)** $y = 4x + 1$

> **Tip**
>
> Use your table of values to help you decide on the size of your y-axis. You may wish to consider using a different scale on the y-axis.

> **Think about**
>
> Can you think of a quicker method for drawing the graph of a line like $y = 4x + 3$ without drawing a table to generate lots of coordinates?

7 For each part, draw a table of values for values of x between –3 and 3 and then plot the graphs on separate axes.

a) $y = 3 - x$ **b)** $y = 0.5x$ **c)** $y = 1 - 2x$ **d)** $y = 3 - 4x$

8 Which of the coordinates **a)** to **e)** lie on the line $y = 2x - 3$?

a) (2, 7)   **b)** (–1, –5)   **c)** (8, 15)   **d)** (15, 27)   **e)** (20, 37)

Explain your answers.

9 Which of the coordinates **a)** to **e)** lie on the line $y = 5x - 7$?

a) (–3, –8)   **b)** (–7, –42)   **c)** (9, 32)   **d)** (12, 53)   **e)** (30, 147)

Explain your answer.

10 Which of these equations will be straight-line graphs when plotted?

$y = x^2$ $y = 2x + 1$ $y = 3$ $x = -1$ $y = 5 - 4x$

$y = \frac{1}{2}x$ $y = x - 6$ $y = \sqrt{x}$ $y = 4 - x$ $x - 8 = y$

Now check your answers using graphing software.

Explain how you can tell if a line is straight from the equation of the line.

11 Use graphing software to plot the graphs of:

- $y = 2x$ • $y = 2x + 5$ • $y = 2x - 3$.

If you do not have graphing software, then draw the lines on graph paper.

What do you notice about where each of your graphs crosses the y-axis?

Can you predict what the graph of $y = 2x + 10$ will look like?

Check your answer.

12 Use graphing software to plot the graphs of:

- $y = x$ • $y = 2x$ • $y = 3x$.

If you do not have graphing software, then draw the lines on graph paper.

What do you notice about where each of your graphs crosses the y-axis?
What do you notice about the steepness of the lines?

Can you predict what the graph of $y = 4x$ will look like?

Can you predict what the graph of $y = \frac{1}{2}x$ will look like?

Check your answers.

13 Vocabulary feature question

Complete the sentences using words from the box.

linear	axis	formula	coordinate	equation

A mathematical relationship between 2 or more variables is _____

x- _____ or y- _____

In a _____ the first number tells you how far to move in the x-direction and the second number tells you how far to move in the y-direction

Straight line graphs are also known as _____ graphs

The _____ of a line is usually in the form $y = mx + c$.

End of chapter reflection

You should know that ...	You should be able to ...	Such as ...
The points that lie on a line can be described using an equation.	Plot a graph of a given equation.	Plot the graph of $y = 2x - 1$ for values of x between -3 and 3.
An equation describes the relationship between the x-coordinate and the y-coordinate.	Say whether a coordinate lies on a given line.	Does the coordinate $(2, 3)$ line on the line $y = 3x - 5$?
Straight-line graphs have an equation in the form $y = mx + c$.	Say whether a graph is a straight-line graph from the equation of the line.	Which of the following equations are not straight lines? Explain your reasoning. • $y = 3x + 1$ • $y = x^2$ • $y = 4 - 2x$ • $y = 4$ • $x = -2$

Nets and constructions

You will learn how to:

- Draw simple nets of solids, e.g. cuboid, regular tetrahedron, square-based pyramid, triangular prism.
- Use a straight edge and compasses to construct:
  - the midpoint and perpendicular bisector of a line segment
  - the bisector of an angle.

Starting point

Do you remember …?

- how to use a ruler, set square and protractor to:
  - measure and draw straight lines
  - measure and draw different types of angles
  - draw parallel and perpendicular lines
  - construct a triangle given two sides and the included angle (SAS) or two angles and the included side (ASA)?

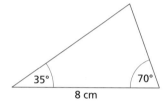 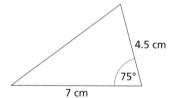

For example,

- construct squares and rectangles
- construct regular polygons, given a side and the internal angle.

This will also be helpful when you:

- learn to calculate surface areas and volumes in right-angled prisms.
- learn how to construct the perpendiculars from a point to a line and from a point on a line.

Hook

Mystic rose?

Begin by drawing a circle.

Next mark six equally spaced points around the edge of the circle (the easiest way to do this is to leave your compass radii the same size).

Next draw straight lines between each pair of points.

Keep going until you have joined all of the points.

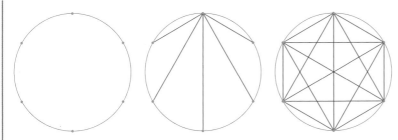

- Can you identify and name some of the shapes that you can see in the mystic rose?
- Can you work out how many lines there are altogether?
- Now investigate with different numbers of points around the edge.

Can you find a link between the number of points around the edge and the number of lines in the mystic rose?

Nets of 3D shapes

Key terms

A **prism** is a 3D shape with the same cross-section all the way along its length. We name a prism using the name of the shape on its cross-section.

For example, triangular prism or octagonal prism.

A **pyramid** is another special type of 3D shape.

Pyramids can have different shaped bases. The other faces of a pyramid are all triangles which meet at a single vertex.

For example, hexagonal pyramid.

A pyramid with a triangle for a base is called a **tetrahedron,** which means four-faced shape, but you could call it a triangular pyramid.

A **net** is a flat shape that can be folded to make a three-dimensional shape. The net of a shape can be folded to make the shape.

A solid can have more than one net.

For example, here are two nets of the same triangular prism.

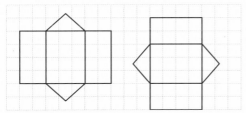

Worked example 1

Draw an accurate net of this shape.

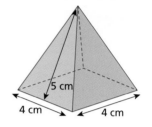

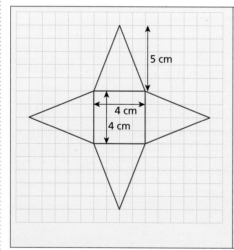

The shape has a square base with side length 4 cm.

All of the other faces are identical triangles with a height of 5 cm.

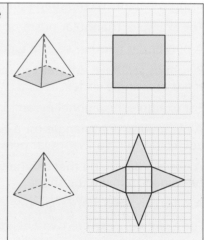

Exercise 1

1 Draw as many different nets of this cuboid as you can.

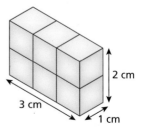

2 This is a tetrahedron.

Which of these nets will make a tetrahedron?

Copy these nets onto isometric (triangular dotty paper), cut them out and check if you were correct.

a)

b)

c)

3 The diagram shows the net of a solid. What is the name of the solid?

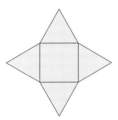

> **Think about**
>
> If you cut off one triangles from the edge of the square, where else could you place the triangle and still make the same 3D shape?

> **Tip**
>
> There are six different possibilities.

4 Here is a triangular prism. Draw a sketch of the net of the shape.

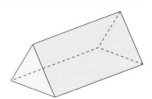

5 Draw an accurate net of this shape.

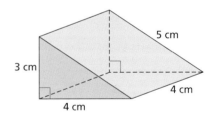

3 cm

5 cm

4 cm

4 cm

6 A net is made from six identical shapes.
Ben says that the 3D shape must be a cube.
Is Ben correct? Explain your answer.

7 Is this statement sometimes true, always true or never true?
  'A prism has a triangular face at each end'.
Explain your answer.

8 Is this statement sometimes true, always true or never true?
  '3-dimensional shapes have more than 5 faces.'
Explain your answer.

9 Is this statement sometimes true, always true or never true?
  'A pyramid has one face that is not a triangle.'
Explain your answer.

10 Here is a triangular prism.

Draw an accurate net of this shape using a scale 1cm : 4 cm.

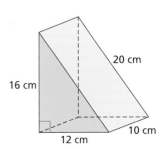

20 cm

16 cm

12 cm

10 cm

11 Draw a sketch of the net of a 3D shape made from two identical square-based pyramids placed together. This shape is called an octahedron.

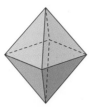

Constructing bisectors

Key terms

A **straight edge** is like a ruler but without any markings. If you are asked to construct using a straight edge, that means you should use your ruler only for drawing straight lines, and not for measuring lengths.

Perpendicular means at right angles to or at 90°.

The **midpoint** of a line segment is the point that is the same distance from both end points. It is halfway along the line segment.

A **bisector** is a line which cuts a shape in half.

A **line segment** is a section of a line. It has two end points.

A pair of **compasses** are used to draw circles or part of a circle called an **arc**.

Worked example 2

a) Construct, using a pair of compasses and a ruler, the perpendicular bisector of an 8 cm line.

b) Construct the angle bisector of a 70° angle.

a) You need to draw a line 8 cm long.

Set your pair of compasses so that the point of the pair of compasses and the pencil are over half of the length of the line apart.

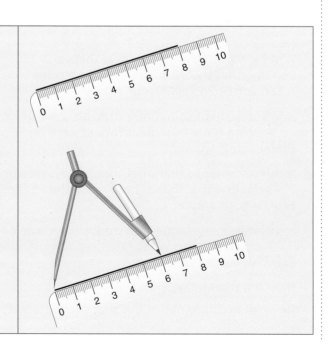

Place the point of the pair of compasses on one end of the line and draw a large arc.

Do not adjust your pair of compasses. Now place your pair of compasses on the other end of the line and again draw a large arc. The two arcs should cross twice. If they do not cross twice, replace the pair of compasses on the ends of the line and extend your arcs.

Draw a straight line through the two points where your arcs meet. This is the **perpendicular bisector**.

Do not rub out your construction lines.

This is the midpoint of the line

b) You need to use your protractor to draw an angle of 70°.

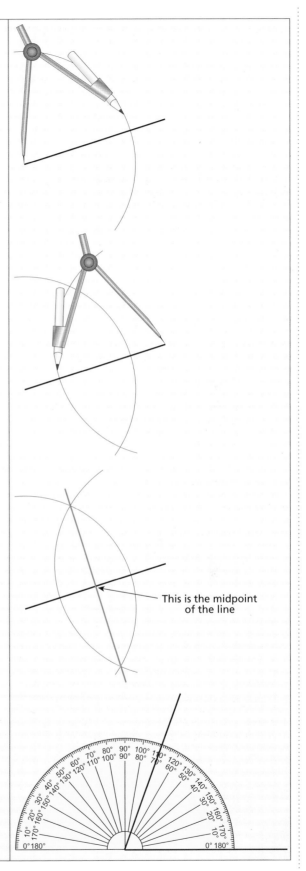

Place the pair of compasses on point *A* and draw an arc.

Now place the pair of compasses on point *B* and draw another arc.

Now place the pair of compasses on the point *C* and draw a final arc.

Finally draw a straight line through the points where your arcs meet and point *A*.
This is the **angle bisector**.

Do not rub out your construction lines.

Think about

What size angles can you construct by combining the two techniques from Worked example 2?

Exercise 2

1. Draw a 12 cm line on plain paper and construct the perpendicular bisector.

2. Draw a 9 cm line on plain paper. Find the midpoint of the line by constructing the perpendicular bisector.

3. Use a protractor to draw a 50° angle. Construct the angle bisector. Use your protractor to check that you have done this accurately.

4. Use a protractor to draw a 130° angle. Construct the angle bisector.

5. Draw a 10 cm line, construct the perpendicular bisector and then bisect the angle between the original line and the perpendicular bisector.

6. Draw a triangle (it does not matter what size). Bisect each angle. Label the points where the angle bisectors meet the triangle *A*, *B* and *C* respectively. Label the point where the three bisectors meet *O*. Measure the lengths *OA*, *OB* and *OC*.

   What do you notice about the lengths *OA*, *OB* and *OC*?

   Draw a different triangle and again bisect each angle. Does the same thing happen? What is special about the triangles created by the angle bisectors?

> **Tip**
>
> You can check your angle bisectors are accurate using your protractor or by cutting out your triangle and folding each of the angles in two.

7. Draw a triangle (it does not matter what size). Construct the perpendicular bisector of each side.
   Draw a different triangle and again construct the perpendicular bisector of each side.
   Can you draw an example where the bisectors meet outside the original triangle?

8. Use a dynamic geometry software to draw a triangle and extend two of the sides.

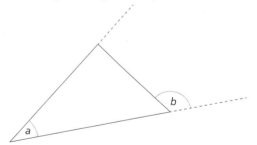

Construct bisectors of angles *a* and *b*.

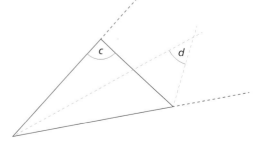

Now measure the angles *c* and *d* on your triangle.

What do you notice about angles c and d?

Now draw a different triangle, bisect the angles and measure as before. Is the relationship the same?

What about if you use special types of triangles, such as equilateral, obtuse or isosceles triangles?

Can you explain why this relationship works?

End of chapter reflection

You should know that ...	You should be able to ...	Such as ...
Nets of • **tetrahedron** have 4 triangular faces. • **square-based pyramids** have 4 faces which are triangular and one which is a square. • **triangular prisms** have 2 faces which are triangular and 3 which are rectangular.	Identify nets of solids such as • cuboids • regular tetrahedrons • square-based pyramids • triangular prisms.	Draw a sketch of the net of a tetrahedron. What is the name of the solid which has this net?
Construct means produce an accurate drawing (using equipment). A pair of **compasses** is used for drawing arcs. **Bisect** means to cut in half.	Use a straight edge and a pair of compasses to construct the midpoint and perpendicular bisector of a line segment.	Draw a line 8 cm long. Construct the perpendicular bisector and label the midpoint.
	Use a straight edge and a pair of compasses to construct the bisector of an angle.	Draw a 70° angle and construct the angle bisector.

Symmetry and transformations

You will learn how to:
- Identify all the symmetries of 2D shapes.
- Transform 2D shapes by rotation, reflection and translation, and simple combinations of these transformations.

Starting point

Do you remember …?

- how to draw lines of symmetry and identify the order of rotation symmetry in 2D shapes and patterns?
- how to transform points and shapes by reflecting in a given line, rotating about a given point and translating?
- that shapes are congruent after they have been rotated, translated or rotated?

This will also be helpful when you:

- use the coordinate grid to solve problems involving translations, rotations, reflections and enlargements.

Did you know?

Rangoli patterns are an art form, originating from India, in which **patterns** are created on the floor in living rooms or courtyards using materials such as coloured rice, dry flour, coloured sand or flower petals. Rangoli patterns usually have either lines of symmetry or rotational symmetry.

Here are some examples of Rangoli patterns.

Hook

Create your own Rangoli pattern by following the steps below.

Draw a horizontal and vertical line with an equal number of squares in each quadrant.

Draw a pattern with straight lines in the top left hand corner.

Then reflect your pattern in the both the horizontal and vertical lines to create a pattern with two lines of symmetry.

Colour this pattern to create your own Rangoli pattern. Your colours should also be symmetrical.

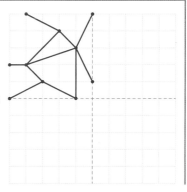

You could experiment further by:

- rotating the pattern in the top left-hand corner to create a pattern with rotational symmetry.

- using four lines of symmetry.

- using three lines of symmetry on isometric paper.

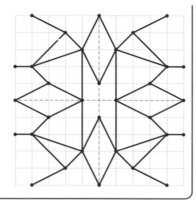

Symmetry

Key terms

A shape has **line symmetry** if it can be folded in half exactly along a straight line. The straight line is called a **line of symmetry**.

A shape has **rotational symmetry** if it fits into its outline more than once as you rotate it a full turn.

The **order of rotational symmetry** is the number of times a shape fits into its outline in a full turn.

Worked example 1

For each shape, state how many lines of symmetry it has and whether or not it has rotational symmetry. If it has rotational symmetry, state the order of that rotational symmetry. State 'no rotational symmetry' if it does not have rotational symmetry.

a)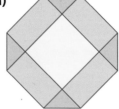

b)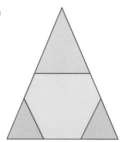

c)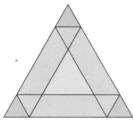

a) It has four **lines of symmetry** as it can be folded in half along a vertical line, horizontal line and along both diagonals

It has **rotational symmetry order 4** as it will fit back onto its outline four times in a full turn.

> **Tip**
>
> Use tracing paper, trace the shape, then rotate the object about the centre for one full turn. The shape fits back, exactly, into its outline four times.

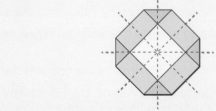

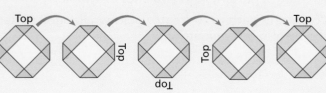

b) It has one line of symmetry as it can be folded in half vertically.

It has **no rotational symmetry** as it will not fit back onto its outline more than once in a full turn.

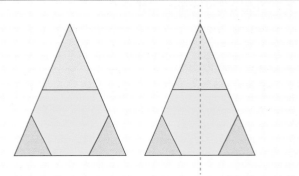

c) It has three lines of symmetry.

It has **rotational symmetry order 3** as it will fit back onto its outline three times in a full turn.

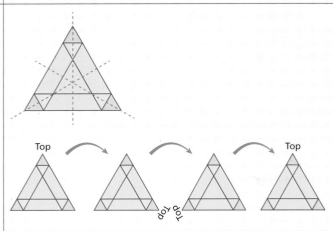

Exercise 1

1 For each shape:

a) State the number of lines of symmetry.

b) State the order of rotational symmetry.

i)   ii)    iii) 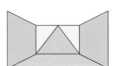   iv)

v) 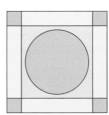   vi) 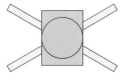   vii) 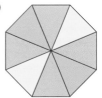   viii)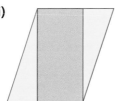

2 Copy this grid and shade 4 more squares so that the shape has order of rotational symmetry 4.

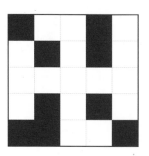

3 Use a spreadsheet to create a pattern with order of rotational symmetry 4.

To create squares, click on the top left-hand corner to highlight all cells, then adjust the column width until you have the same width as the height of the cells. To be more accurate you will need to look at the row height and column width.

Click here to highlight all cells

	A	B	C	D	E	F
1						
2						
3						
4						
5						
6						
7						
8						

e.g.

	A	B	C	D	E	F
1						
2						
3						
4						
5						
6						

4 Copy this shape and shade 4 more triangles so that the shape has order of rotational symmetry 3.

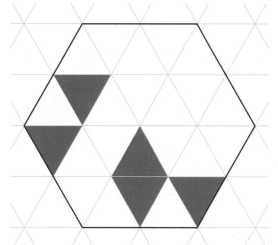

5 Jane says that a parallelogram has two lines of symmetry.

Do you agree? Explain you answer.

6 Create your own shape which has order of rotational symmetry 3.

Try to make your design intricate and colourful.

Tip

You may want to use isometric paper.

Key terms

A **reflection** is a mirroring or flipping of a shape. You usually state or draw the line in which the shape is reflected.

A **rotation** is the turning of shape. You usually state the angle and direction of the rotation as well as the centre point around which the shape turns.

A **translation** is a movement of a shape. You usually state the size and direction of the movement horizontally (left/right) and vertically (up/down).

You call reflections, rotations and translations **transformation** because they transform or change one shape into another.

You call the shape you start with the **original** shape.

When you move this shape around you, call the resulting shape an **image**.

Worked example 2

a) Reflect shape A in the mirror line and label this shape B.

b) Rotate shape B about the point shown 90° anti-clockwise and label this shape C.

c) Translate the shape C 2 squares to the left and 5 squares up.

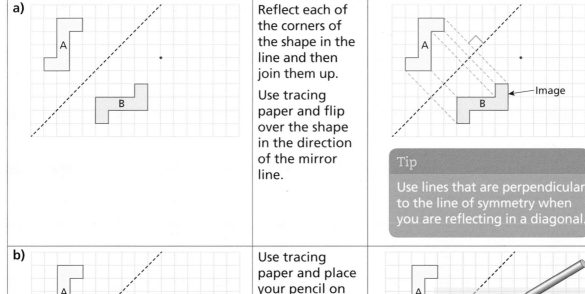

a)

Reflect each of the corners of the shape in the line and then join them up.

Use tracing paper and flip over the shape in the direction of the mirror line.

Tip

Use lines that are perpendicular to the line of symmetry when you are reflecting in a diagonal.

b)

Use tracing paper and place your pencil on the centre of rotation and turn the paper through 90° anti-clockwise.

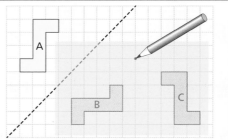

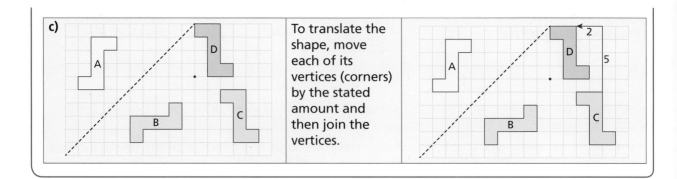

| c) | | To translate the shape, move each of its vertices (corners) by the stated amount and then join the vertices. | |

1 Reflect shape A in the mirror line and label this shape B.

a)
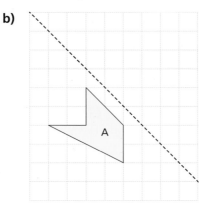

b)

Discuss

How could you create a delta/dart using a reflection?

2 a) Rotate shape A about the point shown 90° anti-clockwise and label this shape B.

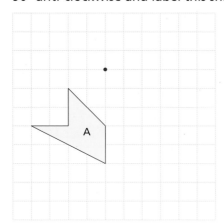

b) Rotate shape A about the point shown 90° clockwise and label this shape B.

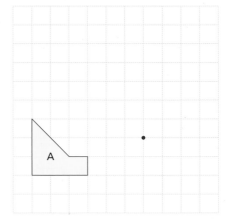

c) Rotate shape A about the point shown 180° and label this shape B.

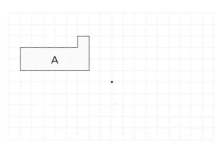

d) Rotate shape A about the point shown 90° anti-clockwise and label this shape B.

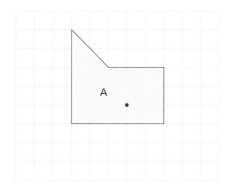

3 Reflect the shape in both mirror lines.

a)

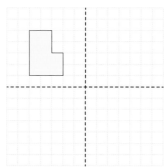

b)

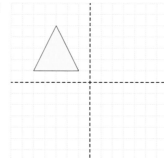

c)

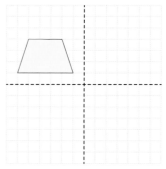

d)

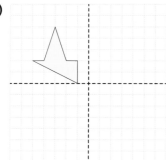

e)

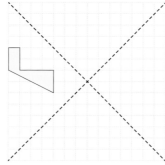

> **Tip**
>
> Once you have reflected in both mirror lines you should have 4 shapes in each grid.

4 **a)** Reflect shape A in the mirror line and label this shape B.

b) Rotate shape B about the point shown by 180° and label this shape C.

c) Translate the shape C 2 squares to the right and 4 squares up.

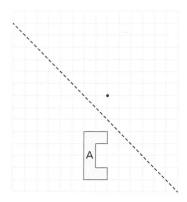

5 **a)** Reflect shape A in the mirror line and label this shape B.

   b) Rotate shape B about the point shown 90° clockwise and label this shape C.

   c) Translate the shape C 1 square up and 3 squares to the right.

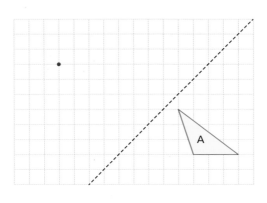

Think about

If you change the order of the transformations would shape D be in the same place?

6 Julie says that if you reflect a right-angled triangle you always get a square. Do you agree? Explain your answer.

7 Draw a shape that when you reflect it in two mirror lines the resultant picture has order of rotational symmetry 2.

Make sure you show the mirror lines. Your mirror lines can either be perpendicular or parallel to each other.

End of chapter reflection

You should know that …	You should be able to …	Such as …
An object has **line symmetry** if it can be folded in half exactly along a straight line.	Identify all symmetries of a 2D shape.	State how many lines of symmetry this shape has and whether or not it has rotational symmetry.
The order of **rotational symmetry** is the number of times a shape or pattern fits back onto its own outline when rotated through a full turn.		
If the order of rotational symmetry of a shape or pattern is less than 2 then it has **no rotational symmetry**.		
Reflection is the process of mirroring or flipping a shape in a mirror line.	Transform a shape using simple combinations of rotations, reflections and translations.	Reflect shape O in the line shown and label this shape P.
Rotation is the process of turning a shape around a **centre** point by a specified **angle** and **direction**.		Rotate shape P 90° clockwise about the point shown and label this shape Q.
Translation is the process of moving a shape horizontally and vertically a specified number of squares.		Translate shape Q 3 squares left and 2 squares down and label this shape R.

The order in which multiple **transformations** are completed can alter the finishing position of the shape.	Say whether the order of the sequence of transformations does or does not alter the finishing position of the shape.	If I alter the sequence of transformations as follows: Rotate shape O 90° clockwise about the point shown and label this shape P. Reflect shape P in the line shown, label this shape Q. Translate shape Q 3 squares left and 2 squares down and label this shape R. Does shape O finish in the same place as when you reflected first, then rotated and then translated?

Unit 2C
Handling data and measures

What it's all about?

- Imperial measures of distance
- Area, surface area and volume
- Statistical diagrams for displaying data
- Drawing conclusions from data
- Listing all the possible outcomes for two events

You will learn about:

- miles as a measure of distance
- calculating the area of a triangle, parallelogram and trapezium
- finding the volume of cuboids and surface area of 3D shapes
- drawing frequency diagrams, pie charts, line graphs and stem-and-leaf diagrams
- interpreting diagrams and statistics and making conclusions
- how to list outcomes from two events in a systematic way

You will build your skills in:

- using everyday measurement systems
- drawing accurate diagrams for displaying a set of data
- forming and explaining conclusions
- solving problems involving measures and probability using logical argument

Imperial units of measurement

You will learn how to:
- Use that 1 kilometre is about $\frac{5}{8}$ of a mile to convert between distances in miles and distances in kilometres.

Starting point

Do you remember ...?

- how to convert between kilometres (km), metres (m), centimetres (cm) and millimetres (mm)?
  For example, how many cm are in 4.3 m?
- how to multiply a whole number by a fraction?
  For example, multiply 8 by $\frac{1}{2}$.
- how to calculate fractions of quantities?
  For example, find $\frac{3}{4}$ of 32 cm.
- how to round decimals to the nearest whole number?

Hook

Before there were accurate measuring instruments, such as rulers, units of measurement were often based on parts of the body – usually parts of the arm and hands.

One of the oldest measurements is the cubit – the distance between the elbow and the tip of the middle finger in an adult male. It was used in ancient Egypt almost 5000 years ago in the construction of the pyramids.

The cubit was divided into 7 palms – the width across the palm below the 4 fingers – and each palm was then divided into 4 fingers – the width of the middle finger. Measuring sticks, such as the one shown below used by King Tutankhamen's Minister of Finance, show a cubit divided into 7 palms and 28 fingers.

Working in groups, find three things that you can reach to measure using your own arms and hands for cubits, palms and fingers. Choose one large object such as a wall or door, one medium object such as a table or desk and one small object such as a book and take it in turns to be the measuring stick.

Converting between miles and kilometres

Key terms

Approximately equal to means almost equal, but not exactly equal to. The symbol ≈ means approximately equal to.

Worked example 1

a) What is the approximate value of 72 km in miles?

b) What is the approximate value of 35 miles in km?

c) What is the approximate value of 38 miles in km?

a) $72 \text{ km} \approx 72 \times \frac{5}{8} \text{ miles}$ $72 \times \frac{5}{8} = 72 \div 8 \times 5$ $= 45$ $\therefore 72 \text{ km} \approx 45 \text{ miles}$	There are approximately 8 km in 5 miles. To convert approximately from km to miles, divide the number of km into blocks of 8 km and then multiply the number of blocks by 5.	<table><tr><td colspan="9">72 km</td></tr><tr><td>8 km</td><td>8 km</td><td>8 km</td><td>8 km</td><td>8 km</td><td>8 km</td><td>8 km</td><td>8 km</td><td>8 km</td></tr><tr><td>5 miles</td><td>5 miles</td><td>5 miles</td><td>5 miles</td><td>5 miles</td><td>5 miles</td><td>5 miles</td><td>5 miles</td><td>5 miles</td></tr><tr><td colspan="9">45 miles</td></tr></table>
b) 35 miles $\approx 35 \times \frac{8}{5} \text{ km}$ $35 \div 5 \times 8 = 56$ $35 \text{ miles} \approx 56 \text{ km}$	To convert approximately from miles to km, divide the miles into blocks of 5 miles and then multiply the number of blocks by 8.	<table><tr><td colspan="7">35 miles</td></tr><tr><td>5 miles</td><td>5 miles</td><td>5 miles</td><td>5 miles</td><td>5 miles</td><td>5 miles</td><td>5 miles</td></tr><tr><td>8 km</td><td>8 km</td><td>8 km</td><td>8 km</td><td>8 km</td><td>8 km</td><td>8 km</td></tr><tr><td colspan="7">56 km</td></tr></table>
c) $38 \text{ miles} \approx 38 \times \frac{8}{5} \text{ km}$ $38 \div 5 = 7.6$ $7.6 \times 8 = 60.8$ $38 \text{ miles} \approx 60.8 \text{ km}$ or $38 \text{ miles} \approx 38 \times 1.6 \text{ km}$ $38 \times 1.6 = 60.8$ $38 \text{ miles} \approx 60.8 \text{ km}$	To convert approximately from miles to km, divide the miles into blocks of 5 and multiply the number of blocks by 8. In this case there are 7 complete blocks and $\frac{3}{5}$ or 0.6 of a block.	<table><tr><td colspan="8">38 miles</td></tr><tr><td>5 miles</td><td>5 miles</td><td>5 miles</td><td>5 miles</td><td>5 miles</td><td>5 miles</td><td>5 miles</td><td>0.6 × 5</td></tr><tr><td>8 km</td><td>8 km</td><td>8 km</td><td>8 km</td><td>8 km</td><td>8 km</td><td>8 km</td><td>0.6 × 8</td></tr><tr><td colspan="7">56 km</td><td>4.8 km</td></tr><tr><td colspan="8">60.8 km</td></tr></table>

In this exercise take 8 km to be approximately equal to 5 miles or 1 km to be approximately equal to $\frac{5}{8}$ mile.

1 Work out, in your head, the approximate number of km in each of the following.

   a) 10 miles   **b)** 25 miles   **c)** 45 miles   **d)** 250 miles

2 Work out, in your head, the approximate number of miles in each of the following.

   a) 24 km   **b)** 32 km   **c)** 48 km   **d)** 800 km

3 Which is the greater distance in each of these pairs?

   a) 320 km or 250 miles

   b) 800 km or 480 miles

   c) 545 miles or 850 km

4 A road sign in France says that the distance to Paris is 296 km.

   How far, approximately, is this in miles?

5 Calculate the approximate number of miles in each of the following. Give your answers as decimals.

   a) 26 km   **b)** 40 km   **c)** 130 km   **d)** 250 km   **e)** 1000 km

6 If 1 mile is $\frac{8}{5}$ or 1.6 km, calculate the approximate number of km in each of the following. Give your answers as decimals.

   a) 36 miles   **b)** 42 miles   **c)** 108 miles   **d)** 273 miles   **e)** 1000 miles

7 Write a distance between 90 km and 100 km that is easy to convert approximately to miles. Explain what makes it easy.

8 Jamila is checking her sister's work. Without any calculations, she says that all of the following calculations are wrong. Explain how she knows that each calculation is incorrect and correct the calculation.

   a) 160 miles ≈ 100 km   **b)** 30 miles ≈ 60 km   **c)** 85 km ≈ 47 miles

9 Explain the mistake that Jamila's sister has made when working out her answer to question 8a).

10 You are allowed to use your calculator to work out the approximate value of only two of the following distances in miles. You must work out the rest without a calculator. Which two would you choose to use your calculator for?

   a) 80 km   **b)** 188 km   **c)** 64.8 km   **d)** 376 km   **e)** 602 km

> **Tip**
>
> To convert approximately from km to miles you multiply the number of km by $\frac{5}{8}$ or 0.625.

11 Look at the diagram below which is a rough conversion chart for miles and km.

a) Which side of the line represents km and which represents miles?

b) Use the scale to find the approximate value of each of the following.

i) 4 km in miles   **ii)** 3 miles in km   **iii)** 30 miles in km

End of chapter reflection

You should know that ...	You should be able to ...	Such as ...
The ≈ symbol means 'approximately equal to'. This tells us that the answer is approximate, not accurate. The usual approximations used for converting between miles and kilometres are: **8 km ≈ 5 miles** 1 km ≈ $\frac{5}{8}$ mile 1 km ≈ 0.625 miles **5 miles ≈ 8 km** 1 mile ≈ $\frac{8}{5}$ km 1 mile ≈ 1.6 km	Convert approximately between miles and kilometres.	Complete the following: **a)** 15 miles ≈ ___ km **b)** 150 miles ≈ ___ km **c)** 16 km ≈ ___ miles **d)** 320 km ≈ ___ miles

Area, surface area and volume

You will learn how to:
- Derive and use formulae for the area of a triangle, parallelogram and trapezium; calculate areas of compound 2D shapes, and lengths, surface areas and volumes of cuboids.
- Use simple nets of solids to work out their surface areas.

Starting point

Do you remember …?

- the meaning of area as a measure of the space inside a 2-dimensional shape?
  For example, what is the area of this shape?

  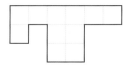

- how to find the area of a rectangle from its length and width?
  For example, what is the area of a rectangle of length 11 cm and width 3 cm?

- the properties of triangles, parallelograms and trapezia?
  For example, describe the properties of the sides and angles of a parallelogram.

- the meaning of volume as a measure of space inside a 3-dimensional shape?
  For example, what is the volume of this shape?

  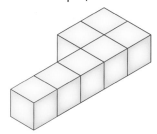

- how to find the volume of a cuboid?
  For example, what is the volume of this cuboid?

  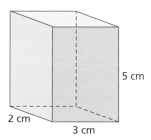

  5 cm

  2 cm

  3 cm

- what the net of a shape is?
  For example, sketch the net of a square-based pyramid.

This will also be helpful when you:

- learn more about finding the area of circles and shapes made from circles, as well as the volume and surface area of prisms and more complex 3D shapes.

Hook

Look at this sequence of **parallelograms.**

- Explain why the first shape is a parallelogram.
- Can you draw the next two parallelograms in the sequence?
- Find the **area** of each of the parallelograms by counting squares.
- What do you notice?
- Predict the area of this parallelogram.

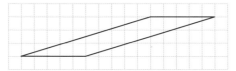

- Can you write what you have discovered as a **formula** that is true for any parallelogram?

> ## Tip
> You can pair parts of squares together to make whole squares.

Key terms

A **parallelogram** is a quadrilateral with two pairs of parallel sides.

The **area** of a 2-dimensional shape is a measure of the amount of space lying within it. We measure this space in squares, such as square metres (m^2) or square centimetres (cm^2).

A **formula** is a way of expressing a general rule using letters to stand for the variables involved. For example, the formula for the area of a rectangle, A, is $A = l \times w$, where l is the length and w is the width of the rectangle.

Area of 2D shapes

Key terms

A **trapezium** is a quadrilateral with one pair of parallel sides. This shape is sometimes also called a trapezoid. Two or more trapeziums are called **trapezia.**

The **perpendicular height** is the height of the shape measured at right angles to the base of the shape as shown in the diagram.

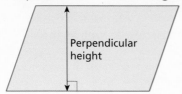
Perpendicular height

Worked example 1

Find the area of:

a)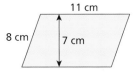

b)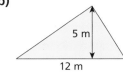

c)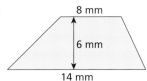

a) Area = length × **perpendicular height** = 11 × 7 = 77 cm²	The parallelogram can be rearranged into a rectangle as shown. So, the area covered by the parallelogram is the same as that of a rectangle with length 11 cm and width 7 cm. Hence, the area of the parallelogram = 11 × 7 = 77 cm² (We do not need the 8 cm measurement provided.)	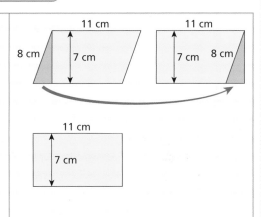
b) Area = $\frac{1}{2}$ base × height = $\frac{1}{2}(12 \times 5)$ = $\frac{1}{2}(60)$ = 30 m²	The triangle is exactly half of a parallelogram as shown. This parallelogram has length 12 m and perpendicular height 5 m. Therefore, the area of the parallelogram is 12 × 5 = 60 m². Since the triangle is half this parallelogram, the area of the triangle is = $\frac{1}{2}(12 \times 5)$ = $\frac{1}{2}(60)$ = 30 m²	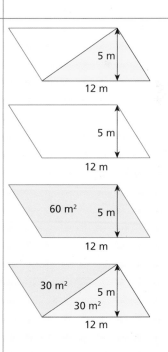

c) Area

$$= \frac{1}{2}(a + b)h$$

$$= \frac{1}{2}([14 + 8] \times 6)$$

$$= \frac{1}{2}(22 \times 6)$$

$$= \frac{1}{2}(132)$$

$$= 66 \text{ mm}^2$$

The **trapezium** is exactly half of a parallelogram as shown

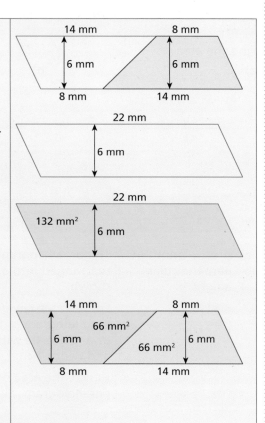

This parallelogram has length 8 + 14 = 22 mm and perpendicular height 6 mm.

Therefore, the area of the parallelogram

$$= (14 + 8) \times 6$$

$$= 22 \times 6$$

$$= 132 \text{ mm}^2$$

Since the trapezium is half the parallelogram, the area of the trapezium

$$= \frac{1}{2}([14 + 8] \times 6)$$

$$= \frac{1}{2}(22 \times 6)$$

$$= \frac{1}{2}(132)$$

$$= 66 \text{ mm}^2$$

Discuss

How many different parallelograms are there with an area of 24 cm²?

Exercise 1

1 Find the area of each rectangles.

a)

11 cm
3 cm

b)

4 m
13 m

c)

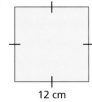

12 cm

d)

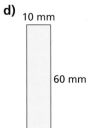

10 mm
60 mm

e)

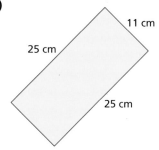

11 cm
25 cm
25 cm

2 Find the area of each parallelograms.

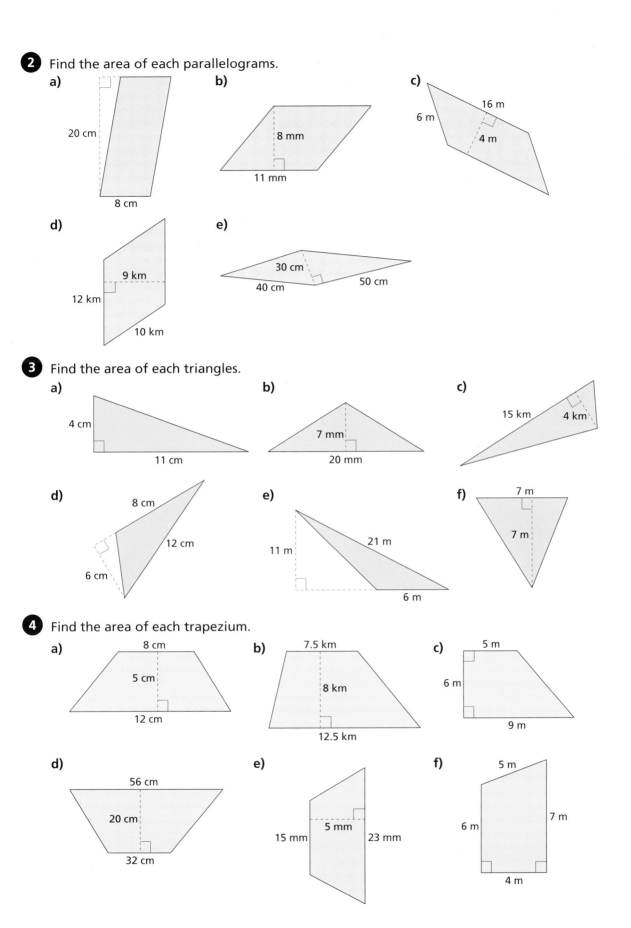

a)

20 cm
8 cm

b)

8 mm
11 mm

c)

16 m
6 m
4 m

d)

9 km
12 km
10 km

e)

30 cm
40 cm
50 cm

3 Find the area of each triangles.

a)

4 cm
11 cm

b)

7 mm
20 mm

c)

15 km
4 km

d)

8 cm
12 cm
6 cm

e)

11 m
21 m
6 m

f)

7 m
7 m

4 Find the area of each trapezium.

a)

8 cm
5 cm
12 cm

b)

7.5 km
8 km
12.5 km

c)

5 m
6 m
9 m

d)

56 cm
20 cm
32 cm

e)

15 mm
5 mm
23 mm

f)

5 m
6 m
7 m
4 m

5 Look at the triangle.

    a) Show how two of these triangles fit together to form a parallelogram.

    b) Write an expression for the area of this parallelogram.

    c) Hence write an expression for the area of this triangle in terms of a and h.

6 Look at the trapezium.

    a) Show how two of these trapezia fit together to form a parallelogram.

    b) Write an expression for the area of this parallelogram.

    c) Hence write an expression for its area of this trapezium in terms of a, b and h.

7 Eleanor is calculating the area of this triangle: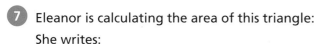

    She writes:

$$\text{Area} = \tfrac{1}{2}(6 \times 4) = 12 \text{ cm}^2$$

    Do you agree with Eleanor? Explain your answer.

8 Which of these shapes is the odd one out? Explain how you know.

a) 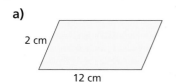   **b)** 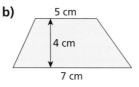   **c)** 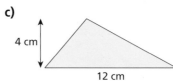   **d)**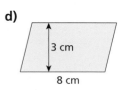

So we have discovered that:

Area of a parallelogram = length × perpendicular height = ah	Area of a triangle = $\tfrac{1}{2}$ base × height = $\tfrac{1}{2}ah$	Area of a trapezium = average length × perpendicular height = $\tfrac{1}{2}(a + b)h$

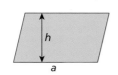 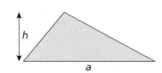 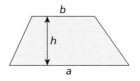

Area of compound shapes

Key terms

A **compound** shape is one that is made from connecting together other named shapes, such as triangles and parallelograms.

To find the area of a compound shape, split it into its connecting shapes and then find the sum of the separate areas.

Find the area of this shape.

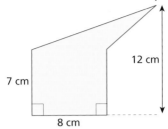

Split the shape into shapes A and B.

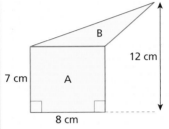

Shape A is a rectangle of base 8 cm and height

7 cm so Area A = 8 × 7 = 56 cm²

Shape B is a triangle of base 8 cm and height = 12 − 7 = 5 cm

So Area B = $\frac{1}{2}(8 \times 5) = 20$ cm²

Therefore,
Total area

= Area A + Area B

= 56 + 20

= 76 cm²

This is a **compound** shape.

So we need to split the shape up into shapes that we can find the area, such as

a rectangle and a triangle as shown:

The area of the rectangle

= length × width

= 8 × 7

= 56 cm²

The area of the triangle

= $\frac{1}{2}$ base × height

We know the base is 8 cm, but we need to find the height, the difference between 12 cm and 7 cm, i.e. 5 cm.

So the area of the triangle

= $\frac{1}{2}$ base × height

= $\frac{1}{2}(8 \times 5)$

= $\frac{1}{2}(40)$

= 20 cm²

Therefore, the total area

= 56 + 20

= 76 cm²

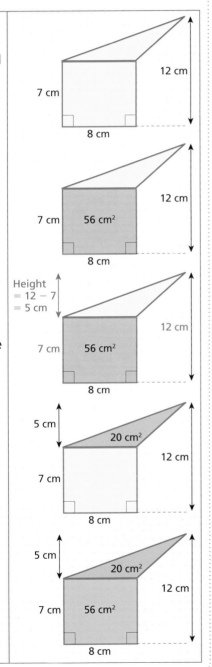

Think about

Do you always have to find a compound area by adding smaller areas together?

What strategy could you use to find the white area in this shape?

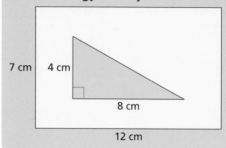

Exercise 2

Find the area of each of the following compound shapes.

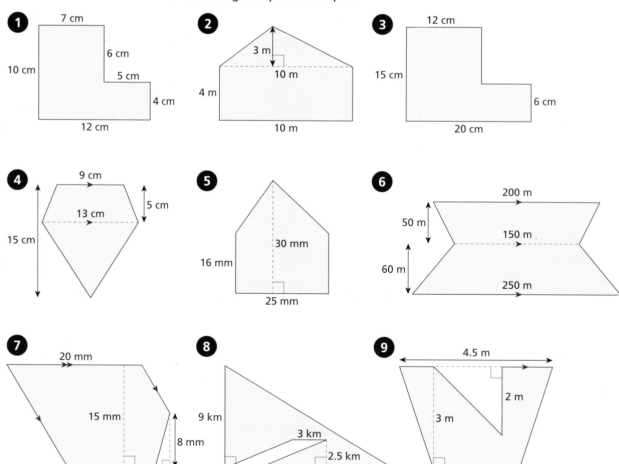

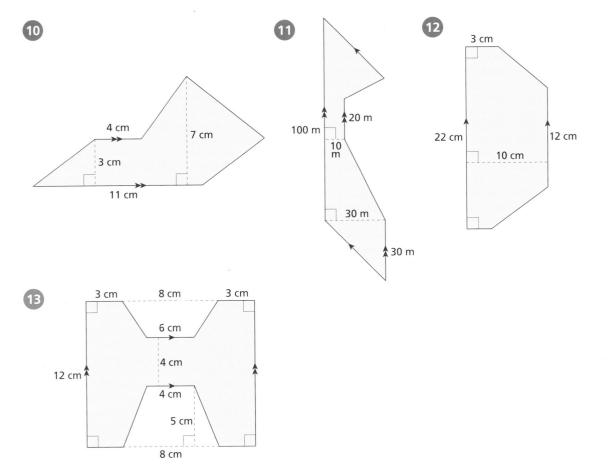

10 4 cm · 7 cm · 3 cm · 11 cm

11 100 m · 20 m · 10 m · 30 m · 30 m

12 3 cm · 22 cm · 10 cm · 12 cm

13 3 cm · 8 cm · 3 cm · 6 cm · 4 cm · 12 cm · 4 cm · 5 cm · 8 cm

14 Josephine is calculating the area of this compound shape.

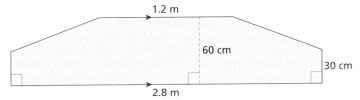

1.2 m · 60 cm · 30 cm · 2.8 m

She writes:

Area = 2.8 × 30 + $\frac{1}{2}$(1.2 + 2.8) × 60

= 84 + 120

= 204 cm²

Josephine has made a mistake in her solution. Find the mistake Josephine has made and correct her solution.

Volume, surface area and lengths of 3D shapes

Key terms

The **volume** of a three-dimensional shape is the measure of the amount of space inside it.
We measure this space in cubes, such as cubic metres (m³) or cubic centimetres (cm³).

The **surface area** of a three-dimensional shape is the measure of the sum of the areas of all its faces.

Look at this cuboid.

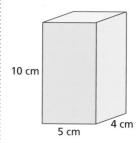

10 cm

5 cm   4 cm

a) Calculate the volume of the cuboid.

b) Calculate the surface area of the cuboid.

a) Volume of a cuboid = length × width × height = 5 × 4 × 10 = 200 cm³	Split this shape into cubic centimetres. There are 10 layers of cubes making the cuboid (because the height is 10 cm).	
	In each layer, there are 4 rows of 5 cubes (because the width is 4 cm and the length is 5 cm). Altogether, this is 5 × 4 = 20 cubes per layer.	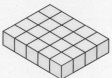
	Since there are 10 layers, this is 20 × 10 = 200 cubes altogether. So the volume of the cuboid is 200 cubes of size 1 centimetre or 200 cm³.	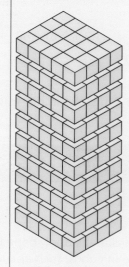

b) Surface area
= 2(5 × 10 + 4 × 5 + 4 × 10)
= 2(50 + 20 + 40)
= 2(110)
= 220 cm²

The surface area is the sum of the area of all the faces.

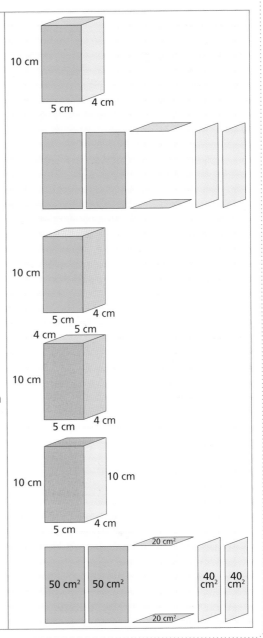

As this is a cuboid, there are six rectangular faces for which we must find the area, although some of them are the same.

The area of the front face
= 5 × 10
= 50 cm²
and this is the same as the back face.

The area of the top face
= 5 × 4
= 20 cm²
and this is the same as the bottom face.

The area of the right face
= 4 × 10
= 40 cm²
and this is the same as the left face.

So altogether we have surface area
= 50 + 50 + 20 + 20 + 40 + 40
= 220 cm²

Exercise 3

1 Calculate the volume of each cuboid.

a)

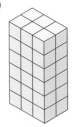

b)

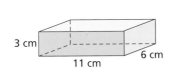

3 cm
11 cm
6 cm

c)

100 mm
20 mm
25 mm

d)

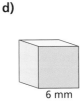

6 mm

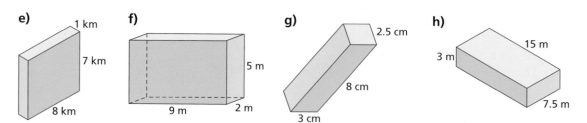

e) 1 km / 7 km / 8 km

f) 5 m / 9 m / 2 m

g) 2.5 cm / 8 cm / 3 cm

h) 3 m / 15 m / 7.5 m

2 Calculate the surface area of each of the cuboids in Question 1.

3 This cuboid has a volume of 280 cm³.

20 cm / 4 cm

Calculate the height of the cuboid.

4 Each of these cuboids have a volume of 360 cm³.

Calculate the length marked *x* in each one.

a)

x / 20 cm / 9 cm

b)

12 cm / *x* / 6 cm

c)

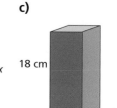

18 cm / *x* / 5 cm

d)

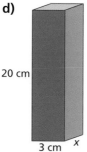

20 cm / 3 cm / *x*

5 A cuboid has a volume of 72 cm³. All the dimensions of the cuboid are a whole number of centimetres. The height of the cuboid is 3 cm. List all the possible pairs of values of the length and width of the cuboid.

6 Amy wants to find the volume of this cuboid:

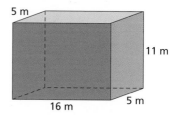

5 m / 11 m / 16 m / 5 m

She says, 'All I need to do is multiply all the lengths together, so the volume is 16 × 5 × 11 × 5 = 4400 m².'

Do you agree with Amy? Explain your answer.

7 Jack wants to find the surface area of this cuboid:

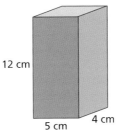

12 cm

5 cm 4 cm

He writes: Surface area = 6 × area of one face = 6 × 60 = 360 cm².

Do you agree with Jack? Explain your answer.

8 Write down the dimensions of each cuboid with its volume and surface area.

Work out the missing values to produce six matching pairs.

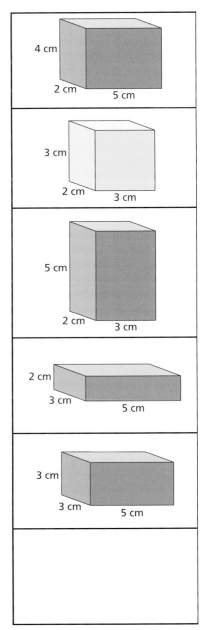

4 cm, 2 cm, 5 cm	30 cm³	62 cm²
3 cm, 2 cm, 3 cm	60 cm³	76 cm²
5 cm, 2 cm, 3 cm		72 cm²
2 cm, 3 cm, 5 cm	18 cm³	74 cm²
3 cm, 3 cm, 5 cm	45 cm³	
	36 cm³	78 cm²

9 A cuboid has a volume of 64 cm³ and a length of 8 cm.

What could its other dimensions be?

Use a spreadsheet to list some possible pairs. Then calculate the surface area of each of the cuboids.

Which one has the biggest surface area? And the smallest?

> **Tip**
>
> Your values for the width and height do not need to be whole numbers.

Did you know?

Doctors use the surface area of a patient to estimate how much anaesthetic to give for an operation. They have special formulae to help them estimate someone's surface area such as the Mosteller Formula.

Surface area of other solids

Key terms

The **net** of a 3 dimensional shape is a 2-dimensional diagram of the faces, edges and vertices of the shape that will fold up to become the shape if cut out.

Worked example 4

Here is the net of a square-based pyramid. Use the net to calculate the surface area of the pyramid.

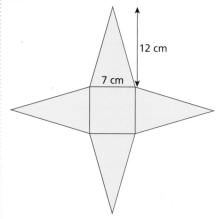

12 cm

7 cm

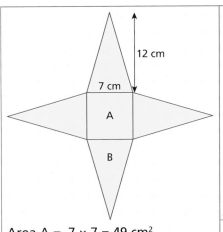

Area A = $7 \times 7 = 49$ cm^2

Area B = $\frac{1}{2}(7 \times 12) = \frac{1}{2}(84) = 42$ cm^2

Surface area of the pyramid

= area A + 4(area B)

= 49 + 4(42)

= 49 + 168

= 217 cm^2

The surface area of the pyramid so the sum of the individual areas of each of the five faces.

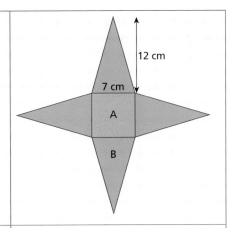

We know from the question text that the base of the pyramid is a square.

So area of base

= length × width

= 7×7

= 49 cm^2

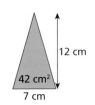

Because this is a pyramid, the four triangle faces will have equal lengths and hence equal areas.

The area of the triangles = $\frac{1}{2}$(base × height)

= $\frac{1}{2}(7 \times 12)$

= $\frac{1}{2}(84)$

= 42 cm^2

So the total surface area

= area of square base + 4 × area of triangular face

= 49 + 4 × 42

= 49 + 168

= 217 cm^2

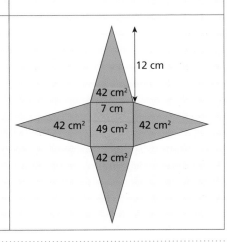

1 Work out the surface area of the shape made by each net.

a)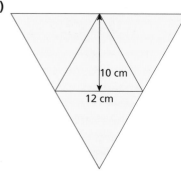

10 cm
12 cm

b)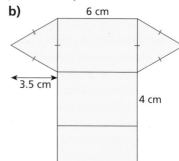

6 cm
3.5 cm
4 cm

c)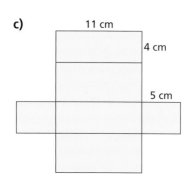

11 cm
4 cm
5 cm

d)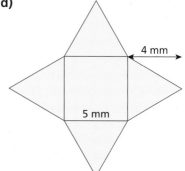

4 mm
5 mm

e)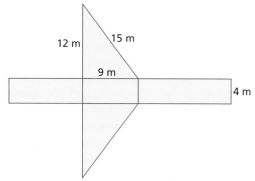

12 m
15 m
9 m
4 m

f)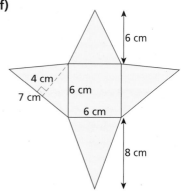

6 cm
4 cm
7 cm
6 cm
6 cm
8 cm

g)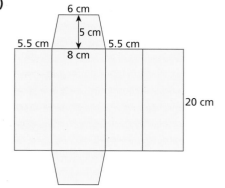

6 cm
5 cm
5.5 cm
5.5 cm
8 cm
20 cm

2 **a)** Sketch the net of a scalene triangular prism.

b) How many different lengths do you need to know to be able to calculate the surface area of a scalene triangular prism from its net? Explain your answer.

3 Draw the net of a shape with a surface area of 120 cm².

Can you find more than one solution?

4 Vocabulary feature question

Match each key term with the correct description.

Volume	A 3-dimensional shape with six rectangular faces
Compound shape	The amount of space inside a 2-dimensional shape, measured in squares
Area	A 2-dimensional diagram that can be folded up to form a 3-dimensional shape
Net	A 3-dimensional shape where all but one face are triangular, and these all meet at a vertex
Length	A quadrilateral with two pairs of parallel sides
Formula	A 1-dimensional quantity
Surface area	A 3-dimensional shape with a fixed cross-section
Perpendicular height	A rule connecting variables, usually expressed using algebra
Parallelogram	The total area of all the faces of a 3-dimensional shape
Pyramid	A quadrilateral with one pair of parallel sides
Trapezium	A shape formed by joining other (named) shapes together
Prism	The distance from the base to the top of a shape, measured at right-angles to the base
Cuboid	The amount of space inside a 3-dimensional shape, measured in cubes

End of chapter reflection

You should know that ...	You should be able to ...	Such as ...
The area of a 2-dimensional shape or surface is the amount of space inside it, measured in squares.		
Area of a triangle $= \frac{1}{2}$ base × height $= \frac{1}{2}ah$ 	Calculate the area of a triangle.	Find the area of:
Area of a parallelogram = length × perpendicular height $= ah$ 	Calculate the area of a parallelogram.	Find the area of:
Area of a trapezium = average length × perpendicular height $= \frac{1}{2}(a + b)h$ 	Calculate the area of a trapezium.	Find the area of:
A compound area can be found by breaking it up into its constituent shapes.	Calculate the area of a compound shape.	Calculate the shaded area: Calculate the area:

The volume of a shape is the amount of space inside a 3-dimensional shape, measured in cubes. The volume of a cuboid = *lwh*	Calculate the volume of a cuboid.	Calculate the volume: 15 cm, 5 cm, 8 cm
	Calculate a missing length of a cuboid, given its volume.	The volume of the cuboid is 60 cm³. Calculate its height. 2 cm, 6 cm
The surface area of a 3-dimensional shape is the total of the areas of each of its faces.	Calculate the surface area of a cuboid.	Calculate the surface area: 15 cm, 5 cm, 8 cm
A net of a shape is a 2-dimensional diagram that can be folded up to form the 3-dimensional shape. The area of a net = the surface area of the 3D shape it represents	Calculate the surface area of a 3-dimensional shape from its net.	Calculate the surface area of the prism represented by this net: 12 m, 13 m, 5 m, 5 m

Displaying and interpreting data

You will learn how to:
- Draw and interpret:
  - frequency diagrams for discrete and continuous data
  - pie charts
  - simple line graphs for time series
  - stem-and-leaf diagrams.
- Interpret tables, graphs and diagrams for discrete and continuous data, and draw conclusions relating statistics and findings to the original question.
- Compare two distributions, using the range and one or more of the mode, median and mean.

Starting point

Do you remember …?

- how to draw and interpret bar charts, bar-line graphs, pictograms and simple bar charts?
  For example, how many students scored less than 8 marks in the spelling test?

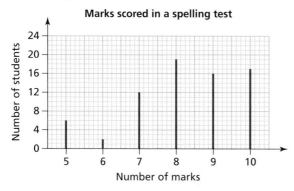

Marks scored in a spelling test

- how to find the mean, median and mode for a set of data?
  For example, what are the mean, median and mode of the numbers 11, 6, 17, 8, 6, 11 and 7?

- how to find the range for a set of data?
  For example, what is the range of these measurements: 12 cm, 19 cm, 24 cm, 10 cm, 17 cm and 25 cm?

This will also be helpful when you:

- learn how to draw back to back stem-and-leaf diagrams for comparing two sets of data.
- learn how to draw scatter graphs to see if there is a relationship between two sets of data.

Hook

In June 2018, the population of the world was estimated to be 7.6 billion.

The diagram shows some facts about the people that live on this planet.

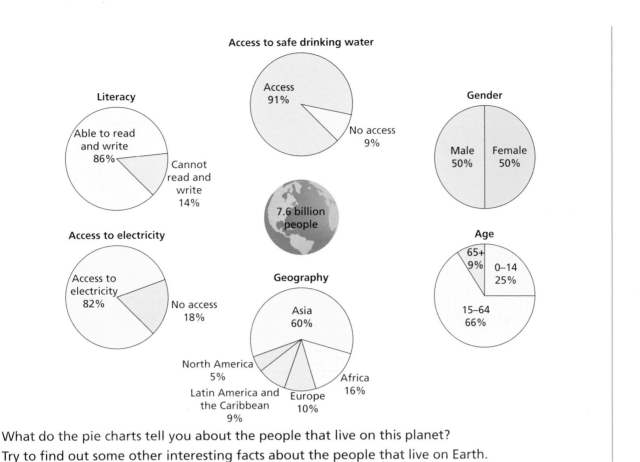

Access to safe drinking water

Literacy

Gender

Access to electricity

Geography

Age

7.6 billion people

What do the pie charts tell you about the people that live on this planet?

Try to find out some other interesting facts about the people that live on Earth.

Frequency diagrams and stem-and-leaf diagrams

Key terms

Frequency diagrams are a type of diagram that can be drawn for grouped discrete or continuous data.

Grouped discrete data

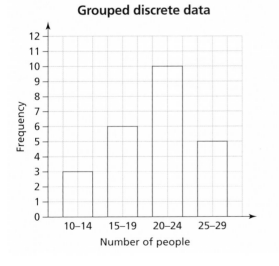

Grouped continuous data

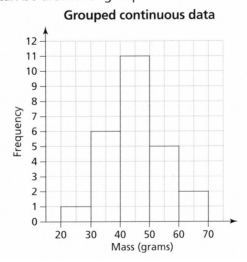

Stem-and-leaf diagrams are a way of displaying data so that the actual data values can still be seen.

A stem-and-leaf diagram to show the ages of 16 people

Stem	Leaf
1	2 5
2	0 4 7
3	1 1 4 6 9
4	3 8
5	0 2 5 5

Key: 5 | 2 = 52 years old

Note that:

- the leaf values are written in order of size.
- the leaf values are written in columns.
- a key is given to explain what each value represents.

Because the numbers in a stem-and-leaf diagram are in order of size, the **median** value can easily be found.

Think about

In what ways do frequency diagrams for continuous data differ from frequency diagrams for discrete data?

Worked example 1

The diagram shows the distances (in kilometres) that 50 students travel to school.

The final bar has not been drawn.

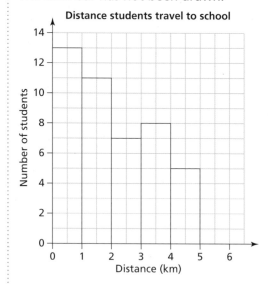

Distance students travel to school

a) Complete the frequency diagram by drawing the bar for students that travel between 5 and 6 km to school.

b) What percentage of the students travel less than 2 km to school?

a) 13 + 11 + 7 + 8 + 5 = 44 students are represented on the diagram. The final bar needs to represent the remaining 6 students. 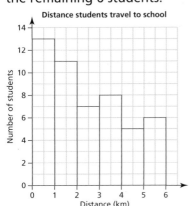	Read off the number of students represented by each of the 5 bars that have been drawn. Subtract these from the total number of students (50) to find the frequency for the final bar.	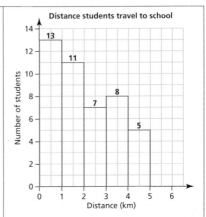 13 + 11 + 7 + 8 + 5 = 44 students 50 − 44 = 6 students
b) The number of students that travel less than 2 km to school is 13 + 11 = 24. The fraction of students who travel less than 2 km is $\frac{24}{50}$. This is the same as 48%.	It is the first two bars that represent students who travel less than 2 km to school. Express these students first as a fraction of the 50 students. Then convert this to a percentage.	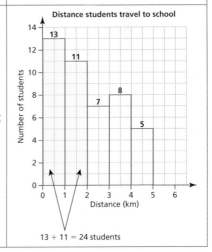 13 + 11 = 24 students

Worked example 2

A shop records the number of jars of coffee it sells each day.

Here are the numbers for the last 20 days.

46	52	71	67	55	72	63	60	48	54
49	61	56	58	52	64	48	45	65	57

a) Draw a stem-and-leaf diagram to show these data.

b) Use the stem-and-leaf diagram to find the median number of jars of coffee the shop sells each day.

a) Stem	Leaf		Start by writing the data values in order of size.	Ordered list of data values:
4	5 6 8 8 9			
5	2 2 4 5 6 7 8		Split each number into two parts, the stem (here the tens digit) and the leaf (here the units digit).	45 46 48 48 49
6	0 1 3 4 5 7			52 52 54 55 56 57 58
7	1 2			60 61 63 64 65 67

Key: 4 | 5 = 45 jars

Make sure that in the stem-and-leaf diagram:

71 72

- you write the leaf values in order of size

- you write the leaf values in columns

- you give a key to explain what each value represents.

b) The 10th value is 56.
The 11th value is 57.

The median is half-way between the 10th and 11th values.

So, the median is 56.5 jars of coffee.

The median is the value that is half-way through the data.

There are 20 data values, so the median will be half-way between the 10th and the 11th values.

Stem	Leaf
4	5 6 8 8 9
5	2 2 4 5 (6 7) 8
6	0 1 3 4 5 7
7	1 2

Key: 4 | 5 = 45 jars

Did you know?

Stem-and-leaf diagrams became a popular way to display data in the 1980s. They were used as they could easily be drawn on early computers.

Exercise 1

1 Draw a frequency diagram to show each set of data.

a)

Length of lorry, *x* (metres)	Number of lorries
$8 \leq x < 10$	9
$10 \leq x < 12$	16
$12 \leq x < 14$	8
$14 \leq x < 16$	7

Tip

Think carefully about whether each table shows discrete or continuous data.

b)

Number of insects	Frequency
0 – 4	6
5 – 9	11
10 – 14	14
15 – 19	9

c)

Temperature, t (°C)	Number of days
$20 \le t < 21$	11
$21 \le t < 22$	4
$22 \le t < 23$	9
$23 \le t < 24$	6
$24 \le t < 25$	1

2 Donna records the heights of 50 trees.

Height, h (m)	Number of trees
$2 \le h < 6$	6
$6 \le h < 10$	10
$10 \le h < 14$	15
$14 \le h < 18$	12
$18 \le h < 22$	7

Draw a frequency diagram to show the information.

3 Pedro draws a frequency diagram to show the height (h cm) of some children.

a) Write down what is wrong with how Pedro has drawn his diagram.

b) Draw Pedro's frequency diagram correctly.

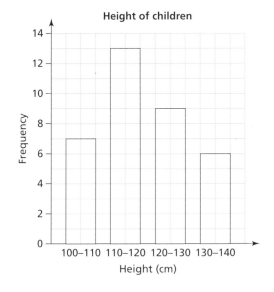

4 The frequency diagram shows the number of books sold by a book shop each day for 40 days.

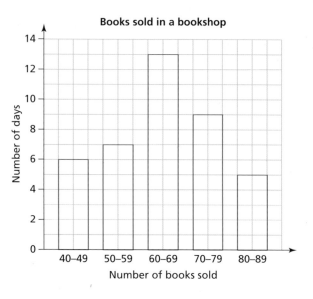

Books sold in a bookshop

a) On how many days were at least 60 books sold?

b) Write down the modal class.

c) On what fraction of the days were less than 50 books sold?

5 The frequency diagram shows the times taken by a group of students to run a race.

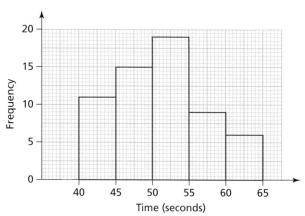

a) Work out how many of the students took less than 50 seconds to run the race.

b) How many students took part in the race altogether?

c) What percentage of the students took more than one minute to run the race?

6 Draw a stem-and-leaf diagram to show each set of data. Remember to include a key.

a) 56   57   59   61   64   65   67   69
   70   75   77   77   79   81   82

b) 19   24   45   35   53   26   38
   27   36   34   52   35   33   41

c) 13.1   12.5   14.7   12.8   13.6   13.4
   15.2   12.5   13.4   14.3   14.8   13.9

> **Tip**
>
> In question 6c, the whole number part of each data value should be in the stem column. The numbers after the decimal point should form the leaves.

> **Discuss**
>
> How could you find the median for each data set in Question 6?

7 The stem-and-leaf diagram shows the masses of 25 apples.

a) How many apples have a mass less than 100 grams?

b) Find the fraction of the apples that have a mass between 120 grams and 130 grams.

c) Write down the mass of the heaviest apple.

d) Find the range of masses of the apples.

e) Write down the mass that is the mode.

f) Find the median mass of the apples.

Stem	Leaf
9	2 4 5 6
10	0 2 4 5 5 8 8
11	1 1 4 4 4 7
12	2 3 5 6 8
13	1 4 9

Key: 9 | 2 represents a mass of 92 grams

8 The stem-and-leaf diagram shows the lengths of 30 insects.

a) How many insects were 4.5 cm long?

b) Work out the percentage of the insects that have a length greater than 3.8 cm.

c) Work out the range of the lengths of the insects.

d) Work out the median length of the insects.

Stem	Leaf
1	2 5 6 8 9
2	1 3 5 6 7 8
3	1 1 2 3 5 6 7 9
4	1 5 5 5 6 7
5	0 4 5 5 8

Key: 1 | 2 represents 1.2 cm

9 The stem-and-leaf diagram shows the number of passengers on each of 30 buses.

a) What was the smallest number of passengers on these buses?

b) Draw a frequency diagram to show these data.

c) What advantage does a stem-and-leaf diagram have over a frequency diagram?

Stem	Leaf
0	6 7 9
1	1 1 2 5 6 7 8
2	0 2 3 4 5 6 6 7 9
3	1 1 2 6 7 8
4	0 1 4 5 6

Key: 3 | 1 represents 31 passengers

Pie charts and line graphs

Key terms

A **pie chart** is a circular diagram. Each category of data is represented as a slice (or sector) of the circle.

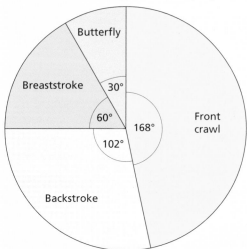

Favourite swimming stroke of 60 people

A **line graph** shows trends over time – data may show an increasing trend or a decreasing trend.

The crosses on this line graph have been connected with a dashed line as intermediate points on the line do not have any meaning.

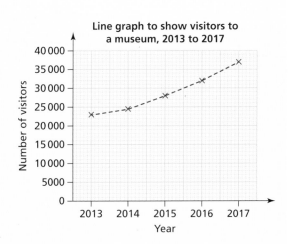

Worked example 3

The table shows how 80 students travel to school.

Draw a pie chart to show the information.

Method of travel	Number of students
walk	38
car	22
bus	10
train	4
bicycle	6

Walk $\frac{38}{80} \times 360 = 171°$

Car $\frac{22}{80} \times 360 = 99°$

Bus $\frac{10}{80} \times 360 = 45°$

Train $\frac{4}{80} \times 360 = 18°$

Bicycle $\frac{6}{80} \times 360 = 27°$

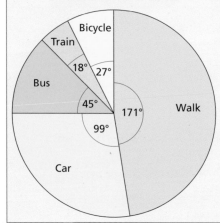

Find the fraction of the students who use each method of travel.

Work out the angle for each sector by multiplying this fraction by 360°.

Measure the angle of each sector using a protractor.

Remember to label each sector.

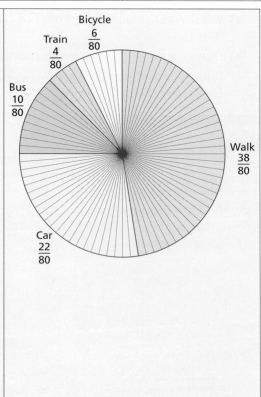

Worked example 4

The line graph shows the depth of water in a tank at different times.

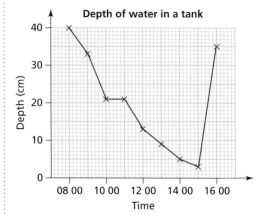

The points in this line graph are joined with solid lines as values between the plotted points do have meaning.

a) By how much did the depth of water fall between 08 00 and 13 00?

b) Between what times did the depth of water stay constant?

c) Estimate the first time when the depth of water was 11 cm.

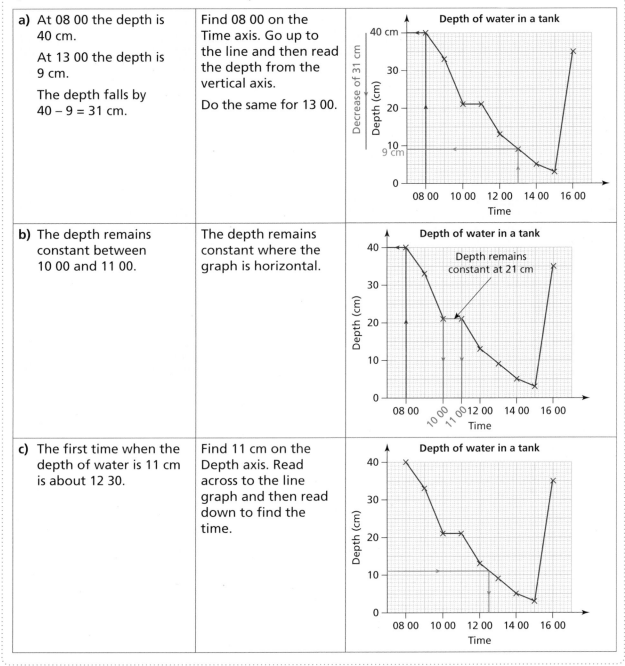

a) At 08 00 the depth is 40 cm. At 13 00 the depth is 9 cm. The depth falls by 40 − 9 = 31 cm.	Find 08 00 on the Time axis. Go up to the line and then read the depth from the vertical axis. Do the same for 13 00.	
b) The depth remains constant between 10 00 and 11 00.	The depth remains constant where the graph is horizontal.	
c) The first time when the depth of water is 11 cm is about 12 30.	Find 11 cm on the Depth axis. Read across to the line graph and then read down to find the time.	

1 A hotel has four types of room. The table shows the number of rooms of each type.

Type of room	Frequency	Angle on a pie chart
Single	11	
Twin	14	
Double	42	
Family	23	

a) Copy and complete the table to show the angle that would represent each type of room on a pie chart.

b) Draw a pie chart to show the information.

2 The table shows the favourite types of fruit for 72 people.

Type of fruit	Frequency	Angle on a pie chart
Apple	26	
Banana	17	
Orange	10	
Grapes	8	
Other	11	

a) Copy and complete the table to show the angle that would represent each type of fruit on a pie chart.

b) Draw a pie chart to show the information.

3 All 30 children in a class choose a club to take part in on a Monday lunchtime. The table shows some information about the choices these children made.

Choice of club	Frequency	Angle on a pie chart
Cookery	7	84°
Choir		108°
Art		72°
Sport		
TOTAL	30	360°

a) Copy and complete the table.

b) Draw a pie chart to show the information.

4 The pie chart shows the sales of different types of sandwich in a café one day.

The café sold a total of 144 sandwiches on that day.

a) Find the angle for Other.

b) What was the most popular type of sandwich sold on that day?

c) Find the fraction of sandwiches sold that were cheese salad. Give your answer in its simplest form.

d) How many turkey sandwiches were sold on that day

e) The café manager says that 40 more egg salad sandwiches were sold than cheese salad sandwiches. Is the manager correct? Give a reason for your answer.

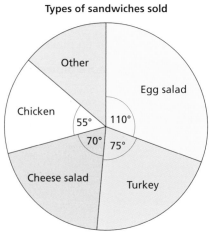
Types of sandwiches sold

5 The table shows the temperature of a cup of hot water at different times.

Time since boiled (minutes)	0	5	10	15	20	25
Temperature (°C)	100	79	61	47	37	30

a) Draw a line graph to show these temperatures.

b) Use your line graph to estimate the temperature after 12 minutes.

6 The diagram shows the population of Nigeria from 2012 to 2018.

a) Write down the population of Nigeria in 2012.

b) Write down the first year in which the population was greater than 190 million.

c) Describe the trend in the population of Nigeria.

> **Tip**
>
> A trend is the general direction in which something is moving – the trend can be increasing or decreasing.

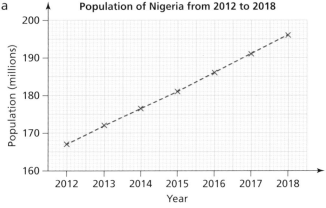

d) Find the difference in the population between 2015 and 2018.

7 Hakima records the rainfall in her garden each month. She shows her results in a line graph.

a) Which month had the most rainfall?

b) How much rainfall fell in Hakima's garden in August?

c) Hakima says that more rain fell in April than fell in total in January, February and March. Is she correct? Explain your answer.

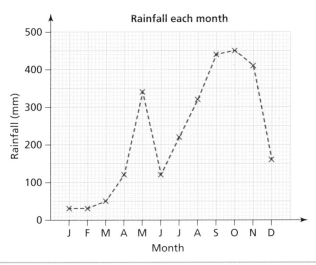

8 The pie chart shows the colours of the shirts sold in a shop one week.

The shop sold 64 black shirts.

How many more blue shirts than white shirts were sold?

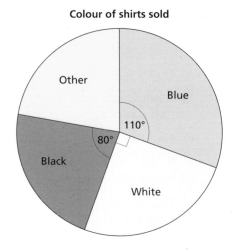

Colour of shirts sold

Drawing conclusions from graphs

A **hypothesis** is an idea that you want to investigate by collecting data.

A statistical investigation has several stages.

Stage 1: Decide on a **hypothesis** or a question to explore.

Stage 2: Collect relevant data.

Stage 3: Display the data in graphs and do calculations.

Stage 4: Make conclusions.

In this section you will make conclusions from statistical graphs.

Worked example 5

A football coach wants to investigate the fitness of his players.

He plans to make every player run a race.

The coach has this hypothesis:

Less than half of the players will be able to run the race in under 1 minute.

The times of each of the 32 players in the race are shown in the stem-and-leaf diagram.

Investigate the coach's hypothesis.

Stem	Leaf
4	5 6 7 8 9 9
5	0 1 2 2 4 5 6 7 8 9 9
6	1 1 2 3 3 3 4 5 5 6 7 8
7	0 2 5

Key: 4 | 5 represents 45 seconds

17 players completed the race in less than 1 minute. Half of the 32 players is 16. So the coach's hypothesis is not true. More than half of the players were able to run the race in under 1 minute.	First find how many players completed the race in under 60 seconds. Then make a conclusion by referring to the coach's hypothesis.	**Stem | Leaf** 4 | 5 6 7 8 9 9 5 | 0 1 2 2 4 5 6 7 8 9 9 6 | 1 1 2 3 3 3 4 5 5 6 7 8 7 | 0 2 5 **Key:** 4 | 5 represents 45 seconds The times in red are all less than 1 minute = 60 seconds.

1 Preema carries out a survey to investigate the types of books that are borrowed from a library.

She draws a pie chart to show her results.

Decide whether these conclusions are true or false or whether you cannot tell from the graph. Give a reason for each answer.

a) More people borrowed non-fiction books than biographies.

b) More than twice as many fiction books were borrowed than non-fiction books.

c) 50 people borrowed a biography from the library.

d) One third of the books borrowed from the library were non-fiction books.

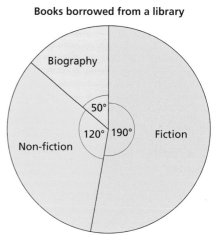

Books borrowed from a library

2 Greg investigates the number of students that are learning a musical instrument in each school in his area. The stem-and-leaf diagram shows his results

Make two conclusions about the number of students learning instruments in the 24 schools.

Stem	Leaf
0	0 7
1	2 3 5 5 9
2	0 1 2 4 5 6 7
3	1 2 6 7 8 9
4	1 3 5
5	2

Key: 1 | 2 means 12 students

3 The diagram shows the speeds of all the cars passing a school between 8 a.m. and 9 a.m. one morning.

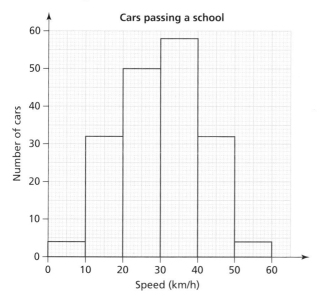

a) The headteacher wants to know if any cars passed the school travelling at more than 50 km/h. Make a conclusion from the graph about this.

b) The speed limit passing the school is 40 km/h. A parent wants to know if more than one quarter of cars go faster than 40 km/h. Make a conclusion from the graph about this.

4 Emanuel owns a small gym. Emanuel makes this claim:

The number of members at the gym more than doubled between 2012 and 2018.

He draws this line graph to show how the number of members at the gym has changed.

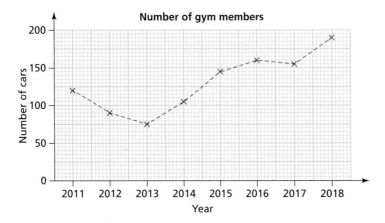

Comment on Emanuel's claim.

5 Silvia is investigating this hypothesis:

The median height of adult women is greater than 155 cm.

She records the height of a random sample of 35 women.

Make a conclusion about Silvia's hypothesis. Use the data to explain your answer.

Stem	Leaf
13	6 9
14	3 4 6 6
15	2 2 3 4 6 7 8 9
16	0 1 1 2 4 5 5 6 7 8
17	1 3 5 6 6 8
18	2 3 4 5
19	1

Key: 13 | 4 means 134 cm

6 A company makes and sells bracelets.

They sell the bracelets in a shop and online.

The table shows the sales of bracelets each month in 2017.

Month	Jan	Feb	Mar	Apr	May	Jun	Jul	Aug	Sep	Oct	Nov	Dec
Sales in the shop	340	115	120	109	132	127	137	97	104	117	290	484
Sales online	134	145	146	136	138	130	143	102	111	118	135	155

a) The manager makes this conclusion from the table:

In most months in 2017, the company sold more bracelets online than it did in the shop.

Comment on the manager's conclusion.

b) Write a different conclusion that can be made from the table.

7 Tom investigates the favourite meals for children in his school.

There are 300 boys and 300 girls in the school.

He has this hypothesis:

Pizza is the favourite meal for more boys than girls in the school.

He draws these diagrams to show the data he collects.

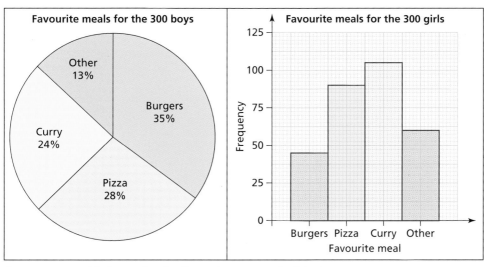

Favourite meals for the 300 boys

Favourite meals for the 300 girls

Comment on his hypothesis. Show how you decided on your answer.

8. Investigate how the population of the world has changed over the past 100 years. Collect relevant data from the internet.

Use a spreadsheet package to draw a line graph to show your data.

Draw some conclusions from your data.

Comparing sets of data using averages and the range

Key terms

Averages are used to decide whether the values in one set of data are typically larger or smaller than the values in a second set of data. The measures of average are the **mean**, the **median** and the **mode**.

The **range** is a measure of **spread**. It is used to compare variations within the values of a data set. A set of data is more consistent than a second set if its values are less spread out.

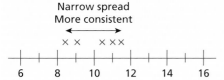

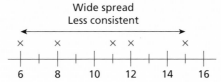

Worked example 6

A team plays football matches on Wednesdays and Saturdays.

The table summarises the attendances at 16 Wednesday matches and 16 Saturday matches.

	Wednesday	Saturday
Median	17 250	31 418
Mean	19 315	34 192
Range	14 336	7 515

a) Compare the average attendances at the matches on the two days.

b) On which day were attendances more varied? Use the data in the table to explain your choice of answer.

a) The median and mean attendance is higher on Saturday. So on average attendances at the matches are higher on Saturday.	The median and the mean are both measures of average. Compare the values of these for the two days.	
b) The range is greater on Wednesday, so attendances are more varied on Wednesday.	The range measures how varied the data are. Compare the value of the range for Wednesday with the value for Saturday.	Wednesday range = 14 436 Saturday range = 7515

Exercise 4

1 Nusrat and Heera take part in dance competitions.

The table shows the median and range of the points they have scored in each of their past 12 competitions.

	Median score	Range of scores
Nusrat	63.5	16.0
Heera	72.0	11.5

Copy and complete these sentences choosing words from the box.

lower   higher   less   more

Heera scored _____ than Nusrat on average in her dance competitions.

Nusrat's scores are _____ consistent than the scores of Heera.

2 Dom can take two different routes to work.

He records how long (in minutes) it takes him to travel to work by each route on 20 different occasions.

His journey times are summarised below.

Route A	Route B
Mean time: 18 mins	Mean time: 16 mins
Median time: 19 mins	Median time: 18 mins
Range of times: 7 mins	Range of times: 4 mins

Decide if each of these statements is true or false. Give a reason for each answer.

a) Journeys made using Route B take less time on average than journeys made using Route A.

b) Journey times using Route A are less varied than the journey times using Route B.

c) More than half of journeys made using Route A took less than 20 minutes.

3 Fabian records the numbers of words in 15 books written by each of two authors. The table summarises his results.

	Author A	Author B
Median	38 136 words	43 815 words
Mean	41 587 words	44 109 words
Range	17 397 words	12 765 words

a) Compare the average number of words in the books written by the two authors.

b) Which author writes books that are more consistent in length? Use the data in the table to explain your answer.

4 The table summarises the ages of people attending two concerts.

	Concert X	Concert Y
Median age	38 years	37 years
Mean age	38.4 years	39.2 years
Range of ages	64 years	48 years

a) Compare the spread of ages of the people attending the two concerts.

b) Amy wants to know which of the concerts had younger people attending on average. What difficulty will Amy have in making a conclusion?

5 Henri and Claudia sell cars. The manager records how many cars they sell each week.

The table shows the mode, mean and range for the number of cars they sold each week over the past year.

	Henri	Claudia
Mode	4 cars	3 cars
Mean	3.8 cars	3.9 cars
Range	5 cars	9 cars

The manager wants to give a bonus to either Henri or Claudia.

a) Henri thinks that he should be given the bonus. Use the numbers in the table to explain why he might think that.

b) The manager actually gives the bonus to Claudia. How can the manager justify his decision?

6 A class takes tests in Geography and Science.

The marks in the Geography test are shown in the stem-and-leaf diagram.

```
Stem | Leaf
  4  | 5
  5  | 0  2  6
  6  | 4  5  6  6  8  9
  7  | 0  1  4  7  8
  8  |
  9  | 2
```
         Key: 4 | 5 represents 45%

The mean and range of the marks in the Science test were:

mean = 68%   range = 31%

Compare the marks the class got in the two tests. Show your working.

End of chapter reflection

You should know that ...	You should be able to ...	Such as ...
Grouped data can be shown in a frequency diagram.	Draw and interpret a frequency diagram for grouped discrete or continuous data.	Draw a frequency diagram to show the data in the table. **Age, *a* years** | **Frequency** $0 < a \leq 20$ | 7 $20 < a \leq 40$ | 9 $40 < a \leq 60$ | 5 $60 < a \leq 80$ | 1
In a stem-and-leaf diagram the data values can still be seen.	Draw and interpret a stem-and-leaf diagram.	The stem-and-leaf diagram shows the lengths (in minutes) of 10 films. Stem | Leaf 9 | 3 10 | 0 5 6 8 11 | 5 9 12 | 1 3 5 **Key:** 9 | 3 = 93 minutes How many of the films are over 2 hours in length?
In a pie chart each category of data is represented by a sector of a circle.	Draw and interpret a pie chart.	Draw a pie chart to show the type of magazine that 45 people most like to read. **Type of magazine** | **Number of people** News | 7 Fashion | 13 Sport | 15 Technology | 10
A line graph can show trends in data over time.	Draw and interpret a line graph.	Draw a line graph to show the number of members of a tennis club. **Year** | **Number of members** 2013 | 47 2014 | 61 2015 | 69 2016 | 73 2017 | 74

The final stage of a statistical investigation involves drawing conclusions.	Draw conclusions from a range of statistical diagrams.	Amy wants to know the ages of people who use the local swimming pool on Saturday mornings. She collects the following data. **Age of people at a pool** *(frequency diagram showing frequencies: 80, 50, 70, 40, 20, 10 across age intervals from 0 to 60 years)* Make some conclusions about the ages of people at the pool.
The mean, median and mode are all averages, whereas the range measures the variability of the data.	Compare two sets of data using the range, mean, median and mode.	The table summarises the daily temperatures in two cities in June. |	City A	City B
Mean	19.3°C	17.7°C
Median	19°C	16°C
Range	5.5°C	8°C | Compare the temperatures of the two cities.

Mutually exclusive outcomes

You will learn how to:
- Find and list systematically all possible mutually exclusive outcomes for single events and for two successive events.

Starting point

Do you remember …?

- how to list the outcomes for a single event?

  For example, list all of the possible outcomes when you roll a fair six-sided dice.

- how to calculate probabilities for a single event?

  For example, find the probability of rolling a 2 on a fair six-sided dice.

This will also be helpful when you:

- begin to draw two-way tables and sample space diagrams in order to show all possible outcomes of two or more successive events.

Hook

Draw a triangle and two circles on three identical cards and turn them over so that only you know which one the triangle is.

Ask your partner to guess which card they think the triangle is on but do not yet reveal it.

Instead, reveal a card which has a circle on it.

Ask your partner if they wish to stick with their original choice or switch to the other remaining card. They win if they select the triangle.

Repeat the game several times and record the results.

Do they win more games if they switch or if they stick?

What are the outcomes for this game?

Are both outcomes equally likely?

What is the probability that the first card selected is the triangle?

Listing outcomes

Key terms

The **event** of flipping a coin has two **outcomes**: heads or tails.

Two outcomes are **mutually exclusive** if they cannot happen at the same time. For example, you cannot roll a 4 and a 6 on a single roll of a six-sided dice.

When you work through a problem **systematically** you should follow a logical order to ensure that nothing gets missed. For example, when flipping a coin twice list all the possibilities of getting a head first before moving on to list all the possibilities of getting a tail first.

Successive events occur one after the other or at the same time. For example, you flip a coin twice or you roll two dice at the same time.

Worked example 1

There are two bags of sweets at a party. Mitchel takes one sweet from each bag at random.

Bag A   Bag B

a) List all the possible combinations of sweets.

b) Find the probability that Mitchel takes two sweets of the same colour.

c) Find the probability that Mitchel does not take a blue or a green sweet.

a) The outcomes are:	It can be useful to draw a table so you remember which bag of sweets you are thinking about.	
red, red		
red, blue	You can write your list in any order, but it is a good idea to do it systematically. You could first list all possibilities when taking a red from the first bag, and follow the same order (red, blue, yellow) with the second bag.	
red, yellow		
blue, red		
blue, blue		
blue, yellow		
yellow, red		
yellow, blue		
yellow, yellow		
green, red		
green, blue		
green, yellow		
There are 12 combinations.		

Bag A	Bag B
Red	Red
Red	Blue
Red	Yellow
Blue	Red
Blue	Blue
Blue	Yellow
Yellow	Red
Yellow	Blue
Yellow	Yellow
Green	Red
Green	Blue
Green	Yellow

b) $\frac{3}{12}$ or $\frac{1}{4}$	There are 3 out of 12 outcomes which have the same colour sweet being chosen.	Bag A	Bag B

Bag A	Bag B
Red	Red
Red	Blue
Red	Yellow
Blue	Red
Blue	Blue
Blue	Yellow
Yellow	Red
Yellow	Blue
Yellow	Yellow
Green	Red
Green	Blue
Green	Yellow

Three of the rows have the same colour sweet twice.

c) $\frac{4}{12}$ or $\frac{1}{3}$	There are 4 out of 12 outcomes which do not have a blue or a green sweet being chosen.

Bag A	Bag B
Red	Red
Red	Blue
Red	Yellow
Blue	Red
Blue	Blue
Blue	Yellow
Yellow	Red
Yellow	Blue
Yellow	Yellow
Green	Red
Green	Blue
Green	Yellow

Four of the rows do not include a blue or green sweet.

Exercise 1

1 Here is a spinner.

List all the possible outcomes when the spinner is spun once.

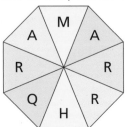

2 A game is played by spinning each of these spinners once.

Spinner 1   Spinner 2

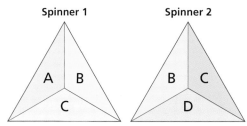

a) Copy and complete the table to show all the possible outcomes.

Spinner 1	Spinner 2
A	B
A	C

You score a point by getting the same letter on both spinners.

b) What is the probability that you score a point on your turn?

3 An outdoor activity centre runs morning and afternoon sessions.
Daisy picks one morning and one afternoon activity.

Morning	Afternoon
archery	raft building
zip wire	canoeing
climbing wall	

a) Complete the list to show all the possible combinations.

(archery and raft building), (archery and canoeing)...

b) What is the probability that she chooses zip wire and raft building?

c) What is the probability that she chooses climbing wall for the morning activity?

d) What is the probability that she does not chose canoeing?

> **Tip**
>
> You can reduce your work by using abbreviations: (A, RB) could be used instead of writing out each word in full. Make sure that your abbreviations are clear. You could write a key to be certain.

4 Vocabulary feature question

a) Complete the sentence:

Two outcomes which cannot happen at the same time are known as _____ _____ events.

b) Write down the outcomes that are mutually exclusive.

Getting a 6 and a 5 on a single roll of a dice

Getting a 3 and a 4 when you roll a pair of dice

Getting a 1 and a head when you roll a dice and flip a coin

Choosing a tea and a coffee when selecting one drink

5 There are 4 doughnuts in a bag.

2 are jam filled.

1 is chocolate filled.

1 is cream filled.

Augustus picks out a doughnut and eats it. He then takes another doughnut.

a) Complete the table to show all possible combinations.

b) What is the probability that he takes two jam doughnuts?

c) What is the probability that he takes a cream doughnut?

d) What is the probability that he takes two chocolate doughnuts?

1st doughnut	2nd doughnut
jam	jam
jam	chocolate

6 Lucy has a fair four-sided dice with sides labelled: 1, 2, 3 and 4.

She rolls the dice twice and adds the score together.

a) Copy and complete the list to show all the possible outcomes.

(1, 1), (1, 2), (1, 3) …

b) What is the probability that she scores a total of 5?

c) What is the probability that she gets a total greater than 6?

7 A restaurant serves a choice of the two starters and three main meals as shown on the menu.

Mikael says that there are 9 possible combinations of choosing a starter and a main meal and he writes them all down.

Explain what mistake Mikael has made when listing his combinations.

Menu

Starter	Main
Garlic prawns	Roast chicken
Melon	Beef Wellington
	Stuffed peppers

(GP, RC), (GP, BW), (GP, SP)
(M, RC), (M, BW), (M, SP)
(M, GP), (RC, BW), (BW, SP)

8 Aeeza has three children.

Find the probability that she has three girls.

Tip

Write a list of all the possible outcomes, starting with: Boy Boy Boy (BBB), Boy Boy Girl (BBG) etc.

End of chapter reflection

You should know that ...	You should be able to ...	Such as ...
Mutually exclusive events cannot happen at the same time.	Recognise which outcomes are mutually exclusive.	Which of the following outcomes are mutually exclusive? Getting a 3 and a 4 when you roll a pair of dice. Choosing 'raspberry ripple' and 'mint choc chip' when selecting one scoop of ice-cream.
	List all the mutually exclusive outcomes of a single event.	Write down all the possible outcomes when you roll an ordinary six-sided dice.
The outcomes of two successive events are not mutually exclusive.	List all of the outcomes of two successive events. Calculate probabilities of two successive events by considering all of the possible outcomes.	This spinner is spun twice and the scores are added together. **a)** List all of the possible outcomes. **b)** Find the probability of getting a total of 9.

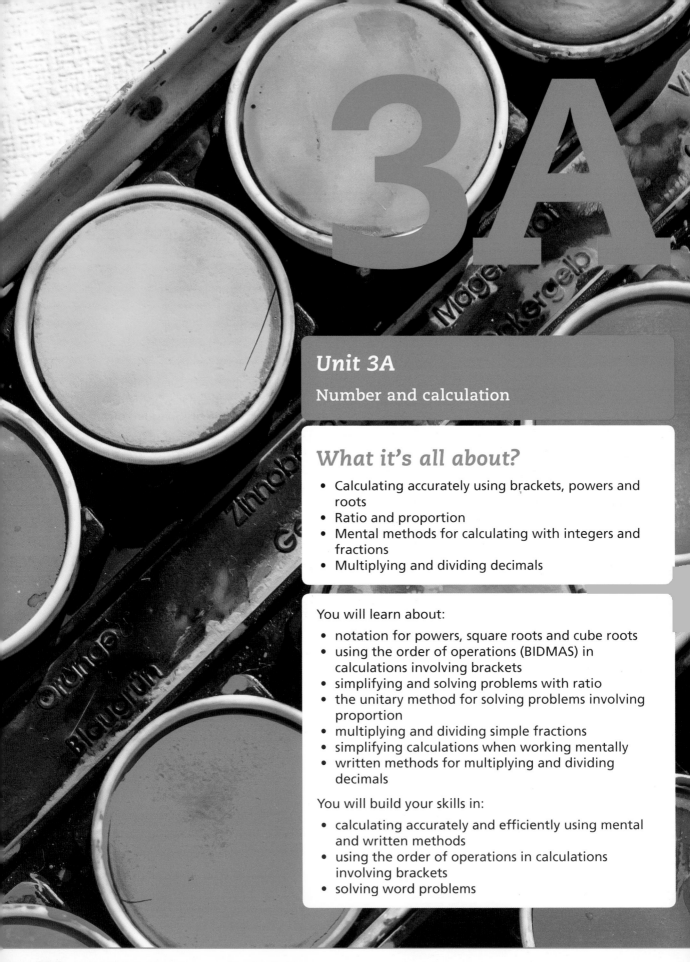

Unit 3A

Number and calculation

What it's all about?

- Calculating accurately using brackets, powers and roots
- Ratio and proportion
- Mental methods for calculating with integers and fractions
- Multiplying and dividing decimals

You will learn about:

- notation for powers, square roots and cube roots
- using the order of operations (BIDMAS) in calculations involving brackets
- simplifying and solving problems with ratio
- the unitary method for solving problems involving proportion
- multiplying and dividing simple fractions
- simplifying calculations when working mentally
- written methods for multiplying and dividing decimals

You will build your skills in:

- calculating accurately and efficiently using mental and written methods
- using the order of operations in calculations involving brackets
- solving word problems

Calculations

You will learn how to:
- Calculate squares, positive and negative square roots, cubes and cube roots; use the notation $\sqrt{49}$ and $\sqrt[3]{64}$ and index notation for positive integer powers.
- Use the order of operations, including brackets, with more complex calculations.

Starting point

Do you remember ...?

- how to find multiples and factors?

  For example, can you name a multiple of 20? Can you name a factor of 20?
- how to write a number in terms of its prime factors?

  For example, $500 = 2^2 \times 5^3$.
- how to recall squares to 20×20, cubes to $5 \times 5 \times 5$, and corresponding roots?

  For example, what is: 11^2? 5^3?
- how to use a calculator to find squares and square roots?

  For example, $\sqrt{1156} = ?$
- how to use indices?

  For example, $8 \times 8 = 8^2$.

This will be helpful when you:

- estimate square roots and cube roots.
- use Pythagoras theorem to find distances.
- learn about writing numbers in standard form.
- learn about indices and index law.

Hook

Have you heard of **happy numbers**? If you add the squares of their digits, then keep repeating, the answer will be 1. Otherwise they are called **sad** numbers.

For example:

$129 \rightarrow 1^2 + 2^2 + 9^2 = 86 \rightarrow 8^2 + 6^2 = 100 \rightarrow 1^2 + 0^2 + 0^2 = 1$

$145 \rightarrow 1^2 + 4^2 + 5^2 = 42 \rightarrow 4^2 + 2^2 = 20 \rightarrow 2^2 + 0^2 = 4 \rightarrow 4^2 = 16 \rightarrow 1^2 + 6^2 = 37 \rightarrow$

$3^2 + 7^2 = 58 \rightarrow 5^2 + 8^2 = 89 \rightarrow 8^2 + 9^2 = 145$

Game: Finding **happy numbers**!

Work in pairs.

Think of a 2 or 3 digit number. Write it down. Do this 5 times. Ask your partner to check whether the number is a **happy number**. The person that finds the most **happy numbers** wins the game.

Think about

Have you noticed what happens to the **sad** numbers when you add the squares of their digits?

Powers and roots

Key terms

A number multiplied by itself one or more times is called a **power** of that number. You use indices to show **powers**. For example, $2^2 = 2 \times 2 = 4$. This is 2 **squared** or the square of 2.

A **cube number is** a number raised to the power of 3. For example, $3 \times 3 \times 3 = 3^3 = 27$.

A **square root** is the number you multiply by itself to make a square number. A positive number has both a positive and negative square root. $\sqrt{\ }$ means the positive square root of the given number. For example, 3 is the square root of 9, $\sqrt{9} = 3$.

A **cube root** is the number you raise to the power of 3 to make a cubed number. For example, 3 is the cube root of 27, $\sqrt[3]{27} = 3$.

> ### Discuss
>
> $1^2 = 1$
>
> $11^2 = 121$
>
> $111^2 = 12\ 321$
>
> Predict 1111^2.
>
> What would $111\ 111^2$ be?
>
> Use a calculator to check your predictions.

Worked example 1

Work out:

a) the positive and negative square root of 400

b) $3 \times 3 \times 3 \times 5 \times 5$ using power notation.

a) The square roots of 400 are 20 and −20.	400 has two square roots because 20^2 and $(-20)^2$ both equal 400.
b) $3 \times 3 \times 3 \times 5 \times 5$	3 is multiplied by itself three times.
$= 3^3 \times 5^2$	5 is multiplied by itself two times.

Did you know?

Powers are very useful when studying bacteria. For example, if some bacteria double every half an hour, then the number of bacteria after 3 hours can be shown as:

Time period	Time passed	Number of bacteria
0	0	1
1	0.5 hours	$2^1 = 2$
2	1 hour	$2^2 = 4$
3	1.5 hours	$2^3 = 8$
4	2 hours	$2^4 = 16$
5	2.5 hours	$2^5 = 32$
6	3 hours	$2^6 = 64$

238 Unit 3A: Number and calculation

1 Write down the value of:

a) 13^2
b) $(-7)^2$
c) 15^3

d) $(-3)^3$
e) $(-5)^3$
f) $3^3 + 4^3$

g) $(-15)^2 - (14)^2$
h) $\sqrt[3]{64} + (-2)^2$

> **Tip**
>
> Remember that when two negative numbers are multiplied, the answer is positive.

2 Write down the positive and negative value of:

a) $\sqrt{100}$
b) $\sqrt{400}$
c) $\sqrt{225}$
d) $\sqrt{256}$

3 Use a calculator to find the value of the following, giving your answers correct to two decimal places.

a) $\sqrt[3]{216}$
b) $\sqrt[3]{-512}$
c) $7.31^2 - 1.3^3$
d) $\sqrt[3]{13.31} - \sqrt{0.8}$

e) $\sqrt[3]{-343} + \sqrt[3]{4096}$
f) $\sqrt[3]{4.6} - \sqrt[3]{-3.7}$
g) $8.3^3 - 8.3^2$
h) $\sqrt[3]{-5.8} + \sqrt{5.8}$

4 Write each number using power notation.

a) $3 \times 3 \times 3$
b) $5 \times 5 \times 5 \times 5$
c) $4 \times 4 \times 6 \times 6 \times 6$
d) $3 \times 3 \times 10 \times 10 \times 11 \times 11 \times 11$

5 Which of these numbers is larger? Explain your reasoning.

a) 5^2 or 2^5
b) 3^5 or 5^3
c) 4^3 or 3^4
d) 10^1 or 1^{10}

6 True or false? Correct the statements that are false.

a) $\sqrt[3]{1} = 1$ or -1
b) $(-2)^4 = 16$
c) $(-3)^3 = 27$
d) $\sqrt[3]{-64} = -4$

7 Find the missing powers.

a) 1 hundred is $10^{\square}$
b) 1 thousand is $10^{\square}$

c) 10 thousand is $10^{\square}$
d) 1 million is $10^{\square}$

e) 1 billion is $10^{\square}$
f) 10 billion is $10^{\square}$

Did you know?

A googol is 10 to the power of 100. A googolplex is 10 to the power of googol, which is 10 to the power of 10 to the power of 100. There is not enough space in the known universe to write the whole number out on paper.

Order of operations

Worked example 2

Work out:

a) $5 \times (12 - (8-3))$ **b)** $(20 \div 4 + 2 \times 5) \times 3$

Tip

When calculations involve more than one operation, always make sure you use BIDMAS.

BIDMAS can help remember the order of operations.

BIDMAS stands for Brackets, Indices (powers or roots), Division and Multiplication, Addition and Subtraction. Always work out the Brackets and Indices first, followed by Division and Multiplications, and finally Additions and Subtractions.

a) $5 \times (12 - (8 - 3))$	Work out the bracket $(8 - 3)$ first.
$\quad = 5 \times (12 - 5)$	Work out the bracket $(12 - 5)$.
$\quad = 5 \times 7$	Multiply 5 by the result.
$\quad = 35$	
b) $(20 \div 4 + 2 \times 5) \times 3$	Start with the bracket.
$\quad (5 + 10) \times 3$	Multiply and divide first. Work out $20 \div 4$ and 2×5.
$\quad = 15 \times 3$	Add the results.
$\quad = 45$	Multiply the answer by 3.

Discuss

Brackets and the order of operations are very important in real life. Suppose two classes of 18 and 13 children are going to visit the Blue Mountains in Australia on a school trip.

The teacher takes two bottles of water for each child. The calculation is $2 \times (18 + 13) = 62$ bottles.

What mistakes could the teacher make if there were no brackets?

Think about other examples where brackets and order of operations are important in real life.

1 Work out:

a) $5 + 3 \times 10$ b) $27 - 18 \div 9$ c) $4 \times 9 + 2 \times 8$ d) $2 \times 8 - 4 \times 3$

e) $(28 - 2 + 9) \times 3$ f) $(10 - 5 + 3) \div 4$ g) $8 \div (7 - 5 + 2)$ h) $(7 \times 4 - 5) \times 9$

2 Find the answers. Which of these calculations is the odd one out?

a) $3 \times 8 \div 4 - 1$ b) $27 - 2 \div 1 + 4$ c) $5 \times (7 - 5 - 1)$ d) $(81 - 3 \times 7) \div 12$

3 Put these calculations in order of size of answer starting from the smallest.

a) $(12 \div 3 + 3) - (3 \times (12 - 10))$ b) $100 \div (3 + 2)^2$

c) $\sqrt{9^2 - 5 \times \left(20 \div 2 + 3^2\right)}$ d) $\sqrt[3]{3 \times 5 + 2 \times (10 - 4)}$

4 Work out:

a) $30 \div (3 \times (9 - 5) + 3)$ b) $10 \times ((12 - 8) + 1)$

c) $20 \div ((11 - 6) \times 2)$ d) $(5 \times (14 - 11)) \div 3 + 2$

5 Use a calculator to work out the value of:

a) $2.7 - (4.1 + 2.1) + 5 \times 0.05$ b) $2.1 \times ((12.7 - 8) + 1.3)$

c) $20 \div ((11 - 6) \times 2)$ d) $0.3 \times ((3.4 - 0.7 \times 2) + 1.6)$

> Check your answer. Does it make sense? Does your calculator follow the order of operations?

6 True or false? Explain your answers.

a) $(4 + 6 \times 2) \times 5 = 100$ b) $60 \div (16 - 4 \div 2) = 10$

c) $(5 \times (14 - 8)) \times (11 - 7) = 120$ d) $50 \times 3 - 1 \times (3 \times 2 - 1) = 500$

7 Farzana buys 3 boxes of juice at \$1.80 each, 2 snack bars at \$1.15 each and 1 apple at 50c. She pays with \$10. Which of these statements show the change that she gets?

a) $10 - 3 \times 1.80 + 2 \times 1.15 + 0.50$ b) $10 - (3 \times 1.80 + 2 \times 1.15 + 50)$

c) $10 - (3 + 2 + 1) \times (1.80 + 1.15 + 0.5)$ d) $10 - (3 \times 1.80 + 2 \times 1.15 + 0.5)$

8 a) Find the missing numbers.

i) $25 + (\blacksquare - 3 \times 5) = 100$ ii) $(85 - 4 \times 2) \div \blacksquare = 7$

b) Use numbers 9, 11, 20 and 45 to make this calculation true.

$(\blacklozenge + \blacklozenge) \div (\blacklozenge - \lozenge) = 6$

9 Insert brackets to make the statements true.

a) $48 + 12 \div 4 \times 1 + 2 = 50$ b) $48 + 12 \div 4 \times 1 + 2 = 49$

c) $48 + 12 \div 4 \times 1 + 2 = 17$ d) $48 + 12 \div 4 \times 1 + 2 = 5$

End of chapter reflection

You should know that ...	You should be able to ...	Such as ...
A positive integer has two square roots, one positive and one negative.	Calculate square numbers and square roots, cube numbers and cube roots. Use known square roots and cube roots to find related ones. Use a calculator to find square numbers and square roots, cube numbers and cube roots.	Work out the value of: $\sqrt{9} =$ $\sqrt[3]{64} =$ Work out the value of: $\sqrt[3]{8000} =$ Use your calculator to find: $4.9^3 + \sqrt{3.5} - 2.8^2 =$
A number multiplied by itself several times is called a power of that number.	Use indices to show powers.	Write $5 \times 5 \times 5 \times 5 \times 5$ using power notation.
In more complex calculations first you start with brackets, then powers or indices, followed by multiplication and division, and finally addition or subtraction.	Use the order of operations, including brackets, with more complex calculations. Use a calculator for more complex calculations.	Calculate: $7 - (1 + 2) \times 3 =$ Use a calculator to find: $2.9 \times (4.1 - 2.1) + 8 =$

Ratio and proportions

You will learn how to:
* Simplify ratios, including those expressed in different units; divide a quantity into more than two parts in a given ratio.
* Use the unitary method to solve simple problems involving ratio and direct proportion.

Starting point

Do you remember ...?

* how to express a ratio.

  For example, there are 6 girls and 4 boys in a class, write down the ratio of boys to girls.

* the relationship between ratio and proportion.

  For example, if the ratio of apples to oranges is 1 : 3, what fraction of the fruits are apples?

* how to use direct proportion in real-life contexts such as cooking.

  For example, if you need 1 cup of flour and 2 cups of milk to make 5 pancakes, how much of each do you need to make 20 pancakes?

* how to solve simple problems using ratio and direct proportion.

  For example, a bag of 25 sweets contains 10 red sweets and the rest are yellow. What is the ratio of red to yellow sweets? What proportion is yellow?

* how to find the highest common factor of two numbers.

  For example, find the highest common factor of 20 and 50.

This will also be helpful when you:

* compare two ratios and solve problems involving ratios in different context.

* solve problems involving converting between different currencies.

Hook

The Summer Solstice is the day when the sun reaches its highest position in the sky as seen from the north or south pole. In the Northern hemisphere, this happens on the 21st of June.

The ratio of daylight to darkness is different throughout the year in different countries. The table below shows the results of the ratio of daylight and darkness on 21 June for a selection of countries. Complete the table.

	Ratio of hours of daylight: hours of darkness	Hours of daylight	Hours of darkness
Argentina	7 : 17	7 hours	17 hours
Beijing	5 : 3		
Sydney	5 : 7		
Stockholm	3 : 1		
Equator	1 : 1		

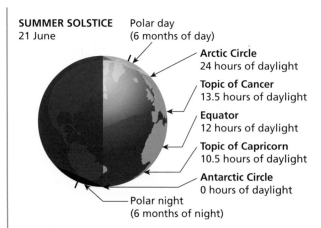

SUMMER SOLSTICE
21 June

Polar day
(6 months of day)

Arctic Circle
24 hours of daylight

Topic of Cancer
13.5 hours of daylight

Equator
12 hours of daylight

Topic of Capricorn
10.5 hours of daylight

Antarctic Circle
0 hours of daylight

Polar night
(6 months of night)

When was the longest night of the year in your country? What was the ratio of hours of daylight to hours of darkness that day?

Ratio

Key terms

A **ratio** compares the relative sizes of two quantities. We write a ratio using a **colon (:)** between the two relative sizes of each quantity, in the order they appear in the text. You can **simplify** a ratio by dividing the quantities by a **common factor**. For example, 30 : 70 can be simplified by dividing both sides by 10 (the highest common factor of 30 and 70) to give 3 : 7.

Worked example 1

a) A soup pack contains 300 g meat to every 1.5 kg of vegetables. Express this ratio in its simplest form.

b) Share 580 g in the ratio 2 : 3 : 5.

a) 300 g : 1.5 kg 300 g : 1.5 × 1000 g 300 g : 1500 g 300 : 1500 ÷ 300 ÷ 300 1 : 5	Change all of the quantities to the same units. Simplify by dividing by a common factor. The highest common factor (HCF) of 300 and 1500 is 300, so divide both quantities by 300.	300 g 300 g | 300 g | 300 g | 300 g | 300 g 1.5 kg
b) 2 + 3 + 5 = 10 580 ÷ 10 = 58 g	You need to share 580 g into 3 amounts with ratio 2 : 3 : 5. The ratio 2 : 3 : 5 contains 10 parts. Divide 580 g into 10 parts. Each part measures 58 g.	580 g 2 parts | 3 parts | 5 parts 580 g 1 part |1 part|1 part|1 part|1 part|1 part|1 part|1 part|1 part|1 part 58 g | 58 g | 58 g | 58 g | 58 g | 58 g | 58 g | 58 g | 58 g | 58 g

2 × 58 g = 116 g 3 × 58 g = 174 g 5 × 58 g = 290 g So the answer is: 116 g : 174 g : 290 g	Find 2 parts, 3 parts and 5 parts.	*(see tables below)*

580 g									
1 part	1 part	1 part	1 part	1 part	1 part	1 part	1 part	1 part	1 part
58 g	58 g	58 g	58 g	58 g	58 g	58 g	58 g	58 g	58 g

580 g									
1 part	1 part	1 part	1 part	1 part	1 part	1 part	1 part	1 part	1 part
58 g	58 g	58 g	58 g	58 g	58 g	58 g	58 g	58 g	58 g
116 g		174 g			290 g				

Tip

To check your answer, add up the amounts to make sure they make the correct total: 116 g + 174 kg + 290 g = 580 g

Did you know?

When the ratio of the lengths of the sides of a triangle is 3 : 4 : 5, the triangle is a right-angled triangle.

Ancient Egyptians used a square as the base of the pyramid. However, they didn't have tools to measure or check that the angles in the base were right-angles. Instead, they tied knots to divide a rope into 12 equal parts. They then formed a triangle with sides in the ratio of 3 : 4 : 5 to make a right-angled triangle. Once they checked that the angles were a right angle, they made sure all the sides of the base were equal to build a square.

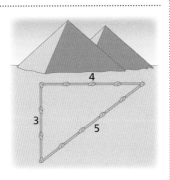

Exercise 1   1–10

1 Express each ratio in its simplest form.

a) 48 : 12
b) 25 : 60
c) 100 : 150
d) 15 : 20 : 10
e) 18 : 15 : 21
f) 24 : 12 : 36
g) 20 : 100 : 140
h) 0.4 : 0.6 : 0.8

Tip

Multiply 0.4 : 0.6 : 0.8 by 10 then simplify.

2 James gets a puzzle pack. It contains 25 cards with sudoku puzzles, 5 cards with crossword puzzles and 10 cards with riddles.

Write each ratio in its simplest form.

a) sudoku : riddle
b) riddle : crosswords
c) sudoku : riddle : crossword

3 For each pattern, write the ratio of **yellow : green : pink** squares in its simplest form.

a)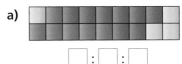

☐ : ☐ : ☐

b)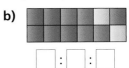

☐ : ☐ : ☐

c)

$\boxed{} : \boxed{} : \boxed{}$

d)

$\boxed{} : \boxed{} : \boxed{}$

4 Simplify fully.
- **a)** 40 cm : 0.36 m
- **b)** 55 mm : 8 cm
- **c)** 800 g : 1.2 kg
- **d)** 6 weeks : 21 days
- **e)** 200 ml : 2 litres : 3 litres
- **f)** 3 minutes : 150 seconds : 2 minutes

5 Divide £480 into these ratios.
- **a)** 3 : 2
- **b)** 5 : 7
- **c)** 1 : 2 : 3
- **d)** 3 : 5 : 8
- **e)** 6 : 7 : 7
- **f)** 2 : 9 : 13

6 Complete these ratios.
- **a)** $2 : 150 cent = ... : .....
- **b)** 1000 g : 3 kg = ... : ......
- **c)** 3 hours : 180 minutes = ... : .....
- **d)** 32 cm : 0.8 m ...... : ......

7 The ratio of windy days: sunny days: rainy days in April is 3 : 2 : 5.
- **a)** How many days were windy?
- **b)** How many more days were sunny than rainy?

8 Complete the missing numbers to form equivalent ratios.
- **a)** 2 : 3 = 16 : $\boxed{}$
- **b)** 3 : 5 = 63 : $\boxed{}$
- **c)** 1 : 3 : 7 = $\boxed{}$: 18 : $\boxed{}$
- **d)** 2 : 5 : 9 = $\boxed{}$: $\boxed{}$:72

9 The table shows the number of students from Years 7, 8, 9, 10 and 11 who take part in a school show.

Year	Frequency
7	12
8	24
9	15
10	35
11	28

Complete the missing words or numbers to make each statement true.
- **a)** Year 7 : $\boxed{}$ = 1 : 2
- **b)** $\boxed{}$: $\boxed{}$ = 3 : 7
- **c)** $\boxed{}$: $\boxed{}$ = 3 : 7
- **d)** $\boxed{}$: $\boxed{}$: $\boxed{}$ = 3 : 6 : 7

10 a) Split this square into 3 parts using 2 dividing lines so that the ratio between the areas is 2 : 3 : 4.

b) In how many different ways can you do this?

11 A cereal contains a mixture of oats, nuts and wheat flakes in the ratio of 3 : 2 : 1. A box contains a total of 660 g. To find the mass of oats, nuts and wheat in the box, Ben uses two different methods. His answers are both wrong.

Answer 1	Answer 2
3 + 2 + 1 = 6	660 ÷ 3 = 220 g oats
660 ÷ 6 = 110	660 ÷ 2 = 330 g nuts
oats = 2 × 110 = 220 g	660 ÷ 1 = 660 g wheat
nuts = 1 × 110 = 110 g	
wheat = 3 × 110 = 330 g	

a) Explain the mistakes in Ben's workings.

b) What should the answer be?

Direct proportion

Key terms

Two values are in **direct proportion** when they increase or decrease in the same ratio. You can use the **unitary method** to solve ratio and proportion problems when the values are in direct proportion. You need to find the value of one part or unit first, then multiply this value by the number of parts or units you need to calculate.

Worked example 2

Mikaela makes bread rolls. A batch of 8 rolls uses 320 g of flour.

How much flour would she need to make 11 rolls?

8 rolls : 320 g
÷ 8   ÷ 8
1 roll : 40 g
× 11   × 11
11 rolls : 440 g

Find how much flour is needed for 1 roll.

Multiply by 11.

320 g							
1 roll	1 roll	1 roll	1 roll	1 roll	1 roll	1 roll	1 roll

320 g							
1 roll	1 roll	1 roll	1 roll	1 roll	1 roll	1 roll	1 roll
40 g							

440 g										
40 g	40 g	40 g	40 g	40 g	40 g	40 g	40 g	40 g	40 g	40 g

Worked example 3

A paint mix uses white and blue paint in the ratio 4 : 3. How much blue paint will be needed to mix with 240 ml of white paint?

white : blue 4 : 3 ⤻ ×60 ×60 ⤺ 240 ml : ? Blue paint = 180 ml 180 ml of blue paint will be mixed with 240 ml of white paint.	The mixture is made of 4 parts of white paint and 3 parts of blue paint. The 4 parts of white paint make 240 ml. Find how many ml one part of white paint is. The blue paint has 3 parts. Each part is 60 ml. Multiply 60 ml by 3.	**Paint mix** [240 ml] [?] **Paint mix** [60 ml|60 ml|60 ml|60 ml] 240 ml ? **Paint mix** [60 ml|60 ml|60 ml|60 ml|60 ml|60 ml|60 ml] 240 ml 180 ml

Exercise 2 1–7, 9

1 If 5 AA batteries have a mass of 115 g, find the mass of:

a) 1 AA battery   b) 8 AA batteries   c) 11 AA batteries

2 The cost of 5 notebooks is 350 cents.

a) Find the cost of 1 notebook.

b) Find the cost of 12 notebooks.

3 The ratio of the length of a car to the length of a van is 2 : 3. If the length of the van is 3.6 m, which of these represents the length of a car?

a) 120 cm   b) 1.2 m   c) 240 cm   d) 1.8 m

4 Make three ratios that are equivalent to 6 : 8 : 12.

5 The ratio of the length and width of a birthday card is 2 : 3. The width of the card is 30 cm. Find the mistakes in the calculations below.

a) 2 + 3 = 5 parts
   30 ÷ 5 = 6 cm
   3 × 6 cm = 18 cm

b) 30 ÷ 2 = 15 cm
   3 × 15 cm = 45 cm

c) 30 cm ÷ 3 = 10 cm
   10 cm × 2 = 20 cm

6 Six sandwiches cost $15. Eight bottles of water cost $6. Jake buys a sandwich and a bottle of water for each of his ten friends. How much does he pay in total?

7 The ratio of copper to silver in a metal is 7 : 4. 168 g of silver is used to make the metal.

a) How much copper is used to make the metal?

b) Use two different methods to find how much more copper than silver is used.

8 Twelve cans of soda cost $16.20.

a) Work out the cost of 5 cans of soda.

b) Sarah buys enough soda for a party. She pays $101.25. How many cans does she buy?

9 80 sweets have a mass of 160 g.

Amy and Tom buy 360 g of sweets. To find out the number of sweets they bought, they do different calculations but reach the same answer. Are both calculations correct?

Amy's answer	Tom's answer
1 sweet = 80 ÷ 160 = $\frac{1}{2}$ g	1 sweet = 160 g ÷ 80 = 2 g
$\frac{1}{2}$ × 360 = 180 sweets	360 g ÷ 2 g = 180 sweets

> **Tip**
> Use a bar model to explain your answer.

End of chapter reflection

You should know that …	You should be able to …	Such as …
You can simplify a ratio by dividing the numbers in the ratio by the same factor. You can write a ratio in its simplest form by dividing the numbers in the ratio by the highest common factor. If the quantities are expressed in different units, you need to change them so all the units are the same.	Simplify ratios, including those expressed in different units.	Express this as a ratio in its simplest terms. 4 km : 450 m : 1 km
When you share an amount in a given ratio, you must divide the amount by the total number of parts.	Divide a quantity into more than two parts in a given ratio.	Share 180 g in the ratio 1 : 2 : 1.
The unitary method means finding the value of one part or one unit first.	Use the unitary method to solve simple problems involving ratio and direct proportion.	A shop is selling 5 tins of beans for $3.00. How much would 12 tins cost?

Mental calculations with fractions and integers

You will learn how to:
- Use known facts and place value to multiply and divide simple fractions.
- Use the laws of arithmetic and inverse operations to simplify calculations with integers and fractions.

Starting point

Do you remember ...?

- how to add and subtract fractions and mixed numbers?
  For example, $1\frac{3}{4} + \frac{1}{5} =$

- how to calculate a fraction of a quantity?
  For example, $\frac{1}{3} \times 2$ kg =

- how to multiply and divide an integer by a fraction?
  For example, $4 \div \frac{1}{3} =$

- how to use known facts to derive new ones?
  For example, $5 \times 6 = 30$, so $30 \div 6 = 5$ and $30 \div 5 = 6$.

This will also be helpful when you:

- solve equations.
  For example, $\frac{2}{5} x = 10$, find the value of x.

- simplify algebraic expressions.
  For example, simplify $2x + 3y + 4x - y$.

- expand algebraic brackets.
  For example, $3(2a + b)$

Hook

Multiplication = addition?

Is $1\frac{1}{2} \times 3 = 1\frac{1}{2} + 3$?

Is $1\frac{1}{4} \times 5 = 1\frac{1}{4} + 5$?

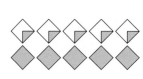

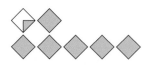

Can you find other fractions and integers that work in the same way?

$$1\frac{\square}{\square} \times \dots = 1\frac{\square}{\square} + \dots$$

What would happen if your fraction was $2\frac{\square}{\square}$?

Make a table to show your results. What do you notice?

Key terms

When you **derive** an answer, you work it out using what you already know. To **multiply a fraction by an integer**, multiply the numerator by the integer.

When dividing an integer by a fraction, invert the fraction and then multiply.

Mental calculations with fractions

Worked example 1

Find:

a) $\frac{1}{3}$ of $\frac{1}{4}$

b) Use your answer to part a) to find $\frac{1}{3}$ of $\frac{3}{4}$

c) Use the known fact that $2 \div \frac{1}{6} = 12$ to find:

i) $2 \div \frac{5}{6}$

ii) $\frac{2}{3} \div \frac{1}{6}$

a) $= \frac{1}{3}$ of $\frac{1}{4}$	Start with $\frac{1}{4}$	
$= \frac{1}{3} \times \frac{1}{4} = \frac{1 \times 1}{3 \times 4}$	Find $\frac{1}{3}$ of it by dividing $\frac{1}{4}$ into thirds. Multiply the numerators. Multiply the denominators.	
$= \frac{1}{12}$	$\frac{3}{4}$ is three times the value of $\frac{1}{4}$. So $\frac{1}{3}$ of $\frac{3}{4}$ will be 3 times the previous answer.	
b) $= \frac{1}{3}$ of $\frac{3}{4}$ $= 3 \times \frac{1}{12}$ $= \frac{3}{12}$ $= \frac{1}{4}$	Simplify the answer	

c) $2 \div \frac{1}{6} = 12$	Start with the known fact that $2 \div \frac{1}{6} = 12$.	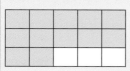
i) $2 \div \frac{5}{6}$ $= 12 \div 5$ $= \frac{12}{5}$ $= 2\frac{2}{5}$	The number 2 has been divided by a fraction that is five times the original fraction. Divide the original answer by 5.	
ii) $= \frac{2}{3} \div \frac{1}{6}$ $= 12 \div 3 = 4$ $=$	Start with the known fact that $2 \div \frac{1}{6} = 12$. The number 2 has been replaced by $\frac{2}{3}$, so it has been divided by 3. The answer should be divided by 3 too.	

Did you know?

Multiplying and dividing fractions can be used when making clothes. For example, if 1m of fabric is used to make normal length trousers, $\frac{3}{4}$ m may be used to make $\frac{3}{4}$ length trousers.

$\frac{3}{4}$ length trousers

Exercise 1 1–9

1 Use the known fact $20 \times \frac{1}{5} = 4$ to work out:

a) $80 \times \frac{1}{5}$ **b)** $20 \times \frac{3}{5}$ **c)** $60 \times \frac{3}{5}$ **d)** $120 \times \frac{3}{5}$

2 Calculate

a) $33 \times \frac{1}{3}$ **b)** $33 \times \frac{2}{3}$ **c)** $66 \times \frac{1}{3}$ **d)** $66 \times \frac{2}{3}$

e) $\frac{1}{8} \times 72$ **f)** $\frac{5}{8} \times 72$ **g)** $\frac{1}{8} \times 144$ **h)** $\frac{5}{8} \times 144$

3 Work out

a) $\frac{1}{2}$ of $\frac{1}{3}$ **b)** $\frac{1}{2}$ of $\frac{1}{6}$ **c)** $\frac{1}{4} \times \frac{1}{6}$ **d)** $\frac{1}{8} \times \frac{1}{6}$

4 Use the known fact that $\frac{1}{8}$ of $\frac{1}{5} = \frac{1}{40}$ to find

which of these answers are not correct.
Explain the reasons for your answer.

> **Discuss**
>
> $\frac{1}{2} \times \frac{2}{3} = \frac{1}{3}$
>
> What known facts can you use to find this product?
> Will the answer be different? Why or why not?

a) $\frac{3}{8}$ of $\frac{1}{5} = \frac{3}{40}$ b) $\frac{1}{8}$ of $\frac{4}{5} = \frac{1}{4}$ c) $\frac{5}{8}$ of $\frac{1}{5} = \frac{1}{8}$ d) $\frac{1}{8}$ of $\frac{1}{10} = \frac{1}{20}$

5 Work out:
a) $8 \div \frac{1}{2}$ b) $4 \div \frac{1}{3}$

c) $2 \div \frac{1}{4}$ d) $5 \div \frac{1}{5}$

6 What is bigger?
a) $\frac{4}{9} \div 2$ or $\frac{4}{9} \div 4$ b) $\frac{6}{11} \div 3$ or $\frac{4}{7} \div 2$ c) $\frac{1}{4} \div 4$ or $\frac{1}{6} \div 4$

7 Use the known fact $1 \div \frac{1}{5} = 5$ to complete these calculations. Find the odd one out:

a) $\frac{1}{9} \div \frac{1}{5}$ b) $\frac{1}{7} \div \frac{1}{5}$ c) $\frac{1}{2} \div \frac{1}{5}$ d) $\frac{1}{8} \div \frac{1}{5}$

8 a) Markus buys $\frac{1}{5}$ kg of candy. He gives $\frac{1}{2}$ of his candy to his brother. Work out the mass
of the candy that Markus' brother receives.

b) Use the known fact $10 \div \frac{1}{10} = 100$ and a calculator to check what other divisions make 100.
At least one of the numbers you are using must be a fraction.
Make a table with your results and discuss the findings.

9 Challenge
Find the mistakes. Correct them.
a) When working out $\frac{6}{10} \div 2$, use the fact that $6 \div 2 = 3$ and $10 \div 2 = 3$.

$\frac{6}{10} \div 2 = \frac{3}{5}$

b) When working out $\frac{3}{8} \div \frac{1}{2}$, use the fact that $3 \div \frac{1}{2} = 6$

and $8 \div \frac{1}{2} = 16$.

$\frac{3}{8} \div \frac{1}{2} = \frac{6}{16}$

> **Think about**
>
> Tom uses the number fact
>
> that $\frac{1}{5} \times \frac{1}{3} = \frac{1}{15}$ to work out $\frac{1}{5} \div \frac{1}{3}$.
> This is his method:
>
> > Known fact: $\frac{1}{5} \times \frac{1}{3} = \frac{1}{15}$, so
> >
> > $\frac{1}{15} \div \frac{1}{3} = \frac{1}{5}$
> >
> > $\frac{1}{5} \div \frac{1}{3} = \frac{3}{15} \div \frac{1}{3} = \frac{3}{5}$
>
> Is he correct?

10 Use numbers 5 and 10 and the number fact

$5 \div \frac{1}{12} = 60$ to make this statement correct.

$\boxed{} \div \dfrac{\boxed{}}{12} = 6$

Key terms

The **commutative** law tells us that for addition and multiplication, you can change the order of the numbers:

$a + b = b + a$ $3 + 7 = 7 + 3$

$a \times b = b \times a$ $3 \times 7 = 7 \times 3$

The **associative** law says that when you add or multiply numbers, you can group them in different ways:

$(a + b) + c = a + (b + c)$ $(2 + 5) + 3 = 2 + (5 + 3)$

$(a \times b) \times c = a \times (b \times c)$ $(2 \times 5) \times 3 = 2 \times (5 \times 3)$

The **distributive** law tells us that you can partition a number and then multiply both parts:

$x(y + z) = (x \times y) + (x \times z)$ $6 \times 13 = 6 \times 10 + 6 \times 3$

$x(y - z) = (x \times y) - (x \times z)$ $6 \times 19 = 6 \times 20 - 6 \times 1$

The distributive law does not work for division.

Partition means to break up a number into different parts. For example, you can partition 7 into $2 + 5$, or $3 + 4$, or $1 + 6$, and so on, if this makes it easier to work with.

Worked example 2

Use the laws of arithmetic to help you simplify these calculations.

a) $907 + 136 + 1003$ **b)** $\frac{6}{7} \times 3$ **c)** $10 \times \frac{1}{3}$

a) $907 + 136 + 1003$ $= 907 + 1003 + 136$ $= 2000 + 136$ $= 2136$	In the order of operations, we can add in any order. $907 + 136 + 1003$ is the same as $907 + 1003 + 136$. Add 907 and 1003 first. Add the result to 136.	

b) $\frac{6}{7} \times \frac{1}{3}$

$= (\frac{2}{7} \times 3) \times \frac{1}{3}$

$\frac{2}{7} \times (3 \times \frac{1}{3})$

$\frac{2}{7} \times 1$

$\frac{2}{7}$

Write $\frac{6}{7}$ as $\frac{2}{7} \times 3$

Use the associative law.

Multiply 3 by $\frac{1}{3}$ first.

Multiply $\frac{2}{7}$ by the result.

c) $10 \times \frac{1}{3}$

$= (9 + 1) \times \frac{1}{3}$

$9 \times \frac{1}{3} = 3$

$1 \times \frac{1}{3} = \frac{1}{3}$

$= 3 + \frac{1}{3}$

$= 3\frac{1}{3}$

Partition 10 as 9 + 1.

Use the distributive law and multiply both 9 and 1 by $\frac{1}{3}$.

Add the results.

Did you know?

Decorators use the distributive law when ordering material. For example, if the cost of 1 tin of paint is $14.50 and they need 2 tins for the kitchen, 3 tins for the bedrooms and 5 tins for the rest of the house, they calculate the cost of paint by working out 10 × $14.50 rather than 2 × $14.50 + 3 × $14.50 + 5 × $14.50.

1 Work out:
   a) $23 + 45 + 27$
   b) $98 + 350 + 102$
   c) $1019 + 2800 + 3071$
   d) $1085 + 278 + 2115 + 3322$

2 Work out:
   a) $\frac{4}{7} + \frac{5}{8} + \frac{3}{7}$
   b) $\frac{2}{3} + \frac{5}{12} - \frac{1}{12}$
   c) $\frac{11}{12} + \frac{1}{2} - \frac{5}{12}$
   d) $1\frac{1}{2} + \frac{7}{8} - \frac{1}{2} + \frac{1}{8}$

> **Tip**
> First, add or subtract fractions with the same denominator. Don't forget to simplify.

3 Match the pairs of calculations that have the same answer.
   a) $1279 + 1086 - 235 - 1086$
   b) $\frac{1}{2} + \left(\frac{2}{5} + \frac{9}{10}\right)$
   c) $\frac{4}{7} \times \frac{5}{8} + \frac{4}{7} \times \frac{3}{8}$
   d) $\left(\frac{1}{2} \times \frac{2}{5}\right) \times \frac{9}{10}$
   e) $\left(\frac{1}{2} + \frac{2}{5}\right) + \frac{9}{10}$
   f) $\frac{4}{7} \times \left(\frac{5}{8} + \frac{3}{8}\right)$
   g) $\left(\frac{9}{10} \times \frac{2}{5}\right) \times \frac{1}{2}$
   h) $1272 + 235 + 7$

> **Tip**
> You don't need to work out the answers.

4 Work out:
   a) $2\frac{1}{2} \times 6 \times 2$
   b) $\frac{2}{3} \times 2 \times 9$
   c) $35 \times 1\frac{2}{3} \div 7$
   d) $24 \times \frac{5}{8} \div 8$

5 Complete the calculations.
   a) $5 \times 28 + 5 \times 28 = 10 \times \text{.......} = \text{.......}$
   b) $3 \times 248 + 7 \times 248 = \text{.......} \times 248 = \text{.......}$
   c) $12 \times 1350 - 2 \times 1350 = \text{.......} \times \text{.......} = \text{.......}$
   d) $4 \times \frac{1}{3} + \text{.......} \times \frac{1}{3} = 9 \times \text{.......} = \text{.......}$
   e) $\frac{3}{8} \times 20 - 20 \times \frac{1}{8} = \text{.......} \times \text{.......} = \text{.......}$
   f) $\frac{1}{9} \times 38 - \frac{1}{9} \times 2 = \frac{1}{9} \times \text{.......} = \text{.......}$

6 Look at these calculations.
$$\frac{1}{2} \times \frac{1}{3} = \frac{1}{2} - \frac{1}{3}$$
$$\frac{1}{3} \times \frac{1}{4} = \frac{1}{3} - \frac{1}{4}$$

Is it always, sometimes or never true that the product of the unit fractions is equal to their difference?

7 The perimeter of the rectangle is equal to the perimeter of the square.

Find the area of the rectangle.

$\frac{1}{4}$ m

$\frac{3}{8}$ m

? m

8 Jane got the following question right, but she used a very long method. Explain an easier way to solve it.

$49 \times \frac{7}{10} - 19 \times \frac{7}{10}$

$= \frac{49 \times 7}{10} - \frac{19 \times 7}{10}$

$= \frac{343}{10} - \frac{133}{10}$

$= \frac{343 - 133}{10}$

$= \frac{210}{10}$

$= 21$

End of chapter reflection

You should know that....	You should be able to ...	Such as ...
Known facts can be used to work out other related calculations. This can include calculations involving multiplication or division of fractions.	Use known facts to derive new facts.	Given that $\frac{1}{2} \times \frac{1}{3} = \frac{1}{6}$ calculate $\frac{1}{2} \times \frac{2}{3}$ Given that $2 \div \frac{1}{5} = 10$ Calculate $\frac{2}{7} \div \frac{1}{5}$
$(a + b) + c = a + (b + c)$ and $(a \times b) \times c = a \times (b \times c)$ $x(y + z) = (x \times y) + (x \times z)$ and $x(y - z) = (x \times y) - (x \times z)$	Use the laws of arithmetic and inverse operations to simplify calculations with integers and fractions.	$(213 + 788) + 87$ $25 \times 9278 \times 4$ $25 \times 7 / 8 + 15 \times 7 / 8$

Calculations with decimals

You will learn how to:

- Multiply and divide integers and decimals by decimals such as 0.6 or 0.06, understanding where to place the decimal point by considering equivalent calculations, e.g. 4.37 × 0.3 = (4.37 × 3) ÷ 10, 92.4 ÷ 0.06 = (92.4 × 100) ÷ 6.

Starting point

Do you remember …?

- how to multiply and divide simple decimals?
  For example, 0.07 × 9 = , 2.4 ÷ 3 = ?
- how to multiply and divide integers and decimals?
  For example, 4.35 ÷ 3 = ?

This will also be helpful when you:

- solve problems involving average speed.

  For example, a cyclist travelled 9.6 km in 0.8 hours. Find the average speed in km per hour.

Hook

Game: **4 in a row**

You need:

12 counters per player (1 colour)

Dice

How to play:

0.08	0.28	0.54	4.2	3.6
0.27	1.8	0.45	0.36	0.32
1.2	0.06	3.5	0.12	0.4
0.5	0.24	0.1	0.16	0.48

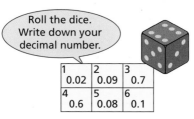

Roll the dice. Write down your decimal number.

1 0.02	2 0.09	3 0.7
4 0.6	5 0.08	6 0.1

- Roll the dice. Write down the decimal number in the table on the right that corresponds to the number your dice shows.
- Roll the dice again. Multiply this number by the decimal from the table.
- Find this number on the grid.
- Use a counter to cover the number on the grid if it is not already covered.
- Aim to place four counters in a row, horizontally, vertically or diagonally.
- The first player to make a row of four counters is the winner.

Did you know?

A gardener uses decimals to calculate the cost of fencing.
For example, to calculate the cost of a fence 8.5 m long when
1 m of fence costs $9, he multiplies 8.5 by 9.

Multiplication and division

Key terms

The **decimal places** or d.p. tells you the number of places after the decimal point. For example, 0.4175 has four decimal places. When you divide a number by a decimal, use the **place values** of the decimal to work out an equivalent calculation. For example, when multiplying or dividing a number by 0.8 consider the multiplication or division of that number by 8, then divide or multiply the result by 10.

Worked example 1

a) 2.64×0.9 **b)** $1.76 \div 0.02$

a)   264
    ×   9
    2376
      5 3
	Start by considering the calculation 264×9.
	
	 2.64 is 100 times smaller than 264.
	
	 0.9 is 10 times smaller than 9.
	
	 The answer to 2.64×0.9 will be $100 \times 10 = 1000$ times smaller than the answer to 264×9.

$264 \times 9 = 2376$

÷100   ÷10   ÷1000

$2.64 \times 0.9 = \ldots\ldots$

2.64×0.9

$= 2376 \div 1000$

$= 2.376$

b) $1.76 \div 0.02$

$176 \div 2 \qquad = 88$

÷100   ÷100

$1.76 \div 0.02 \qquad = 88$

Start by considering the calculation $176 \div 2$.

The answer to $1.76 \div 0.02$ will change by $100 \div 100$ times.

$100 \div 100 = 1$ hence the answer will not change.

1 267 × 8 = 2136. Use this to help you calculate:

a) 2.67 × 8   **b)** 26.7 × 8   **c)** 26.7 × 0.8   **d)** 2.67 × 0.08

2 426 × 5 = 2130. Use this to help you calculate:

a) 4.26 × 5   **b)** 4260 × 0.5   **c)** 42.6 × 0.05   **d)** 0.426 × 0.005

3 You are given 468 ÷ 6 = 78. Work out these calculations and write them in order of size of answer, starting with the smallest.

a) 4.68 ÷ 0.6   **b)** 468 ÷ 0.6   **c)** 46.8 ÷ 0.06   **d)** 4.68 ÷ 0.06

4 5752 ÷ 8 = 719. Use the numbers from the list to complete statements a) to d).

5.752   0.08   0.8   0.008   57.52

a) 575.2 ÷ ...... = 719   **b)** 0.5752 ÷ ...... = 71.9   **c)** 5.752 ÷ ...... = 71.9   **d)** ...... ÷ 0.8 = 7.19

5 Calculate:

a) 84 × 0.6   **b)** 231 × 0.04   **c)** 23.1 × 0.8

d) 3.09 × 0.09   **e)** 24.8 × 0.05   **f)** 0.209 × 0.03

> **Tip**
>
> You can use multiplication to check your answers to question 4.

6 Work out:

a) 16.2 ÷ 0.3   **b)** 1.32 ÷ 0.6   **c)** 94.5 ÷ 0.05

d) 2.45 ÷ 0.7   **e)** 0.28 ÷ 0.08   **f)** 0.207 ÷ 0.09

> **Discuss**
>
> Does dividing one number by another always make it smaller?

7 Explain the mistakes in each calculation. Correct them.

a) 6.9 × 0.7 = 48.3

$$\begin{array}{r} 6.9 \\ \times\ 0.7 \\ \hline 6\ 3 \\ 420 \\ \hline 48.3 \end{array}$$

b) 371 ÷ 0.7 = 53

$$7\overline{)37^21}\ \ 53$$

8 Jackie sells lemonade. She charges \$0.60 for a cup. At the end of the afternoon, she has \$22.80. How many cups of lemonade did she sell?

9 Simon needs to divide a 7.5 m roll of fabric into lengths of 0.6 m. How many pieces can he make?

10 The art teacher has 7.25 kg of clay. She cuts lumps of 0.3 kg out for each of the students in the art class. She has 0.95 kg of clay left. How many students are there in the art class?

Discuss

Discuss two different examples where you have used multiplying and dividing by decimals in real life.

Think about

What multiplication is equivalent to ÷ 0.001?
What about 0.01?

End of chapter reflection

You should know that ...	You should be able to ...	Such as ...
You can use equivalent calculations to help you multiply and divide integers and decimals by decimals.	Multiply and divide integers and decimals by decimals, using equivalent calculations.	2.24 × 0.9 3.12 ÷ 0.08

3B

Unit 3B

Algebra and geometry

What it's all about?

- Solving equations
- Algebraic rules for sequences
- Angles in triangles and quadrilaterals
- Problem solving involving angles

You will learn about:

- solving equations involving brackets and variables on both sides
- constructing an equation to solve a problem
- the nth term of simple sequences
- proofs relating to the sum of the angles in triangles and quadrilaterals
- solving angle problems that involve triangles, quadrilaterals and parallel lines

You will build your skills in:

- using mathematics to represent situations
- solving equations, showing your working step-by-step
- using logical argument to prove geometrical results
- solving geometrical problems, giving geometrical reasons for your answer

Equations

You will learn how to:
- Construct and solve linear equations with integer coefficients (unknown on either or both sides, without or with brackets).

Starting point

Do you remember …?

- the meaning of the words **unknown**, **equation**, and **solve**?
- how to solve an equation with an unknown on one side?
  For example, solve $3x + 5 = 32$ or $22 = 30 - 2x$.
- how to expand a single bracket?
  For example, expand $3(2x - 5)$.

This will also be helpful when you:

- learn how to solve pairs of equations with two unknowns (called simultaneous equations).

Hook

Look at the rectangle.

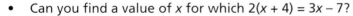

2(x + 4) cm

3x − 7 cm

- When $x = 4$, what is the value of $2(x + 4)$?
- What about $3x - 7$?
- Can this value of x be correct for this rectangle? How do you know?
- What about when $x = 3$?
- Make a table of values for x, $2(x + 4)$ and $3x - 7$.

  You could use a spreadsheet to produce this table using a formula to speed up your calculations.

- Can you find a value of x for which $2(x + 4) = 3x - 7$?
- What must the length of the rectangle be if this is the value of x?
- Are there are any other values of x that make the lengths equal?
- Make up your own expressions for the lengths of a rectangle. Can you find a solution, x, that makes them equal?
- Can you make up an example where this is no solution?

Solving equations with brackets

Worked example 1

Solve $3(3x + 2) = 42$.

$3(3x + 2) = 42$	Start by expanding the brackets to create an equivalent equation. Multiply everything in the bracket by 3.	
$3 \times 3x + 3 \times 2 = 42$ $9x + 6 = 42$	Collect terms to simplify the equation.	$9x + 6 = 42$
$9x + 6 = 42$ $-6 \quad -6$ $\overline{9x = 36}$	Subtract 6 from the $9x + 6$ and from the 42.	$9x = 36$
$9x = 36$ $\div 9 \quad \div 9$ $\overline{x = 4}$	Finally, divide both sides by 9 to find the value of x.	$x = 4$

Exercise 1

1 Solve these equations.

a) $x + 8 = 20$ b) $4x = 12$ c) $7x + 1 = 15$

d) $20 + 2x = 36$ e) $x - 1 = 9$ f) $2x - 5 = 13$

g) $6 = 3x - 9$ h) $15 - x = 11$ i) $30 - 2x = 18$

j) $12 = 33 - 3x$ k) $\frac{x}{3} = 6$ l) $\frac{15}{x} = 3$

2 Solve these equations.

a) $4(x + 2) = 32$ b) $5(x - 3) = 25$ c) $2(3x + 1) = 14$ d) $3(5x + 10) = 90$

e) $7(2x - 1) = 77$ f) $3(3x - 2) = 75$ g) $24 = 2(x + 3)$ h) $54 = 9(5x - 19)$

3 Sofia and Thomas are solving the equation $3(5x - 1) = 42$.
Here are their workings out:

Sofia   Thomas

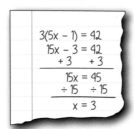

Sofia:
$3(5x - 1) = 42$
$15x - 3 = 42$
$+3 \quad +3$
$15x = 45$
$\div 15 \quad \div 15$
$x = 3$

Thomas:
$3(5x - 1) = 42$
$\div 3 \quad \div 3$
$5x - 1 = 14$
$+1 \quad +1$
$5x = 15$
$\div 5 \quad \div 5$
$x = 3$

a) What has Thomas done differently to Sofia? Is his method correct?

b) Does this method always work?

c) Which method is better to use for an equation like $9(6x - 5) = 63$?

4 Solve $3(x + 2) + 5(x + 4) = 90$.

Solving equations with unknowns on both sides

Worked example 2

Solve these equations.

a) $1 + 2x = 5x - 8$ b) $3(2x + 1) = 4x + 7$

a) $1 + 2x = 5x - 8$ $-2x\quad -2x$ $\overline{1 = 3x - 8}$	We must do the same to each side of the equation. First, subtract $2x$ from each side (or each row in the bar model).	The bar model has $1 + 2x$ on the top row the same length as $5x - 8$ underneath: 
$1 = 3x - 8$ $+8\qquad +8$ $\overline{9 = 3x}$	We now have an equation with an unknown on just one side. Add 8 to both sides (rows in the bar model).	
		$9 = 3x$
$9 = 3x$ $\div 3\quad \div 3$ $\overline{3 = x}$	Finally, divide both sides (rows) by 3.	so $x = 3$
b) $3(2x + 1) = 4x + 7$ $6x + 3 = 4x + 7$	Start by expanding the bracket to create an equivalent equation.	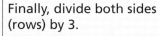 Simplify the top row by collecting the xs together and the numbers together.

$6x + 3 = 4x + 7$ $\underline{-4x \qquad -4x}$ $2x + 3 = 7$	Now subtract $4x$ from both sides (rows) of the equation.	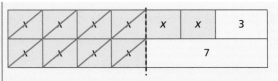
$2x + 3 = 7$ $\underline{-3 \quad -3}$ $2x = 4$	Subtract 3 from both sides (rows).	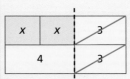
$2x = 4$ $\underline{\div 2 \quad \div 2}$ $x = 2$	Finally, divide by 2 to find the value of a single x.	

Exercise 2

1 Solve:

a) $3x + 1 = 2x + 5$ b) $7x + 2 = 4x + 11$ c) $11x + 13 = 9x + 17$

d) $3x + 13 = 5x + 3$ e) $10x - 3 = 8x + 9$ f) $3x - 7 = x + 11$

g) $6x - 2 = 2x + 14$ h) $4x - 18 = x$ i) $7x + 1 = 10x - 11$

j) $8x - 15 = 4x - 3$ k) $2x - 1 = 7x - 16$

Think about

How can you check whether your solution to an equation is correct?

2 Put these steps for solving the equation $2x + 7 = 19 - 2x$ in the right order.

$4x = 12$

$x = 4$		$4x + 7 = 19$

$-7 \qquad -7$

$+2x \qquad +2x$		$\div 3 \qquad \div 3$

$2x + 7 = 19 - 2x$

3 Solve:

a) $2x + 4 = 13 - x$ b) $6x - 1 = 20 - x$

c) $24 - x = x + 4$ d) $60 - 2x = x + 3$

> **Tip**
>
> Start by adding x to both sides.

4 Solve:

    a) $2(4x + 1) = 7x + 13$ **b)** $3(x - 4) = x + 2$ **c)** $10(5x + 3) = 20x + 60$

    d) $2(3x + 1) = 51 - x$ **e)** $3x + 14 = 2(5x - 21)$ **f)** $2x + 5 = 3(x - 1)$

5 Darlene is solving the equation $3(2x + 4) = 2(3x + 6)$.

    She writes:

$$6x + 12 = 6x + 12$$
$$- 6 \qquad\quad - 6$$
$$\overline{12 = 12}$$
$$- 12 \quad - 12$$
$$\overline{0 = 0}$$

    Is Darlene correct?

    What does this mean about the equation? Is there a solution? Explain your answer.

6 Complete this equation so that it has a solution of $x = 5$.

    $2(3x + 7) = 10x \ldots$

Constructing equations

Worked example 3

Ali and Ben each have the same number of pencils.

Ali has 4 full boxes of pencils and 2 loose pencils.

Ben has 2 full boxes of pencils and 10 loose pencils.

How many pencils are there in a full box?

Let x represent the number of pencils in a full box.	The unknown that we are trying to find is the number of pencils in a full box, so let's give this value a letter to represent it, x.	Visually, number of pencils in a full box x
Ali has $4x + 2$ pencils. Ben has $2x + 10$ pencils.	We can write an expression for the number of pencils that Ali and Ben have in terms of x.	Ali has 4 full boxes and 2 loose pencils and Ben has 2 full boxes and 10 loose pencils.
$4x + 2 = 2x + 10$	Since Ali and Ben have the same total number of pencils, we can make these two expressions equal.	These amounts are equal so have the same length of bar: Ali: x | x | x | x | 2 Ben: x | x | 10

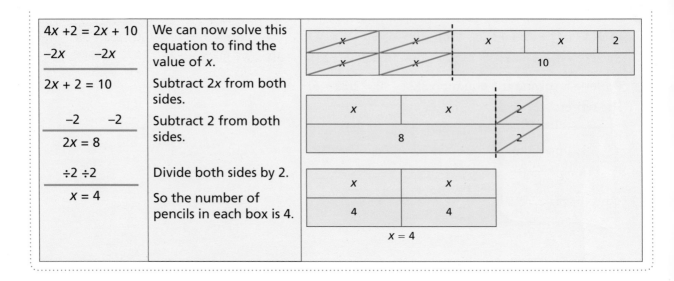

$4x + 2 = 2x + 10$	We can now solve this equation to find the value of x.
$-2x \qquad -2x$	
$2x + 2 = 10$	Subtract $2x$ from both sides.
$-2 \qquad -2$	Subtract 2 from both sides.
$2x = 8$	
$\div 2 \ \div 2$	Divide both sides by 2.
$x = 4$	So the number of pencils in each box is 4.

Exercise 3

1 Agatha's age is x years.

When you multiply Agatha's age by 7 and add 6, you get a result of 83.

a) Construct an equation in terms of x to represent this problem.

b) Solve your equation to find the value of x.

2 Multiplying a number by 3 and then adding 5 gives the same answer as adding the number to 23. What is the number?

3 Meera is thinking of a number, x.

She doubles her number, adds 3 and then multiplies the result by 4.

This gives her a final answer of 52.

a) Construct an equation in terms of x to represent this problem.

b) Solve your equation to find the value of x.

4 A father is 3 times as old as his daughter's age plus one.

The father is 36.

How old is the daughter?

5 Fiona and George each have the same number of sweets.

Fiona has 3 full packets and 12 loose sweets.

George has 2 full packets and 22 loose sweets.

How many sweets are there in a full packet?

6 Quentin thinks of a number.

He multiplies it by 4 and then subtracts 21.

His answer is the same as the number he first thought of.

What number did Quentin think of?

7 Here is an isosceles triangle.

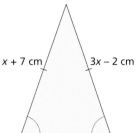

$x + 7$ cm $3x - 2$ cm

Find the value of x.

Tip

The two sides shown are of equal length so you can make an equation using the expressions for their lengths.

8 Here is a square.

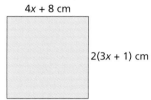

$4x + 8$ cm

$2(3x + 1)$ cm

a) Find the value of x.

b) Find the side length of the square.

9 Jamie is n years old.

Kathryn is 7 years older than Jamie.

Laura is twice as old as Kathryn.

The total of their ages is 57.

By constructing and solving an equation, find the age of each person.

10 By constructing and solving an equation, find the value of x.

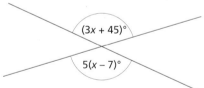

$(3x + 45)°$

$5(x - 7)°$

11 Vocabulary feature question

Complete the text using words from the box.

substituting	construct	simplify	solve
unknown	expand	solution	equation

You can _____ an equation to find the value of an _____ number in a problem.

You _____ the equation by carrying out the same operations to both sides of the equation.

If there is a bracket, you can _____ this first and then _____ if needed.

Once you have found the _____ to the equation, you can check it is correct by

_____ into the original _____ to check it balances.

End of chapter reflection

You should know that ...	You should be able to ...	Such as ...
You must do the same to both sides of an equation to keep it balanced.	Solve an equation with an unknown on one side, with and without brackets.	Solve: **a)** $7x - 3 = 25$ **b)** $23 - 3x = 11$ **c)** $2(5x + 6) = 102$
You can check whether your solution is correct by substituting it back into the equation and making sure the two sides are equal.	Solve an equation with an unknown on both sides with and without brackets.	Solve: **a)** $4x + 2 = 8x - 30$ **b)** $2x + 7 = 31 - 2x$ **c)** $6(4x + 1) = 5(3x + 12)$
	Construct an equation to represent a problem and interpret the solution in the context of the problem.	Esme thinks of a number. She subtracts it from 15 and then multiplies her result by 2. Her answer is the same number she started with. What was Esme's number? A triangle has angles of $x°$, $2x - 40°$ and $90 - x°$. Find the value of the smallest angle.

nth term of sequences

You will learn how to:
- Use a linear expression to describe the *n*th term of a simple arithmetic sequence, justifying its form by referring to the activity or practical context from which it was generated.

Starting point

Do you remember …?

- how to generate a sequence from a term-to-term rule?
  For example, first term 7 and term-to-term rule of 'add 11'
- how to generate a sequence from a position-to-term rule?
  For example, multiply by 3 and then add 2.
- how to find the term-to-term rule for a sequence?
  For example: 9, 14, 19, 24, …
- how to find the position-to-term rule for a sequence?
  For example: 6, 12, 18, 24 …

This will also be helpful when you:

- learn more about sequences that are linked to square and cube numbers.

Hook

Khalid is a gardener. He makes square ponds with a path around the outside.

The smallest pond Khalid can make is a 1 m × 1 m square with a path around it like this:

Khalid needs 8 tiles to build this path.

The second smallest pond Khalid can make is a 2 m × 2 m square with a path around it like this:

- How many tiles does Khalid need to build this pond?
- How many tiles does he need for a 3 m × 3 m pond? Draw a diagram to show how you got your answer.

- Investigate the number of tiles that Khalid needs for different size ponds. Use diagrams and tables to help you.

nth term rules

Key terms

An **arithmetic sequence** is one that goes up or down by the same amount between terms. It has a term-to-term rule of +*a* or −*a*, where *a* is a fixed number.

You can write the **position-to-term rule** for a sequence in words, such as 'multiply by 2 and add 1', or we can write it as an algebraic expression called the **nth term**.

For example, instead of writing 'multiply the position by 2 and add 1', you could write $2n+1$. This expression shows *n* being multiplied by 2 and then 1 being added.

Worked example 1

Here is a pattern made from counters. The first five patterns are shown.

Write an expression for the number of counters in the nth term of the pattern.

The table shows the positions and values of the terms in the sequence.	In the nth pattern, there are n counters in the top row, n counters in the bottom row and 2 counters in the middle row.	The pattern is made out of the numbers in the 2 times table with an extra 2 counters each time:

Position/ Pattern number	Term/ Number of counters
1	4
2	6
3	8
4	10
5	12

The position to term rule is 'multiply by 2 and add 2' or

$n \rightarrow \times 2 \rightarrow + 2$

Therefore, the nth term is $2n + 2$.

So the nth term is $n + n + 2 = 2n + 2$.

2 blue	4 blue	6 blue	8 blue	10 blue
2 red	2 red	2 red	2 red	2 red

So the nth term will be made of $2n$ blue counters and 2 red counters.

Therefore the nth term is $2n + 2$.

Worked example 2

Jane has $1. Every day, her mother gives her $5 for completing jobs around the house. Jane saves all the money.

The sequence of totals of Jane's money each day is $6, $11, $16, $21, $26, ...

Write an expression for the amount of money that Jane has on the nth day.

The table shows the positions and values of the terms in the sequence.	Each day Jane gets $5. Therefore, on the nth day, Jane has received $5 \times n = 5n$ dollars.	Here is the sequence shown in pictures showing the groups of 5s:

Position/ Day	Term/ Money
1	$6
2	$11
3	$16
4	$21
5	$26

She also has an extra $1 from the start.

So the sequence has an nth term of $5n + 1$.

6    $5 \times 1 + 1$

11    $5 \times 2 + 1$

16    $5 \times 3 + 1$

The position to term rule is 'multiply by 5 and add 1' or $n \rightarrow \times 5 \rightarrow +1$ Therefore, the nth term is $5n + 1$.		21 $5 \times 4 + 1$
		26 $5 \times 5 + 1$
		So the nth term will be made of $5 \times n$ or $5n$ red squares and 1 yellow square.

Discuss

Why is a position-to-term rule more useful than a term-to-term rule?

Exercise 1

1 Match each nth term to the sequence it describes.

$3n + 1$	7, 9, 11, 13, …
$3n$	2, 4, 6, 8, …
$2n$	7, 11, 15, 19, …
$2n + 5$	3, 6, 9, 12, …
$4n$	4, 7, 10, 13, …
$5n - 2$	4, 8, 12, 16, …
$4n + 3$	3, 8, 13, 18, …

2 For each sequence:

i) draw the next pattern

ii) find a position-to-term rule

iii) give an expression for the number of squares in Pattern n.

a)
Pattern 1   Pattern 2   Pattern 3   Pattern 4

b)
Pattern 1   Pattern 2   Pattern 3   Pattern 4

c)

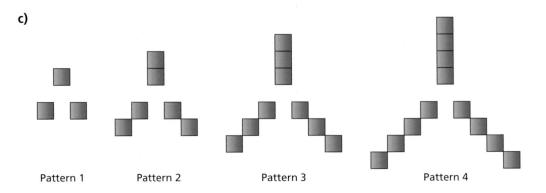

| Pattern 1 | Pattern 2 | Pattern 3 | Pattern 4 |

3 For each sequence:

  i) draw the next pattern

  ii) write an expression for the number of grey squares in Pattern n

  iii) write an expression for the number of white squares in Pattern n

  iv) write an expression for the total number of squares in Pattern n.

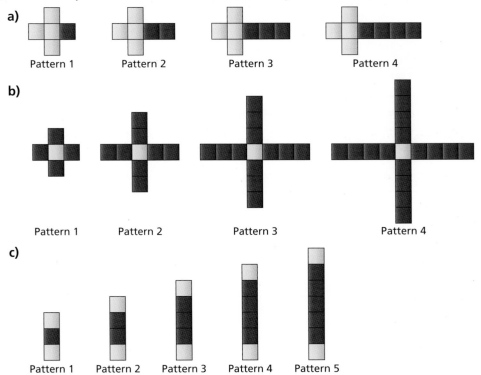

a)

| Pattern 1 | Pattern 2 | Pattern 3 | Pattern 4 |

b)

| Pattern 1 | Pattern 2 | Pattern 3 | Pattern 4 |

c)

| Pattern 1 | Pattern 2 | Pattern 3 | Pattern 4 | Pattern 5 |

4 Write an expression for the number of squares in Pattern n of each sequence.

a)

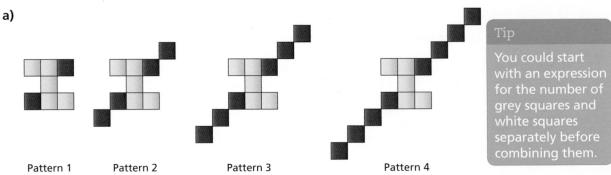

| Pattern 1 | Pattern 2 | Pattern 3 | Pattern 4 |

> **Tip**
>
> You could start with an expression for the number of grey squares and white squares separately before combining them.

b)

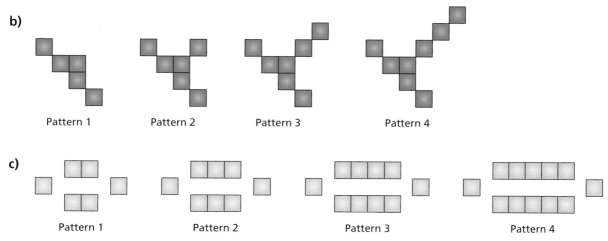

Pattern 1   Pattern 2   Pattern 3   Pattern 4

c)

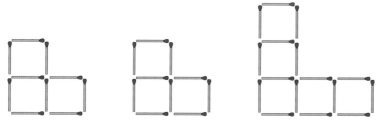

Pattern 1   Pattern 2   Pattern 3   Pattern 4

5 Javinder has $40. Every day she earns $2 for completing her chores at home.

    a) How much money will Javinder have after 4 days?

    b) Write an expression for the amount of money she will have after *n* days.

    c) How much money will she have after 50 days?

> **Tip**
>
> Draw diagrams to show how much money Javinder has.

> **Did you know?**
>
> You can find the value of any term by substituting the position number into your expression for the *n*th term. For example, if your *n*th term is $4n + 10$, the 50th term will be $4 \times 50 + 10 = 210$.

6 Ansar is building a pattern out of matchsticks. Here are the first three patterns.

    a) Draw the 4th pattern.

    b) Write an expression for the number of matchsticks needed to make the *n*th term in the pattern.

    c) Use your expression to calculate the number of matchsticks needed to make the 25th pattern.

7 Jeegar is using a calculator to add multiples of 0.3 to a number to form a sequence. He starts with 6 and keeps adding 0.3.

    a) Try this out yourself with a calculator.

    b) Write down the first 5 terms of Jeegar's sequence.

    c) Write an expression for the *n*th term of the sequence.

    d) Use your expression to find the value of the 100th term in Jeegar's sequence.

How can you use your expression to produce a spreadsheet formula that will calculate any term of your sequence straight away?

8 Helena makes this sequence of squares:

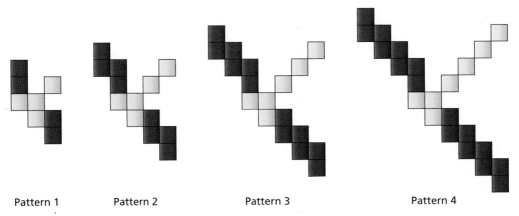

Pattern 1   Pattern 2   Pattern 3   Pattern 4

Write down if the following statements are true or false.

There are 20 grey squares and 8 white squares in Pattern 5.

There are 4n grey squares in Pattern n.

There are n white squares in Pattern n.

The total number of squares in Pattern n is 5n + 3.

There are 40 grey squares and 16 white squares in Pattern 10.

Correct any statements that you say are false.

9 a) Write an expression for the number of squares in Pattern n of this sequence.

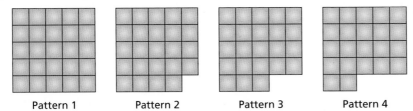

Pattern 1   Pattern 2   Pattern 3   Pattern 4

b) Using your expression, what will the 26th term of the sequence be?

Explain why this is by referring to the pattern above.

10 **Vocabulary feature question**

Complete the sentences using words from the box.

term	pattern n	nth term	term-to-term rule
position-to-term rule	expression	arithmetic sequence	difference

Any sequence that goes up or down by the same amount between terms is called an _____

It has a _____ of +a or –a where a is a fixed number. We say that the terms of the sequence have a fixed _____

You can find the _____ for a sequence in words, such as 'multiply by 2 and add 1' or we can write an algebraic _____ for it, called the _____

When our sequence is a pattern, the nth term tells us the number of items in _____ of the sequence.

You can use your expression to find the value of any _____ in the sequence as long as you know its position.

> **Did you know?**
>
> Halley's Comet is a frozen lump of gas and rock that orbits the sun. It was sighted in 1531, 1607 and 1682. Edmond Halley used arithmetic sequences with these years to predict that the comet would be seen again in 1758.

End of chapter reflection

You should know that ...	You should be able to ...	Such as ...
An arithmetic sequence is one with a term-to-term rule of +a or –a, where a is a constant number.		
The nth term of a sequence is an expression for the value of the term in position n.	Write an algebraic expression for the number of items in pattern n.	Write an expression for the number of squares in pattern n.
You can find any term from the nth term by substituting into the expression.	Explain your expression by linking it to the pattern or problem.	Explain how your expression above relates to the number of orange squares and red squares in each pattern.

Geometrical reasoning and proof

You will learn how to:
- Understand a proof that:
  - the angle sum of a triangle is 180° and that of a quadrilateral is 360°
  - the exterior angle of a triangle is equal to the sum of the two interior opposite angles.
- Solve geometrical problems using properties of angles, parallel and intersecting lines, triangles and special quadrilaterals, explaining reasoning with diagrams and text.

Starting point

Do you remember …?

- the sum of the angles in a triangle and a quadrilateral?
- how to find a missing angle in a triangle or a quadrilateral?

  For example, what is the size of angle *x* in this diagram?

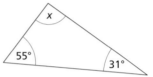

- the sum of angles at a point and on a straight line?
- how to find a missing angle at a point or on a straight line?

  For example, what is the size of angle *x* in this diagram?

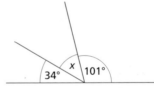

- that vertically opposite angles are equal?
- how to identify alternate and corresponding angles on parallel lines?

  For example, which of these angles are alternate with angle *a*?

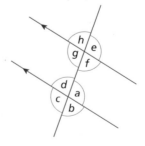

This will also be helpful when you:

- learn how to calculate the interior or exterior angle of any regular polygon.

Hook

Naz is investigating the angles formed by the diagonals of quadrilaterals.

He starts with a square and notices that the diagonals form four right angles.

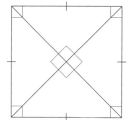

- Which other quadrilaterals have diagonals that meet at right angles?

- Can you find a quadrilateral that has diagonals that do not meet at right angles? What angles do the diagonals form?

- What do you notice about the sum of the angles produced at the point where the diagonals of a quadrilateral intersect? Is this always true? How do you know?

- Naz notices that drawing on the diagonals of a square produces 4 small triangles that meet at the centre.

  What is the sum of all twelve of the angles in these four triangles?

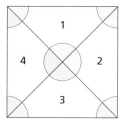

- Use the angle sum from the four triangles and the angle sum at the point where the diagonals intersect to show that the angles in a square must add up to 360°.

- Use a similar approach to show that the angles in a parallelogram must sum to 360°.

Proving angle facts

Key terms

The angles inside a shape are called **interior** angles.

The **exterior** angle of a shape is the angle between one side of the shape and the line created if the next side is extended outwards.

For example:

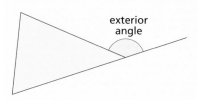

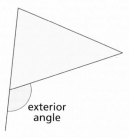

Is there only one position for the exterior angle at each vertex? If there is more than one possibility, where else could the exterior angle be?

Worked example 1

Complete this proof to show that the exterior angle of a triangle is equal to the sum of the two interior opposite angles.

Here is a triangle, with interior angles of size $a°$ and $b°$.

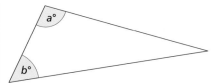

The final interior angle of the triangle is an angle of size $c°$.

a) Write a formula for c in terms of a and b.

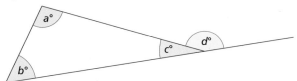

An exterior angle of the triangle of size $d°$ is shown in the diagram.

b) Write a formula connecting angles c and d.

c) Use the two formulae to show that $d = a + b$.

a) The final interior angle of the triangle, c, has size $180 - a - b°$ because the angles in a triangle sum to 180°.	We do not know the sizes of angles a and b but we find the final angle by subtracting these from 180°.
b) Angles c and d lie on a straight line together and the sum of angles on a straight line is **180°**. So the exterior angle, $d = 180 - c$	
c) Using the two expressions above: $d = 180 - (180 - a - b)$ $d = 180 - 180 + a + b$ $d = a + b$	Substituting for c Expanding the bracket Simplifying

You should be able to explain each step of your working out using a geometrical reason or rule.

1 **a)** Use dynamic geometry software to construct a triangle with a line through one vertex that is parallel to the opposite side of the triangle. For example:

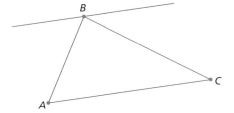

b) Use the software to calculate the size of the angles marked in the diagram below.

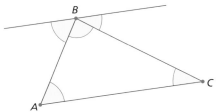

Are any of the angles equal?

c) Drag any of the triangle's vertices to a new position. What do you notice about the angles that were equal before? Are they still equal?

2 Complete this proof to show that the sum of the angles in a triangle is 180°.

Here is a triangle with angles a, b and c and a line drawn parallel to the base through the top vertex. Two further angles, d and e, have been labelled.

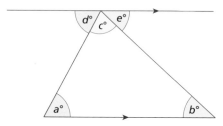

1 $a = d$	(because ....)
2 $b = e$	(because ....)
3 So the sum of the angles in the triangle $= a + b + c$ $= \ldots + \ldots + c$	(substituting for a and b using steps 1. and 2. above)
4 $= 180°$	(because ....)

3 Put these statements in order to produce a proof that the sum of the angles in a quadrilateral is 360°.

Look at triangle *BCD*.

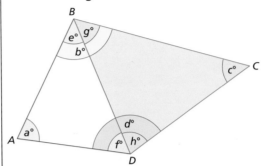

Since this is a triangle, $c + g + h = 180°$ because the angles in a triangle sum to 180°.

Divide the quadrilateral into two pieces using a diagonal from one vertex to the opposite vertex.

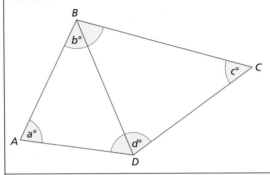

The sum of the angles in the quadrilateral:

$= a + b + c + d$

$= a + (e + g) + c + (f + h)$

$= a + e + f + c + g + h$

$= 180° + 180°$

$= 360°$

Here is a quadrilateral *ABCD*.

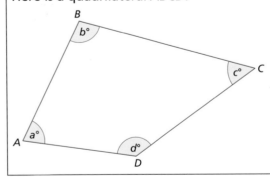

Look at triangle *ABD*.

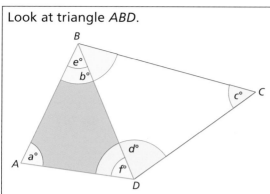

Since this is a triangle, $a + e + f = 180°$ because the angles in a triangle sum to $180°$.

4 Use this diagram to explain why the exterior angle of a triangle must be equal to the sum of the two interior opposite angles.

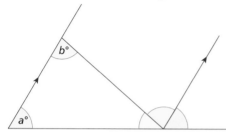

5 Complete this proof to show that the exterior angle of a quadrilateral is equal to the sum of the three interior opposite angles less $180°$.

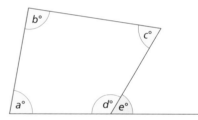

Here is a quadrilateral with angles of sizes *a*, *b*, *c* and *d* and a marked exterior angle of size *e*.

1 $d = 360° - (a + b + c)$	(because ....)
2 $e = 180 - d$	(because ....)
3 $\quad = 180° - (360° - (a + b + c))$	(substituting for *d*)
4 $\quad = ...$	(expanding the brackets)
5 $\quad = a + b + c - 180$	(simplifying)
6 $\quad$ = sum of opposite interior angles $- 180°$	(because ....)

Did you know?

The first person to prove these results and write them down was Euclid, a Greek mathematician. He wrote a set of 13 books about geometry called 'The Elements' around 300 BC which proved all the geometric key facts such as the sum of the angles in a triangle from just five basic statements or axioms.

Worked example 2

ABCDE is a pentagon.

ADE is an isosceles triangle and the lines *AD* and *BC* are parallel.

a) Find the size of angle *DEA*.

b) Find the size of angle *DCB*.

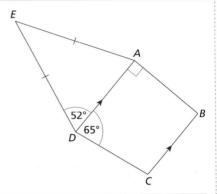

Angle *DEA* and angle *DCB* are marked on the diagram.

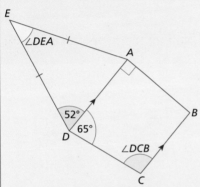

a) angle *DAE* = angle *EDA* = 52° because the triangle is isosceles.

Therefore, angle *DEA* = 180° − 52° − 52° = 76° because the angles in a triangle sum to 180°.

b) If we extend the line *BC*, we can see that angle *ADC* = angle *DCF* because these are alternate angles.

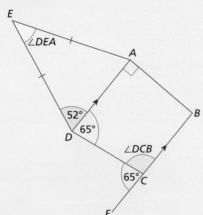

Therefore, angle *DCB* = 180 − angle *DCT* since these angles lie on a straight line and angles on a straight line sum to 180°.

So angle *DCB* = 180 − 65 = 115°.

1 Find the size of the angles marked with letters in each diagram, stating the geometrical reason for each step of your working out.

a)

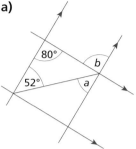

b)

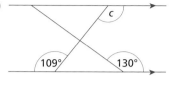

c)

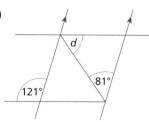

2 Find the size of the angles marked with letters in each diagram, stating the geometrical reason for each step of your working out.

a)

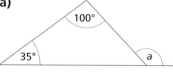

b)

c)

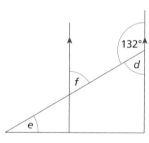

d)

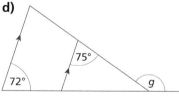

e)

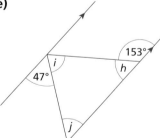

3 ACD and ABE are triangles and the lines EB and DC are parallel.

a) Find all the unknown angles, stating the geometrical reasons for each step of your working out.

b) What is the name of shape BCDE?

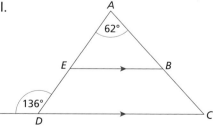

4 Saira is trying to find the value of angle *BCD*.

She says, 'It must be 25° because it is the same as the angle next to it.'

Saira is incorrect.

Explain how she could find angle *BCD* using geometrical reasoning.

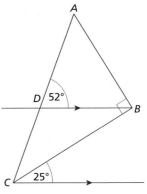

5 Find the size of each of the lettered angles marked below, stating the geometrical reason for each step of your working out.

a)

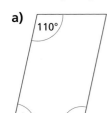

b)

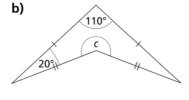

c)

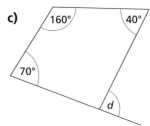

d)

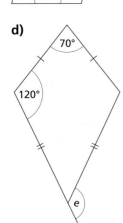

e)

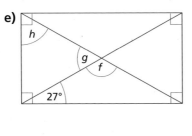

6 *ABDE* is a parallelogram and *BCD* is an isosceles triangle.

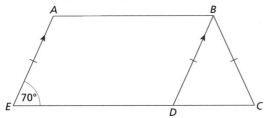

Find the value of angle *DBC*.

7 *ABDE* is a kite and *BCD* is an isosceles triangle. Calculate the size of angle *EAB*.

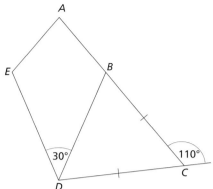

8 Write an angle question for your partner to solve. Draw a diagram with a missing angle, *x*. The answer should be 48°.

Can you make your question into a 2 or 3-step problem that uses several angle facts or rules?

9 Vocabulary feature question

Complete the sentences using words from the box.

exterior angle	angles in a triangle	angles in a quadrilateral
interior angle	alternate	opposite
equal	corresponding angles	vertically opposite

An angle inside a shape is called an _____

The angle formed outside a shape between one side and the extension of the next side is called an _____

The exterior angle of a triangle is _____ to the sum of the _____ interior angles.

We can use angle rules and shape properties to find the value of a missing angle. For example, _____ angles and _____ angles may be found on parallel lines crossed by a transversal and are equal.

When any two lines intersect two pairs of _____ equal angles are formed.

Angles on a straight line and _____ sum to 180°.

Angles around a point and _____ sum to 360°.

End of chapter reflection

You should know that ...	You should be able to ...	Such as ...
The exterior angle of shape is found between one side of the shape and the extension of the next side. The exterior angle of a triangle is equal to the sum of the two opposite interior angles. The angles in a triangle sum to 180°. The angles in a quadrilateral sum to 360°.	Understand a proof that: The angle sum of a triangle is 180° and that of a quadrilateral is 360°. The exterior angle of a triangle is equal to the sum of the two interior opposite angles.	Complete the reasons for each step of the proof that the exterior angle of a triangle is equal to the sum of the two interior opposite angles. **1** $c = 180 - a - b$ (because .....) **2** $d = 180 - c$ (because ....) **3** So $d = 180 - (180 - a - b)$ (substituting for ....) **4** So $d = a + b$ (..........................)
Angle facts can be used to work out missing angles.	Find a missing angle in a diagram, explaining each step using known geometrical facts and rules.	*ABC* is an isosceles triangle. *BCDE* is a kite. Find the value of angle *x*.

Unit 3C

Handling data and measures

What it's all about?

- Constructing triangles
- Comparing pie charts
- Enlarging shapes
- Real life graphs
- Experimental probability

You will learn about:

- using compasses and a ruler to construct circles and triangles
- comparing proportions from pie charts
- drawing the enlargement of a shape
- representing a real life situation as a graph
- comparing results from a probability experiment with those that were expected

You will build your skills in:

- accurate drawing and constructions
- using mathematics to represent real life situations
- making statistical comparisons

Circles

You will learn how to:
- Use a ruler and compasses to construct:
  - circles and arcs
  - a triangle, given three sides (SSS)
  - a triangle, given a right angle, hypotenuse and one side (RHS).
- Define a circle and learn the names of its parts; know and use formulae for the circumference and area of a circle.
- Compare proportions in two pie charts that represent different totals.

Starting point

Do you remember ...?

- how to substitute in formulae?

  For example, if $b = 3a$ find the value of b when $a = 5$.
- the order of operations (BIDMAS)?

  For example, work out 3×5^2.
- how to draw and interpret simple pie charts?

This will also be helpful when you:

- use a straight edge and pair of compasses for other constructions.
- learn about loci.
- solve problems involving the circumference and area of circles.
- find the surface area and volume of cylinders.

Hook

You will need to be in a group of four or more for this activity.

You will need some chalk, a tape measure and some string.

Draw a 2 m straight line on the floor (or playground). One person should stand on each end of the line.

Measure out two 2 m lengths of string. Give one piece to each of the people standing at the end of the line, they should each hold one end of their piece of string.

The third and fourth person in the group should hold the other end of one of the pieces of string and move to a position where the pieces of string are tight.

The third and fourth people should walk around keeping their pieces of string tight. They should stop when they meet.

What type of triangle would you see if you looked down from above?

What shapes were the third and fourth people making as they moved?

If your school has a camera and a tall building then you can get someone to take a picture of the triangle out of one of the windows.

Draw other triangles using this same process but with the chalk line 3 m long and the strings both 2 m long. What type of triangle would you see if you looked down from above?

Investigate for different lengths of chalk line and different lengths of string.

Circles, arcs and constructing triangles

Did you know?

The triangle is the only polygon that cannot be deformed without changing the lengths of one of its sides.

For example, a square is easily deformed to make a rhombus and a rectangle is easily deformed to make a parallelogram.

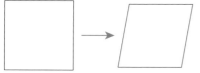

This is why triangles are used a lot in construction.

Use the internet to find other images of triangles being used in construction.

Key terms

A **circle** is a 2-dimensional shape made by drawing a curve where all of the points are the same distance from a centre.

The edge of a circle is called the **circumference**. An **arc** is part of the circumference of a circle.

A **radius** of a circle is a straight line from its centre to its circumference.

The **diameter** of a circle is a straight line that passes through the centre of the circle and has its ends on the circumference.

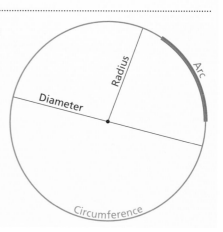

Use a ruler and a pair of compasses to construct a triangle with side lengths of 7 cm, 4 cm and 5 cm.

A ———————— B 7 cm	Start by drawing a 7 cm line using your ruler. Remember to write the lengths on your sides as you draw the triangle.
	Now open your pair of compasses so that the distance between the point and the tip of the pencil is 4 cm.
	Put the point of your pair of compasses at A and draw an arc. Make sure that the pair of compasses stays opened to 4 cm.
	Now open your pair of compasses to 5 cm and draw an arc with the point of the compasses at point B.
	Join the ends of the base line to one of the points where the arcs cross.

Use a ruler and a pair of compasses to construct a triangle with a right angle, a hypotenuse of length 9 cm and a side of length 6 cm.

	Start by drawing a straight line.
	Make a mark part way along the line.
	We need to draw a right angle at the point marked. Open your pair of compasses and use them to make arcs crossing the line on either side of the marked point.
	Open your pair of compasses further and draw an arc from each of points A and B.
	Draw a straight line through the two points where the arcs cross. The angle formed with the horizontal line is 90°. Measure 6 cm along the vertical line and make a mark, labelling this point c.
	Open your pair of compasses to 9 cm (the length of the hypotenuse). Draw an arc from the point c. Join the point c to the point where the 9 cm arc crosses the horizontal line.

Discuss

If you are given three sides is there only one possible triangle?

If you are told that a triangle has a right angle and given the length of a side and length of the hypotenuse is there only one possible triangle?

If you were given three angles is there only one possible triangle?

1 Draw a circle with:

   a) radius 7 cm   **b)** radius 5 cm   **c)** diameter 12 cm.

2 Draw an arc with a centre of *A* passing through *B* and *C*.

B ●   ● *C*

                ●
                A

3 Use some 1 cm squared paper for this question.

   Mark squares with side length 8 cm.

   Draw a circle of radius 4 cm in the centre of each square.

   Draw circles of radius 4 cm on the corner of each square.

   Extend the pattern to cover your sheet of paper.

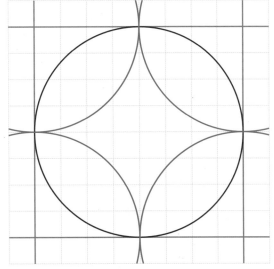

4 Construct this diagram on cm squared paper. The square should have sides of length 4 cm.

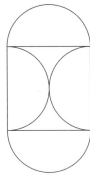

5 Construct a triangle with sides measuring:

a) 8 cm, 6 cm, 5 cm 　　　 b) 3 cm, 4 cm, 5 cm 　　　 c) 6 cm, 8 cm, 6 cm

d) 7.5 cm, 6.3 cm, 4.7 cm 　 e) 7.3 cm, 7.3 cm, 7.3 cm 　 f) 5.4 cm, 8.5 cm, 4.2 cm

g) Identify the types of triangle drawn in parts a) to f).

6 Construct a triangle ABC with:

a) $ABC = 90°$, $AC = 6$ cm, $AB = 10$ cm 　　　 b) $ABC = 90°$, $AC = 4.5$ cm, $AB = 7.8$ cm

7 Amare is constructing a SSS triangle with side lengths 6 cm, 5.5 cm and 7.3 cm

Here is his diagram.

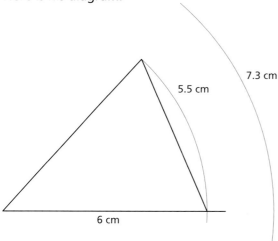

Identify the mistakes in Amare's work and draw an accurate version of the triangle.

8 Write down a set of step-by-step instructions to show a student how to construct a RHS triangle.

9 Roll a 10-sided dice three times.

a) Try to construct a triangle with side lengths in centimetres equal to your three dice rolls.

b) Repeat this process. Which combinations of lengths can you draw a triangle for? Which combinations of lengths do not give triangles?

c) Can you find a rule to check whether three side lengths will give a triangle without having to draw it?

10 Roll a 10-sided dice twice.

a) Try to construct a triangle with a right-angle, a side length in centimetres equal to your smaller dice roll and a hypotenuse equal in length to the larger dice roll.

b) Repeat this process. Which combinations of lengths can you draw a RHS triangle for? Which combinations of lengths do not give RHS triangles?

c) Can you find a rule to check whether two side lengths will give a RHS triangle without having to draw it?

11 Use a ruler and pair of compasses to construct a rhombus with side length 6 cm.

Tip

Think about how to construct equal length sides using a pair of compasses.

Circumference and area of a circle

Key terms

A line that connects any two points on the circumference of the circle is called a **chord**.

A **diameter** is a chord that passes through the centre of the circle.

A diameter divides the circle into two **semicircles**.

A chord divides a circle into two **segments**.

Two radii form a **sector**.

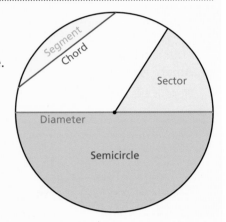

Did you know?

When we calculate the circumference or the area of a circle we use π (pi). Pi has an infinite number of decimal places, so we will never know every single digit of pi. The ancient Chinese were happy to use 3 as a value for π, and the Babylonians (in 2000 B) used the fraction $3\frac{1}{8}$. By 1665, Sir Isaac Newton had calculated pi to 16 decimal places. Later, the use of computers meant that the number of known decimal places of π had increased to 2037 in 1949 and to greater than 1 million digits by 1973. By 2016 Peter Trueb had calculated π to almost 22.5 trillion digits!

The formulae to calculate the circumference, C, and area, A, of a circle are:

$C = \pi d$ or $C = 2\pi r$ $\qquad\qquad A = \pi r^2$

where d is the diameter and r is the radius of the circle.

Worked example 3

A circle has radius 6 cm. Find:

a) the circumference of the circle

b) the area of the circle.

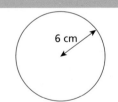

Give your answers correct to one decimal place.

a) $C = 2\pi r$ $\quad C = 2 \times \pi \times 6$ $\qquad = 37.7$ cm (1 d.p.)	To work out circumference, use the formula $C = 2\pi r$ and substitute $r = 6$. Use a calculator to work out the circumference and give our the answer to 1 d.p.
b) $A = \pi r^2$ $\quad A = \pi r^2$ $\qquad = \pi \times 6^2$ $\qquad = 113.1$ cm^2 (1 d.p.)	To work out the area of the circle, use the formula $A = \pi r^2$ and substitute $r = 6$. Use a calculator to work out the area and give the answer to 1 d.p.

Exercise 2

1 Vocabulary feature question

a) Complete the sentences using words from the box.

| radius | diameter | circle | chord | arc |
| semicircles | circumference | segments | sector | |

In a _____ all of the points are the same distance from the centre. The edge of

a _____ is called the _____ . An _____ is part of

the circumference of a circle.

A _____ of a circle is a line from its centre to its circumference.

A line that connects any two points on the circumference of the circle is called a_____ .

If this passes through the centre of the circle then it is a _____ .

A diameter divides a circle into two _____ . A chord divides a circle into two

_____ .

b) One of the words from the box was not used. Write a definition for this word.

2 Work out, correct to 1 decimal place, the circumference of a circle with diameter:

a) 9 cm   **b)** 7.4 cm   **c)** 12.5 m   **d)** 53 mm

3 Work out, correct to 1 decimal place, the circumference of a circle with radius:

a) 5 cm   **b)** 4.2 cm   **c)** 6.1 m   **d)** 37 mm

4 Match each circle to the value of its circumference (rounded to 1 decimal place).

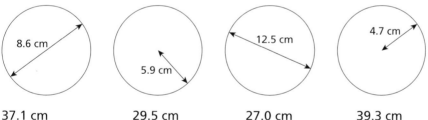

37.1 cm   29.5 cm   27.0 cm   39.3 cm

Discuss

Could you have matched the correct answer to each of the pictures without using a calculator?

5 Work out, correct to one decimal place, the area of a circle with:

a) radius = 5.2 cm   **b)** radius = 3.7 m   **c)** radius = 26 mm

d) diameter = 12.8 cm   **e)** diameter = 7.6 m   **f)** diameter = 86 mm

Tip

The formula for area of a circle is $A = \pi r^2$ where r is the radius.
How can you find the radius if you know the diameter?

6 Copy and complete the table.

Radius	Diameter	Circumference (rounded to 1 decimal place)	Area (rounded to nearest whole number)
6.8 cm			
	11.6 cm		
2.1 m			
	134 mm		

7 Priya has completed her homework on circumference and area of circles.

Are her answers correct?

If her answer is wrong, then explain what mistake she has made.

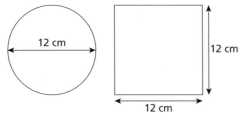

$C = \pi d$ $A = \pi r^2$
$C = \pi \times 4.6$ $A = \pi \times 4.6^2$
  $= 14.5$ cm $= 66.5$ cm

$C = \pi d$ $A = \pi r^2$
$C = \pi \times 12.4$ $A = \pi \times 6.2^2$
  $= 39.0$ cm $= \pi \times 12.4$
    $= 39.0$ cm

8 Find the difference in the areas of these two shapes.

Give your answer correct to one decimal place.

12 cm

12 cm

12 cm

9 For each statement below say whether it is always true, sometimes true or never true. Give reasons for your answers.

The circumference of a circle is greater than its diameter.

The area of a circle is greater than 1 cm².

The area of a sector of a circle is greater than the area of a segment of that circle.

Tip

Try drawing some circles and shading different possible sectors and segments.

10 For each of the shapes shown below find:

i) the perimeter of the shape   **ii)** the area of the shape.

Give your answers correct to one decimal place.

a)

14.6 cm

b)

6.4 cm

c)

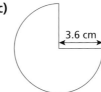

3.6 cm

Think about

How could you find the area of a sector of a circle if you knew the angle formed at the centre of the circle?

11 Find the shaded area of the shape shown below.

Give your answer correct to one decimal place.

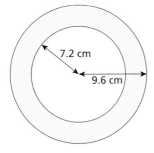

7.2 cm

9.6 cm

Comparing proportions in pie charts

Key terms
....

A **pie chart** shows the proportions of the whole.

Worked example 4

A company that runs holiday cruises has two ships, the Starlight and the Suncatcher.

The Starlight has 120 cabins and the Suncatcher has 600 cabins.

The pie charts show the different types of cabin available on each of the ships.

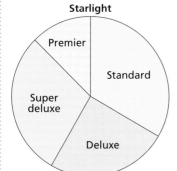

Starlight

Premier

Standard

Super
deluxe

Deluxe

Suncatcher

Standard

Premier

Deluxe

Super
deluxe

a) Write down three comparisons based on the pie charts.

b) Blessy says,

'There are more standard cabins on the Starlight than on the Suncatcher.'

Do the pie charts support what Blessy says?

a) Standard is the most common type of cabin on the Starlight, but super deluxe is the most common type of cabin on the Suncatcher. The deluxe cabin was the same proportion of the cabin types on both the Starlight and the Suncatcher. Premier is the least common type of cabin on the Starlight, but standard is the least common type of cabin on the Suncatcher.	The largest sector of each pie chart shows the most frequent type of cabin for that ship. The pie charts show the proportion of the total number of cabins that are of each type. The sector for deluxe is the same fraction of the pie chart for both Starlight and Suncatcher. The smallest sector of each pie chart shows the least frequent type of cabin for that ship.
b) Blessy has not taken into account the different numbers of cabins represented by each of the pie charts. Standard cabins represent a greater proportion of the cabins on Starlight than on Suncatcher, but there are more cabins on Suncatcher. Around $\frac{1}{3}$ of the cabins on Starlight are standard cabins. $\frac{1}{3}$ of 120 = 40. Around $\frac{1}{8}$ of the cabins on Suncatcher are standard cabins. $\frac{1}{8}$ of 600 = 75. Blessy is incorrect. There are more standard cabins on Suncatcher.	We need to remember that the two pie charts do not represent the same total number. The pie chart for Starlight represents 120 cabins and the pie chart for Suncatcher represents 600 cabins. We can use the approximate fractions of the whole and the total number of cabins represented on each pie chart to check the claim.

> **Tip**
>
> Watch out when comparing two pie charts with different total frequencies. Remember that pie charts show the proportion of the whole.

Exercise 3

1 The pie charts show how Aiko and Tamika spend their pocket money.

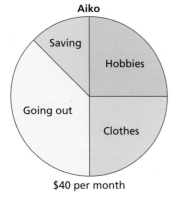

$40 per month

$20 per month

Write down if each of the conclusions below is true or false.

Tamika spends a greater proportion of her monthly pocket money on clothes than Aiko does.

Aiko spends a smaller proportion of her monthly pocket money on going out than Tamika does.

Aiko and Tamika save the same amount of money each month.

Aiko spends more money per month on hobbies than Tamika.

2 The pie charts show how land is used in India and in the UK.

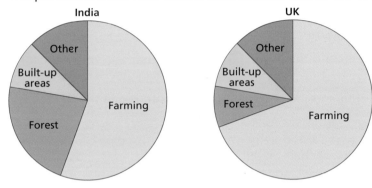

a) Write down three comparisons based on the pie charts.

b) What additional information would you need to be able to compare the amount of land that was used for farming in India and the UK?

3 The pie charts show how students travel to school at Alta Academy and Colham College.

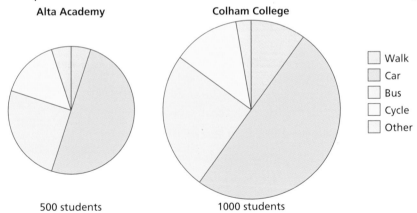

Walk
Car
Bus
Cycle
Other

a) Write down the two methods of transport that were used by the same **proportion** of students at Alta Academy and at Colham College.

   Walk   Car   Bus   Cycle   Other

b) Which school has the larger **number** of students travelling to school by bus?

   Show how you worked out your answer.

4 The pie charts show the favourite type of movie for some children and some adults.

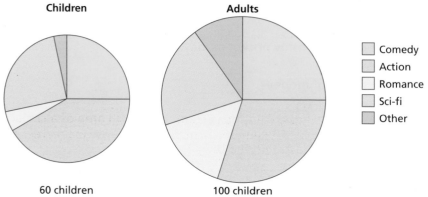

Children

Adults

60 children

100 children

Comedy
Action
Romance
Sci-fi
Other

a) Compare the proportion of children and the proportion of adults that said their favourite type of movie was romance.

b) Compare the proportion of children and the proportion of adults that said their favourite type of movie was action.

c) Compare the number of children who said comedy was their favourite type of movie and the number of adults who said comedy was their favourite type of movie.

d) Give a possible reason why the adults pie chart has been drawn with a larger radius than the pie chart for children.

5 The table gives some information about two pie charts that are to be drawn to represent the types of houses in two towns.

Town	Number of houses	Radius for pie chart
Hachi	1400	5 cm
Kutrah	5600	10 cm

a) Work out the area of each of the two pie charts. Give your answer correct to 1 decimal place.

b) Work out the following calculations:

Number of houses in Kutrah ÷ Number of houses in Hachi

Radius of pie chart for Kutrah ÷ Radius of pie chart for Hachi

Area of pie chart for Kutrah ÷ Area of pie chart for Hachi

Compare your answers. What do you notice?

End of chapter reflection

You should know that ...	You should be able to ...	Such as ...
You can use compasses to construct circles and arcs.	Draw a circle with a given radius. Draw an arc.	Draw a circle with radius 5 cm.

You can use a ruler and compasses to construct a triangle if given three sides (SSS) or given a right angle, hypotenuse and one side (RHS).	Construct a triangle given three sides (SSS). Construct a triangle given a right angle, hypotenuse and one side (RHS).	Use a ruler and compasses to construct a triangle with side lengths 9 cm, 6 cm, 5 cm. Use a ruler and compasses to construct a triangle with a right angle, a hypotenuse of 12 cm and a side of 7 cm.
Parts of a circle can be labelled as the radius, the diameter, the circumference, an arc, a chord, a segment and a sector.	Calculate the circumference and area of a circle given its radius or diameter. Label the different parts of a circle.	Calculate the circumference and area of a circle with diameter 7 cm. Give your answers correct to 1 decimal place. Draw a circle and label it to show the circumference, a radius and a diameter.
You can compare the proportions shown in two pie charts that represent different totals.	Make comparisons between two pie charts representing different totals.	Aiko Tamika Saving Hobbies Saving Hobbies Going out Going out Going out Clothes Clothes $40 per month $20 per month Make **two** comparisons between the spending habits of Aiko and Tamika.

Enlargement

You will learn how to:

• Understand and use the language and notation associated with enlargement; enlarge 2D shapes, given a centre of enlargement and a positive integer scale factor.

Starting point

Do you remember …?

• how to reflect a shape in a mirror line?
• how to rotate a shape about a given point?
• how to translate a shape horizontally and vertically?
• that the image of a reflection, rotation or translation is congruent to the original shape?

This will also be helpful when you:

• learn to use a coordinate grid for combined transformations.

Hook

Here is an investigation for two or more people.

Each person must draw a square onto squared paper independently.

Now compare the squares.

What is the same about every square drawn?

What are the differences?

Can you describe the difference between any two squares using numerical values?

Key terms

An **enlargement** is when you transform a shape to make it either bigger or smaller. The new shape is called an **image**.

The image will be **similar** to the original shape. This means that the side lengths will remain in the same ratio.

The **scale factor** is how many times bigger the **image** will be.

The **centre of enlargement** is the point from which the shape has been enlarged.

The corners of a shape are known as the **vertices**.

Worked example 1

Enlarge each shape with the given scale factor.

a)

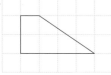

Scale factor 2

b)

Scale factor 4

a) 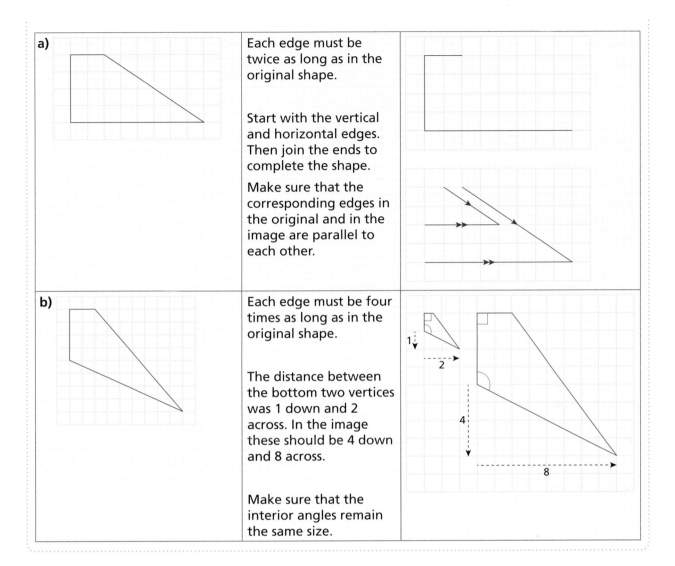	Each edge must be twice as long as in the original shape. Start with the vertical and horizontal edges. Then join the ends to complete the shape. Make sure that the corresponding edges in the original and in the image are parallel to each other.	
b)	Each edge must be four times as long as in the original shape. The distance between the bottom two vertices was 1 down and 2 across. In the image these should be 4 down and 8 across. Make sure that the interior angles remain the same size.	

Key terms

The **centre of enlargement** is the point from which the shape has been enlarged. It determines the final position of the **image**.

Worked example 2

Enlarge the shape by scale factor 3 from the centre of enlargement.

a)

b)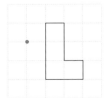

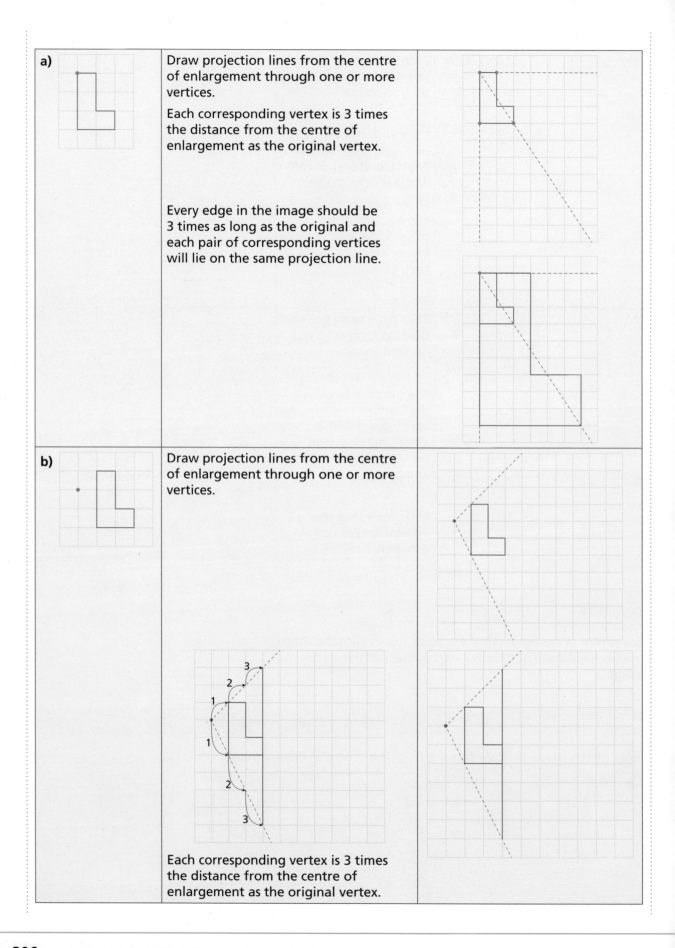

a)

Draw projection lines from the centre of enlargement through one or more vertices.

Each corresponding vertex is 3 times the distance from the centre of enlargement as the original vertex.

Every edge in the image should be 3 times as long as the original and each pair of corresponding vertices will lie on the same projection line.

b)

Draw projection lines from the centre of enlargement through one or more vertices.

Each corresponding vertex is 3 times the distance from the centre of enlargement as the original vertex.

	Every edge in the image should be 3 times as long as the original and each pair of corresponding vertices will lie on the same projection line. Use these facts to complete the image. Do not erase any of your construction lines because these will show your method.	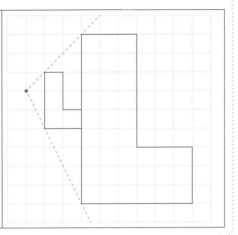

Think about

If you shine a torch onto your hand, you can make a shadow appear on the wall.

What happens to the shadow if you move the torch left, right, up, down, closer to or further away from your hand?

Exercise 1

1 **a)** Write the letters of the shapes that are **not** enlargements of the original rectangle A.

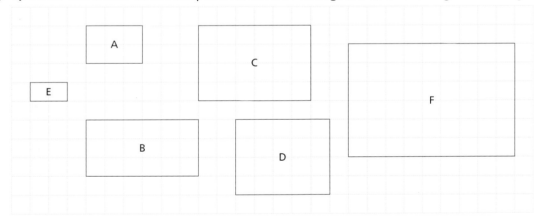

b) Identify the scale factor of any of the shapes which are an enlargement of A.

Tip

When enlarging a slanted line, count the number of squares it covers horizontally and vertically and multiply this by the scale factor for the new line.

For example, 2 right and 1 down becomes 6 right and 3 down when using a scale factor of 3.

Notice that the corresponding lines are parallel.

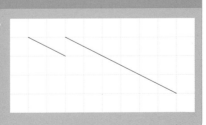

2 The following shapes are drawn onto cm squared paper.

Enlarge each shape by the scale factor given.

a)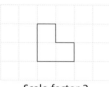

Scale factor 2

b)

Scale factor 3

c)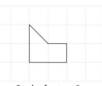

Scale factor 3

d)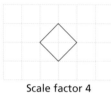

Scale factor 4

e)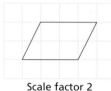

Scale factor 2

f)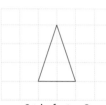

Scale factor 3

Discuss

What would the image look like if you enlarged a rectangle by a scale factor of 1?

3 The quadrilateral is drawn onto cm squared paper.

a) Enlarge the shape by a scale factor of 2.

b) Enlarge the shape by a scale factor of 3.

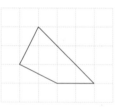

Did you know?

When you resize an image on a word processor by dragging a corner, you are enlarging the image. The corner that stays in the same position is the centre of enlargement.

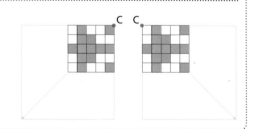

4 Copy each shape onto cm squared paper.

Enlarge each shape by the given scale factor from the centre of enlargement O.

a)

Scale factor 3

b)

Scale factor 2

c)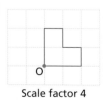

Scale factor 4

d)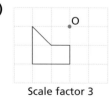

Scale factor 3

5 Eden draws a rectangle with length 3 cm and width 2 cm.

Joel says, 'If you enlarge it by a scale factor of 5 the width will be 15 cm.'

a) Explain why Joel is incorrect.

b) Work out the correct length and the width of the enlargement.

> **Think about**
>
> What is the area of this rectangle?
>
> If you enlarge the rectangle by a scale factor 2, what will the new area be?
>
> Try this out with different scale factors.
>
> What do you notice?
>
> 2 cm ⬜
>
> 3 cm

6 Write down if each statement is always, sometimes or never true.

An enlargement makes a shape bigger.

When a shape is enlarged the angles remain the same size.

An enlargement of scale factor 2 makes each edge 3 times longer.

7 Shape N is **not** an enlargement of shape M.

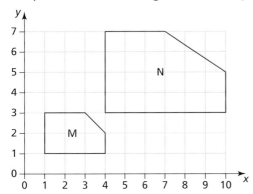

Explain how you could change one vertex of shape N in order to make shape N an enlargement of shape M.

8 Trinity enlarged a shape by a scale factor of 4.

She drew the following image onto cm squared paper.

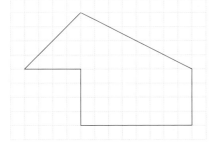

Draw the original shape before the enlargement.

Did you know?

You can have fractional scale factors.

If you enlarge a shape by a scale factor of $\frac{1}{4}$, then the image will be smaller. It will be $\frac{1}{4}$ of the original size.

End of chapter reflection

You should know that ...	You should be able to ...	Such as ...
When a shape is enlarged the image is either bigger or smaller, but the size of all of the interior angles remains the same.	Enlarge a shape by a positive whole number scale factor.	Enlarge the following shapes by a scale factor of 3.
The scale factor is how many times bigger the image will be after the enlargement.	Recognise when one shape is an enlargement of another and identify the scale factor.	What is the scale factor of the enlargement which maps shape A onto shape B?
The centre of enlargement is used to determine the exact location of the enlarged image.	Enlarge a shape by a positive scale factor from a given centre of enlargement.	Enlarge the shape by a scale of 2 from the centre of enlargement, O.

Real-life graphs

You will learn how to:

- Draw and interpret graphs in real-life contexts involving more than one component, e.g. travel graphs with more than one person.

Starting point

Do you remember …?

- how to draw and interpret travel graphs?
- how to draw and interpret scales?
- how to read and plot points on coordinate grid?

This will also be helpful when you:

- learn how to calculate and compare speed and acceleration in real-life contexts.

Hook

Draw the following set of axis onto a mini-whiteboard or sheet of paper.

Draw a continuous line to represent your happiness yesterday from 8 a.m. till 8 p.m.

The line will go up or down (or remain level) throughout the day as your mood changed.

Get your partner to guess what happened at different stages throughout the day.

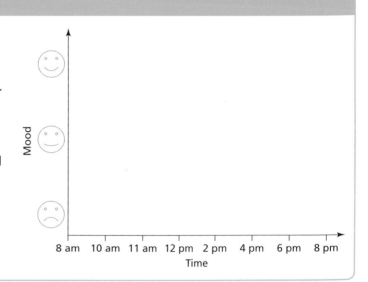

Drawing and comparing real-life graphs

Key terms

Constant speed is when an object travels at a steady pace without speeding up or slowing down.

A **real-life graph** compares changes over time. For example, a travel graph shows how distance changes over time.

Worked example 1

Susan and Owen run to the end of the road, rest and then race back to the start.

Owen twisted his ankle on the way back. The graph shows the full race for both Susan and Owen.

a) Who completed the race in the shortest time?

b) How long did Susan rest for?

c) After how many seconds did Owen twist his ankle?

d) What happened 68 seconds after the start of the race?

e) What was the total distance of the race?

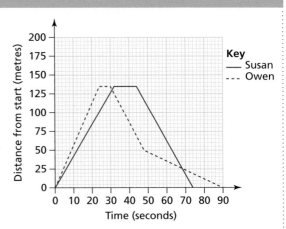

a) Susan completed the race first. Since they both start at 0 metres, the race will end when they get back to 0 metres.	It is clear that Susan's line arrives back at 0 metres before Owen's. 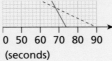
b) 12 seconds Read the scale carefully. Each smaller square represents 2 seconds. 6 small squares, so 6 × 2 = 12	The horizontal line represents the stationary part of the race when they rested.
c) 48 seconds after the start of the race.	Owen's speed significantly decreased at 48 seconds. This is shown by the graph becoming less steep.
d) Susan overtook Owen.	The lines cross when they are both exactly the same distance away from the start/finish.
e) 270 metres 2 × 135 = 270	The distance to the end of the road is 135 m and so the full distance of the race is 2 × 135 since they need to run back to the start.

Exercise 1

1   A train travels from Berlin to Copenhagen. It then returns back to Berlin.
   The graph shows the journey.

) How long did the train stop in Copenhagen for?

   'hat is the distance from Berlin to Copenhagen?

   set off from Berlin at 9 a.m.

c) What happened at 10.24 a.m.?

d) What time did the train arrive back in Berlin?

e) How many times did the train stop on the return journey from Copenhagen to Berlin?

Tip

To work out the scale, divide the time interval by the number of small squares within the interval.

For example, 60 ÷ 10 = 6 minutes per small square.

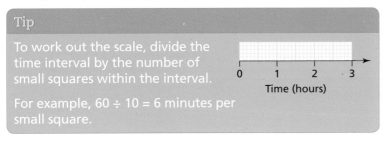

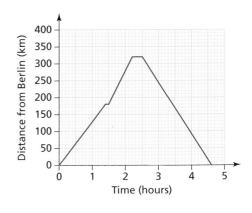

2 A cheetah is sat beneath a tree when it spots a gazelle.

The cheetah then hunts the gazelle. The graph shows the chase.

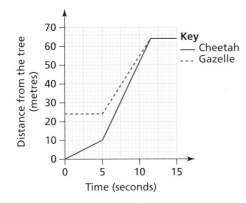

a) How far away from the gazelle is the cheetah when the gazelle starts to run?

b) What happens at 11.5 seconds?

c) What is the gazelle doing between 0 and 5 seconds?

d) How many seconds does the gazelle run for?

e) What is the distance travelled by the gazelle?

f) How can you tell that the cheetah is faster than the gazelle?

Did you know?

The speed of a planet is affected by its distance from the Sun.

Planets which are further away travel more slowly as they orbit the Sun.

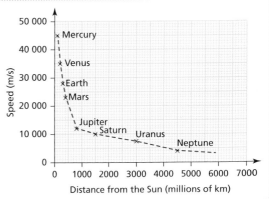

3 A plane flies from London to Paris. It stops in Paris for 30 minutes before flying on to Rome.

This part of the journey is shown on the travel graph.

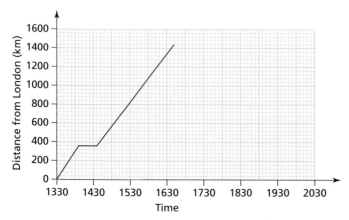

The plane then stops for 36 minutes in Rome before making a $2\frac{1}{2}$ hour return flight to London.

a) Complete the travel graph to show the entire journey.

b) What time does the plane arrive back in London?

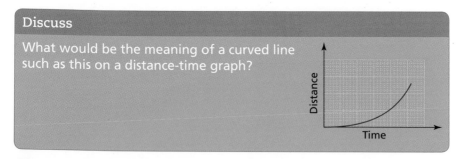

Discuss

What would be the meaning of a curved line such as this on a distance-time graph?

4 A bus sets off from Town A to Town B. It makes two stops along the way.

The journey is shown on the travel graph.

a) How long does the bus wait for at the first stop?

b) What is the distance between the first and second stops?

c) What time does the bus arrive at town B?

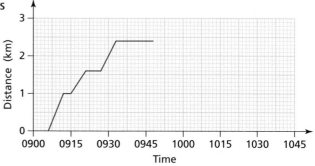

A second bus sets off from town A at 0942. It does not stop at the first stop. It takes 12 minutes to get to the second stop. It is stationary for 6 minutes before taking a further 9 minutes to reach town B.

d) Draw the journey for the second bus onto the graph.

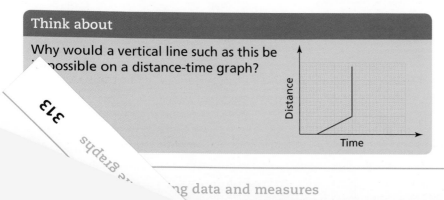

Think about

Why would a vertical line such as this be impossible on a distance-time graph?

5 Kate and Gino go to the same school and live in the same house. They both walk home from school one day.

Gino forgets his lunch box and has to go back to school to pick it up.

Kate stops at the shop on the way home.

Both of their journeys are shown on the travel graph.

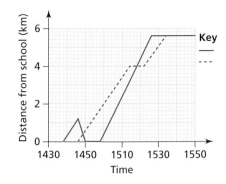

a) Complete the key to show which line represents each person.

b) How long does Kate spend in the shop?

c) What time does Kate arrive home?

d) How far away is the shop from their house?

e) What happens at 1446?

f) Who walks at the faster pace? Give a reason for your answer.

6 Vocabulary feature question

Match the boxes on the left with the boxes on the right in order to accurately describe an object's movement when represented on a distance–time graph.

A straight line		Moving slowly
A steep line		Impossible movement
A vertical line		Stationary
A horizontal line		Moving quickly
A less steep line		Moving at a constant speed

7 Two lifts operate in a hotel with 10 floors. The lifts always travel at the same speed and when they stop they always stop for exactly 7 seconds. Each floor is exactly 3 m high.

The first lift starts at ground level. It goes up to the 2nd floor, then goes up to the fifth floor, then goes down to the fourth flour and then goes back down to the ground floor.

This journey is shown on the travel graph.

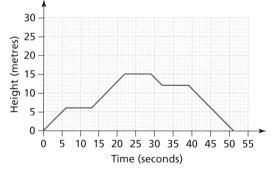

A second lift starts on the tenth floor at same time as the first lift. It goes down to the second floor, then goes up to the fourth floor and then moves up to the sixth floor.

a) Draw this journey on the same graph.

b) For how many seconds are both of the lifts on the same floor at the same time?

8 Three containers Q, P and R are filled up with a steady flow of water.

The graph shows the depth of water in each container as time increases.

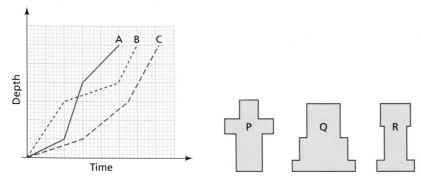

Match the graphs of A, B and C with the containers P, Q and R.

Give a reason for your answers.

End of chapter reflection

You should know that ...	You should be able to ...	Such as...
You can compare one or more components when drawing and interpreting a distance-time graph.	Accurately read and interpret the scales on a distance-time graph. Determine which parts of a distance-graph represent faster and slower speeds by looking at the steepness of the line. Recognise when an object is stationary.	Draw a distance-time graph for two trams which set off along the same route several minutes apart.

Experimental probability

You will learn how to:

- Compare estimated experimental probabilities with theoretical probabilities, recognising that:
  - when experiments are repeated different outcomes may result
  - increasing the number of times an experiment is repeated generally leads to better estimates of probability.

Starting point

Do you remember how to:

- identify all the possible mutually exclusive outcomes of a single event.

  For example, if a bag contains 3 red counters and 4 green counters and a counter is taken out of the bag at random, what are the possible outcomes?

- use experimental data to estimate probabilities.

  For example, a bag contains red counters and green counters A counter is taken out of the bag at random, its colour is noted and the counter is replaced in the bag. This is done a total of 100 times; a red counter is chosen 25 times and a green counter 75 times. Calculate an estimate of the probability of taking out a red counter.

- compare experimental and theoretical probabilities in simple contexts.

  For example, the theoretical probability of throwing a 3 with a dice is $\frac{1}{6}$. John throws a dice 30 times and gets a 3 ten times. Do you think that the dice is fair?

- make a tally chart.

  For example what frequency does represent in a tally chart?   𝍷𝍷𝍷𝍷𝍷 𝍷𝍷𝍷𝍷𝍷 𝍷𝍷

This will also be helpful when you:

- study probabilities for multiple events.

Hook

The probability of throwing a 3 when you throw a dice is the same as the probability of throwing a 6 so if you throw a dice a number of times you should get the same number of 3s and 6s.

Throw a dice and make a tally chart of the numbers of 3s and 6s. After every 20 throws record the totals. Stop after 100 throws. Record your findings on a copy of the chart below.

Number of trials	Number of 3s	Number of 6s
20		
40		
60		
80		
100		

What do you notice about the difference between the number of 3s and 6s as the number of trials increases?

Key terms

An **experimental probability** is an estimate of the probability of a particular outcome of an event based on the outcomes of several repetitions of the event. The formula is:

experimental probability $= \frac{\text{number of successful trials}}{\text{total number of trails}}$

A **theoretical probability** is defined by the formula:

theoretical probability $= \frac{\text{number of favourable events}}{\text{total number of possible outcomes}}$

Worked example 1

A bag contains only green, red and orange sweets. Jan takes a sweet from the bag, notes its colour and then replaces it. He does this a total of 100 times and then makes a table below showing how many times each colour was picked.

Number of trials	Green sweet	Red sweet	Orange sweet
100	22 times	36 times	42 times

a) Calculate the experimental probability of:

   i)   a green sweet being chosen

   ii) a red sweet being chosen

   iii) an orange sweet being chosen.

b) There are actually 5 green sweets, 7 red sweets and 8 orange sweets.

   What is the theoretical probability of choosing:

   i)   a green sweet

   ii) a red sweet

   iii) an orange sweet?

c) Do you think that Jan was choosing at random?

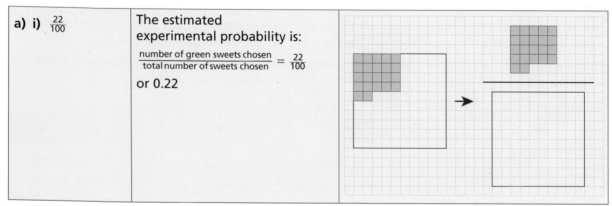

| a) i) $\frac{22}{100}$ | The estimated experimental probability is: number of green sweets chosen / total number of sweets chosen $= \frac{22}{100}$ or 0.22 | |

data and measures

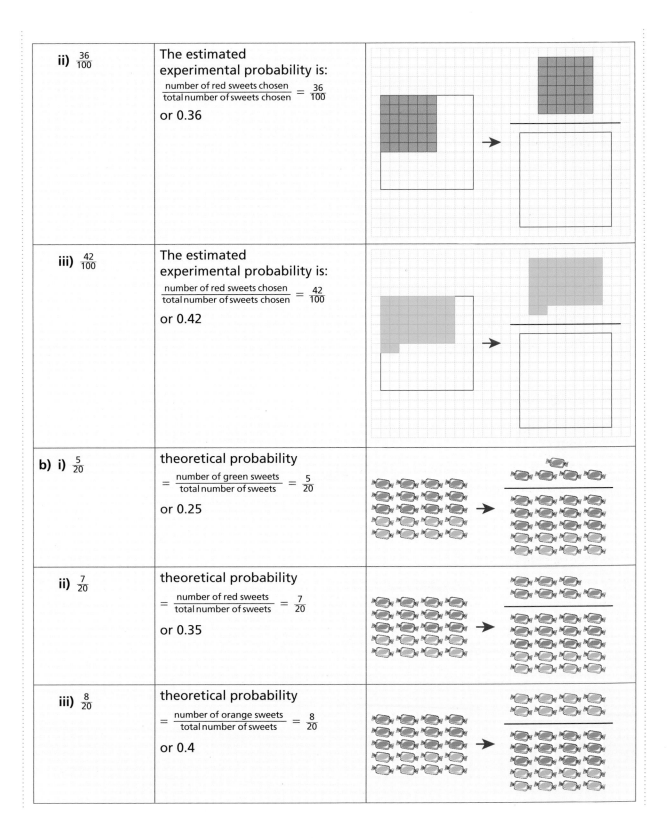

ii) $\frac{36}{100}$	The estimated experimental probability is: $\frac{\text{number of red sweets chosen}}{\text{total number of sweets chosen}} = \frac{36}{100}$ or 0.36	
iii) $\frac{42}{100}$	The estimated experimental probability is: $\frac{\text{number of red sweets chosen}}{\text{total number of sweets chosen}} = \frac{42}{100}$ or 0.42	
b) i) $\frac{5}{20}$	theoretical probability $= \frac{\text{number of green sweets}}{\text{total number of sweets}} = \frac{5}{20}$ or 0.25	
ii) $\frac{7}{20}$	theoretical probability $= \frac{\text{number of red sweets}}{\text{total number of sweets}} = \frac{7}{20}$ or 0.35	
iii) $\frac{8}{20}$	theoretical probability $= \frac{\text{number of orange sweets}}{\text{total number of sweets}} = \frac{8}{20}$ or 0.4	

c) Jan was probably choosing at random because the values for the experimental probability are roughly the same as the values for the theoretical probability.	Check the experimental values against the theoretical value. Put them in order of size and see if they are in the same order and see if they are roughly the same size.	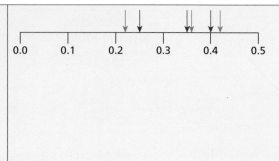

	Theory	Experiment
Green	0.25	0.22
Red	0.35	0.36
Orange	0.4	0.42

Exercise 1

1 A coin is flipped 100 times and the results are shown in the table.

Number of heads	37
Number of tails	63

What is the experimental probability of the coin landing on:

a) a head   **b)** a tail?

2 A spinner with three different colour sections is spun 50 times. It lands on pink 12 times, on purple 23 times and on black 15 times.

a) Giving your answers as decimals, find the experimental probability of the coin landing on:

  i) a pink section   **ii)** a purple section   **iii)** a black section?

b) Which colour section do you think is the largest?

3 **a)** What is the theoretical probability of a fair dice showing a six when it is thrown?

b) A dice is thrown 75 times and shows a six 25 times. What is the experimental probability of throwing a six with this dice?

c) Do you think that the dice in part b) is a fair dice? Explain your answer.

4 A teacher puts some black counters and some red counters into a bag. Sadia and Hala are asked to work out the experimental probability that a counter taken from the bag at random is black. Sadia takes out a counter at random, notes the colour and then replaces the counter into the bag. She does this 50 times and gets 32 black counters.

a) What is Sadia's estimate of the experimental probability of choosing a black counter?

Hala then carries out the same process but repeats it 200 times. She gets 104 black counters.

b) What is Hala's estimate of the experimental probability of choosing a black counter?

**) Which of the two estimates is likely to be closer to the theoretical probability? Explain
     our answer.

Probability

Data and measures

5 A spinner has four different colour sections. The spinner is spun 200 times and the colour section on which it lands is noted.

a) Copy and complete the table.

	Red	Purple	Blue	Black
	36		72	
Experimental probability		0.29	0.36	

b) Which two colour sections are most likely to be the same size?

6 **Discuss**

A fair spinner has 6 sections each a different colour. Jana spins the spinner 100 times and it lands on the red section 18 times. Sara spins the same spinner 100 times. Will she also find that the spinner lands on red exactly 18 times?

7 Jon is planning a picnic. The weather forecast says that there is a 70% probability of rain. Use the internet to find out how this type of weather probability is worked out.

Discuss

If the weather forecast says that there is a 70% chance of rain tomorrow, is this an estimated experimental probability or a theoretical probability?

Did you know?

That probability theory is used in sports such as football to analyse the strengths and weaknesses of teams? You can find details of this on the internet.

End of chapter reflection

You should know that ..	You should be able to ...	Such as ...
You can work out the estimated experimental probability by carrying out trials of the event.	Calculate the estimated experimental probability from results of trials.	A 6-sided dice is thrown 20 times and shows a 5 four times. What is the estimated experimental probability of this dice showing a 5 if it is thrown?
If an experiment or trial is repeated different results can happen.	Recognise that different results are possible when a trial is repeated.	Sema tosses a coin 10 times and it lands on a head 6 times. James then tosses the same coin 10 times. Will he also throw 6 heads?
A larger number of trials will give better results.	Recognise that larger numbers of trials give more accurate results.	Sema tosses a coin 10 times and it lands on a head 6 times so she says that the probability of throwing a head with this coin is 0.6. James then tosses the same coin 100 times and gets 52 heads so he says that the probability of throwing a head with this coin is 0.52. Which of them is likely to have the more accurate result?